R I V E R   T E E T H

RIVER

BANTAM BOOKS

New York
Toronto
London
Sydney
Auckland

TEETH

STORIES AND WRITINGS

DAVID JAMES DUNCAN

RIVER TEETH
A Bantam Book

PUBLISHING HISTORY
Doubleday hardcover edition / June 1995
Bantam trade paperback edition / July 1996

Earlier versions of some of the pieces in this book appeared in the following publications: "River Teeth," "Red Coats," "Rose Vegetables," "A Streetlamp in the Netherlands" and "Giving Normal the Finger" appeared in the anthology *edgewalking on the western rim,* published by One Reel Productions and Sasquatch Press. The author and publisher gratefully acknowledge permission to reprint them here. "River Teeth" and "Red Coats" also appeared in *Pacific Northwest.* "First Native," "Northwest Passage" and *"Not Rocking the Boats"* appeared in *Gray's Sporting Journal.* "Northwest Passage" also appeared in *Left Bank.* *"Molting"* appeared in *Whitefish.* "Lighthouse" appeared in *Zyzzyva.* *"Her Idiots"* appeared in *The North American Review.* "The Mickey Mantle Koan" appeared in *Harper's.*

The excerpt from "The Man on the Dump" from *Collected Poems* by Wallace Stevens, copyright 1942 by Wallace Stevens, is reprinted by permission of Alfred A. Knopf Inc.

ISBN 0-553-37827-9

Published simultaneously in the United States and Canada

Bantam Books are published by Bantam Books, a division of Bantam Doubleday Dell Publishing Group, Inc. Its trademark, consisting of the words "Bantam Books" and the portrayal of a rooster, is Registered in U.S. Patent and Trademark Office and in other countries. Marca Registrada. Bantam Books, 1540 Broadway, New York, New York 10036.

PRINTED IN THE UNITED STATES OF AMERICA

BVG   10 9 8 7 6 5 4

TABLE OF CONTENTS

Italics indicate fiction

RIVER TEETH:

A DEFINITION

WHEN AN ANCIENT STREAMSIDE CONIFER FALLS, FINALLY
WASHED OR BLOWN FROM ITS RIVERBANK DOWN INTO THE
WATER, A COMPLEX PROCESS OF DISINTEGRATION BEGINS. THE
FALLEN TREE BECOMES A NAKED LOG, THE LOG BEGINS TO LEAD
A KIND OF AFTERLIFE IN THE RIVER, AND THIS AFTERLIFE IS, IN
SOME WAYS, OF GREATER BENEFIT TO THE RIVER THAN WAS
THE ORIGINAL LIFE OF THE TREE.

A LIVING TREE STABILIZES RIVERBANKS, HELPS COOL WA-
TER TEMPERATURES, PROVIDES SHADE AND COVER FOR FISH,
SHELTER FOR MAMMALS AND BIRDS. BUT FALLEN TREES SERVE
SOME OF THE SAME PURPOSES, AND OTHER CRUCIAL ONES
BESIDES. THE GRADUAL DISINTEGRATION OF A LOG IN A
STREAMBED CREATES A VAST TRANSFUSION OF NUTRIENTS—A

slow forest to river feast reaching from the saprophytic bottom of the food chain to the predatory, fly-casting, metaphor-making top. Downed trees are also part of a river's filtration system: working in concert in logjams, they become flotsam traps; mud, leaf and carcass traps; Styrofoam, disposable-diaper and beer-can traps. And they're a key element in river hydraulics: a log will force current *down,* digging a sheltering pocket or spawning bed for trout or salmon; *over,* creating a whitewater spill that pumps life-giving oxygen into the stream; or *around,* sometimes digging the salmonid's version of a safe room with a view, the undercut bank.

On the forest streams I know best—those of the Oregon Coast Range clearcuts, "tree farms" and remnant strips of rainforest—the breakdown of even a five- or six-hundred-year-old river log takes only a few decades. Tough as logs are, the grinding of sand, water and ice are relentless. Within a decade or two any drowned conifer but cedar turns punk, grows waterlogged and joins the rocks and crayfish as features of the river's bottom. I often glance down at my feet while fishing and see that the "rock" I'm standing on is really the top of a gigantic log sunk and buried in gravel and sand. And even after burial, decomposition continues. The log breaks into filaments, the filaments become gray mush, the mush becomes mud, washes downriver, comes to rest in side channels. The side channels fill and gradually close. New trees sprout from the fertile muck. The cycle goes on.

There are, however, parts of every drowned tree that refuse to become part of this cycle. There is, in every log, a series of cross-grained, pitch-hardened masses where long-lost branches once joined the tree's trunk. "Knots," they're called, in a piece of lumber. But in the bed of a river, after the parent log has broken down and vanished, these stubborn masses take on a very different appearance, and so perhaps deserve a different name. "River teeth" is what we called them as kids, because that's what they look like. Like enormous fangs, often with a connected, cross-grained root. It took me awhile to realize, when I found my first, that it had once been part of a tree. Having grown up around talk of "headwaters" and "river mouths," it was easier for me to imagine it having washed loose from a literal river's jaw than having once joined a branch to an evergreen.

I don't know how long these teeth last, but even on the rainy coast I'd guess centuries: you sense antiquity when you heft one. Because their pitch content is so high, and hardened pitch outlasts the grainy wood fiber, the oldest teeth lose much of their resemblance to wood. Some look like Neolithic hand tools, others like mammals—miniature seals, otters, manatees. Still others resemble art objects—something intelligently worked, not just worn. And to an extent this is what they become. There is life in rivers, and strength; there are countless grinders and sanders: in a relic the waters have shaped so long, why wouldn't we begin to glimpse the river's mind and blind artistry?

WITH MY TREES, LOGS AND RIVER IN PLACE, I'D LIKE TO PIECE together a metaphor: our present-tense human experience, our lives in the inescapable present, are like living trees. Our memory of experience, our individual pasts, are like trees fallen in a river. The current in that river is the passing of time. And a story—a good, shared story—is a transfusion of nutrients from the old river log of memory into the eternal now of life. But as the current of time keeps flowing, the aging log begins to break down. Once-vivid impressions begin to rot. Years run together. We try to share, with an old friend or spouse, some "memorable" past experience and end up arguing instead about details that don't jibe. Chunks of the log begin to vanish completely. Someone approaches us in a crowd, his face lights up, he says his name, tells us of a past connection—and we shake his hand and grin through our horror, unable to place him at all. Some of us realize, after being endlessly corrected, that there are portions of our pasts we can no longer weave into accurate narratives. Others of us realize, after sharing the same accurate narratives for decades, that we have somehow talked our allotment of stories to death, that no one listens any longer, that when we tell these old tales the room fills with a dark water and our listeners' eyes glaze. So we stop telling them. We let them decompose. The last filaments of memory become gray mush, the mush becomes mud, the mud washes downriver. New life, and new stories, sprout from the silence.

There are, however, small parts of every human past that resist this natural cycle: there are hard, cross-grained whorls of memory that remain inexplicably lodged in us long after the straight-grained narrative material that housed them has washed away. Most of these whorls are not stories, exactly: more often they're self-contained moments of shock or of inordinate empathy; moments of violence, uncaught dishonesty, tomfoolery; of mystical terror; lust; preposterous love; preposterous joy. These are our "river teeth"—the time-defying knots of experience that remain in us after most of our autobiographies are gone.

A true river tooth experience is usually old; until the narrative fiber that surrounded the event turns punk and vanishes, one can't be sure it possesses the adamantine quality that is its chief attribute. Most are also fairly brief—just as actual wooden river teeth are fairly small. In my own such experiences I am more often acted upon than actor; more eye than body; more witness than hero. Yet the emotional impact of such experiences is often huge. Some river tooth experiences, if shared with the wrong person, would certainly wound, and could perhaps even kill. Others, whether shared or not, possess the solidity of a geographer's bearing marker and help us find our way. Almost everyone, I believe, owns scores of these old knots and whorls. Yet—perhaps because they lack a traditional narrative's flow from beginning to middle to end—I hear few people speak of such experiences.

There are many things worth telling that are not quite narrative. And eternity itself possesses no beginning, middle or end. Fossils, arrowheads, castle ruins, empty crosses: from the Parthenon to the Bo Tree to a grown man's or woman's old stuffed bear, what moves us about many objects is not what remains but what has vanished. There comes a time, thanks to rivers, when a few beautiful old teeth are all that remain of the two-hundred-foot spires of life we call trees. There comes a river, whose current is time, that does a similar sculpting in the mind. My hope, in sharing a few personal river teeth here, is to let go of what can't be saved, to honor what can and perhaps to make others more aware of, and more willing to accept and share, the same cycle in themselves.

RED COATS

to the daaman

IT'S A FEW DAYS BEFORE CHRISTMAS, DOWNTOWN PORTLAND.
I AM THREE YEARS OLD. MY MOTHER, TWO BROTHERS, SISTER
AND I HAVE COME IN FROM THE COUNTRY BY BUS. WE'RE
HERE TO SHOP AND, I GUESS, MEET SANTA CLAUS. BUT I'M
NOT INTERESTED IN SANTA. I'M INTERESTED IN SURVIVAL.
THE DOORS OF EVERY CAR, TROLLEY, BUS AND BUILDING IN
TOWN ARE EXTRUDING HUMANS, MOST OF THEM TRAVELING
AT A PACE EQUAL TO MY DEAD RUN, ALL OF THEM BIGGER,
SOME TEN TIMES BIGGER, THAN ME. THE AIR AT MY LEVEL IS
SO THICK WITH SCISSORING THIGHS, SWINGING PURSES AND
JINGLING TROUSER POCKETS THAT I CAN'T EVEN GLANCE AT
THE WINDOW DISPLAYS. MY BROTHER JOHN IS SEVEN, AND
NEARLY COMPETENT TO HANDLE THIS CHAOS. BUT STEVE IS

four and incompetent, so John is under orders to hold Steve's hand and walk directly in front of my mother, whose arms and attention are occupied with a purse, four or five shopping bags, a Christmas list and Katherine, my baby sister. That leaves me to bring up the rear—and I am to maintain my position by clinging to my mother's bright red winter coat.

I am fervently clinging. I know that only by obedience will I survive. We've already walked dozens of blocks, entered revolving or swinging or sliding double doors, traversed the aisle mazes of boiling-hot buildings, ridden fang-stepped escalators and airless, fart-filled elevators, only to shoot, sweating and dizzy, back out into the cram-packed cold. As we head for the Meier & Frank building and rendezvous with Santa, the sidewalk is so thick with percussing shoes that I can scarcely see concrete. One misstep by one of the thousand spiked heels and my foot could end up looking like the foot of Our Lord. On a midblock sidewalk Mom escapes a knot of people by angling us over to the edge of the street—and a delivery truck nearly mows us down. At a crosswalk, moments later, she swims us off the curb with the human current, sees the DON'T WALK sign flash, slams into reverse, smacks her red wool bottom into my face, crushes my head into the keys of some fat guy's pockets, changes her mind, hollers "Run!" and I am barely able to catch the salvific red coat and follow it, dazed, back into the current.

The coat is trolling me now, like a half-drowned herring, through a crush of silhouettes along the shadowed side of a building. The people across the street, in contrast, are ablaze with winter sunlight. Despite sensory overload I am fascinated by their brilliance. It fascinates me, too, to see a woman among them in a fiery red coat who looks a lot like my mother. Tightening my grip on my real mother's coat, I see that the sunlit mother is even carrying a baby. And right in front of her are two boys dressed a lot like my brothers. Funny. The only thing missing is the boy dressed like me. I tug on

Mom's coat, wanting to show her our near-twin family. She feels the tug, turns, gives me a surprised little smile—

—*and something's happened to her face*. It's wrong, wrong! Every piece of it, lips, eyes, nostrils, is different; not ugly, not bad, just hopelessly different. Hoping it's some trick of the shadows, or of makeup, I gasp, "What did you *do?*"

She just stares down at me, then laughs—a strange, nervous titter—and in a strange voice says, "You're holding my coat."

Of course I am. And I keep holding it. But she's lost the baby, lost my brothers, lost her face. Does she want me to let go so she can lose me now, too? Too scared to confront her violent foreignness, I look for the family I'd wanted to show her. There they are, in the beautiful blazing light. And look. The red-coated mother just noticed me here in the shadows. Noticed me, then gaped, then looked behind her. Now she's pointing me out to her boys. They gape, too. The woman and boys start waving and shouting. The Steve-like one starts jumping. The John-like one starts laughing. Even the baby is waving. And I can't understand them, it's way too noisy, but they're acting as if they know me, they're acting as if they *want* me. And though I feel it's a betrayal, I suddenly want them, too.

So I drop the red coat. I let it fall, turn toward the sunlit family, bolt right into the street. But when she sees me coming the sunlit mother screams, tires scream, pavement screams, I feel violent hands, engine heat, my body flying backward, the wind of a speeding car. And I'm back in the shadows, in my weird-faced mother's arms. But she is squeezing me now, she is holding me tight. And strange as she still looks, I know she has just saved my life.

I give her a tentative hug, then grab the sleeve of her red coat and hold it, to show her I remember. She smiles an odd smile in response. But she doesn't laugh or titter. She looks scared now—as scared as I was at first. Yet even scared her face is pretty; maybe prettier than before. I don't know what she did with my brothers or baby sister, but I know by the way she's holding me that they must be okay. "Just wait," she tells me in her quiet new voice—and I like the voice, too. "I'll wait with you. Don't worry. They're coming. See?"

Following the line of her long, elegant finger, I see the sunlit mother herding her boys and baby toward the corner crosswalk. But now I don't understand. I love my changed red-coated mother despite her sudden difference. And the whole time she holds me, the whole time we wait, I believe that I'm about to change families.

ROSE VEGETABLES

In 1960, on one of the hottest June days on record, I went with my family to watch the Grand Floral Parade of Portland's annual Rose Festival. "Rose Vegetable," hippie friends would later dub it, with no argument from me. At age eight, though, one assumes that when a billion flowers get beheaded and thrust on public display, they've died for some noble purpose. So there I hunched, front-row-seated on the curb, watching the edible-looking floats and neurotic clowns; the gymnasts, marching bands and National Guard rockets, the stuntmen, stilt men and sequined majorettes; unicyclists, Indian chiefs, rope-trick artists. White-gloved, admiration-stoned princesses reached toward us through the air, slowly unscrewing invisible jar lids. Beefy Rosarians glad-handed us. Rows of robotic soldiers disdained us. Peanut, ice-cream and bauble vendors hustled us. Magicians and jugglers regaled us. And none of them stuck around long enough to bore us. I grew mesmerized. I can't say for certain that I was having fun, but I was definitely an enthralled little Rose Vegetable, pleased as Pepsi to be a Portlander, wishing I'd a flag, gun or red rose to wave.

The Meadowland Dairy wagon came clomping toward us—a huge, turn-of-the-century bandwagon, drawn by eight enormous black Clydesdales, with a uniformed brass band aboard. The parade abruptly halted, in that inexplicable way parades do, placing the wagon right in front of us. The band lit into some better-than-average Sousa. Parade-goers began bobbing to it like hundreds of happy toilet plungers. Then—in sudden, shocking disagreement with the reigning Rose Vegetable mood—one of the Clydesdales shrieked, and began to rear in its traces. All seven of the other horses began doing the same. The brass band was jerked so violently the Sousa was yanked into silence. And we suddenly knew—as the wagon driver roared his puny "Whoa"s, jerked futile reins, and mothers began gripping kids—that those horses could drag their wagon anywhere they chose, including straight through the marching band in front of them, or into the crowd on either side.

That was when I first noticed a man who'd been trudging along by the Clydesdales from the beginning. Just this bland-faced, pale old bald guy wearing black slacks and a short-sleeved shirt so boring he looked more like a lost salesman than part of a gala parade. Definitely not the guy you'd choose to save a day. But he was holding a riding crop in one hand. And he shuffled back along the rearing team, applied his crop to the trouble horse and managed, in no time, to quell all eight of them. No sooner had he calmed the horses, though, than he fell facedown on the asphalt. And didn't move, though the pavement was blistering hot. Seeing this odd behavior, the horses took a few nervous steps forward, and the wagon's huge wooden-spoked, steel-rimmed wheels turned just once. But once was enough: while we stared as if at another clown stunt or magician's trick, the right front wheel of the Meadowland Dairy wagon rolled, with majestic slowness, not so much over as *through* the old man's head.

The smell of a hospital, the air in a full church—normally these are all it takes to make me faint. But the sense of unreality the parade had engendered in me was so complete that not even the sound of crunching skull or the widening pool of brain made me queasy. When easily twenty-five people, including my father, flopped to the ground as if playing Simon Says with the dead man, the unreality only thickened: I didn't understand till my father recovered and told me, later, that it had been a mass faint.

It betrays my slant on civic pride that I consider this, by far, the most edifying Rose Festival event I've ever witnessed. When I try to this day to grasp the driving force behind words like *karma, destiny* or *fate,* I picture those eight enormous black Clydesdales. And when I first read of the Buddhist symbol of the Great Wheel, you can imagine which wheel's slow turning sprang to mind.

So what a comedown, what a piffle-ization the next morning, to watch my parents paw the daily *Oregonian* from end to end and find that the only mention of this soul-shaking event was a three-sentence piece of denial on the obituary page. The old guy had died a hero; he'd gone down for the Rose Vegetable cause; his actions were the first I'd seen outside a boob tube or movie theater that bore even faint resemblance to Christ's line: "He that loseth his life shall save it." And the paper stated his name, age and ex-address; stated the time and place of his death; called the cause of his death "heat stroke"; and that was that.

The Lord can only giveth. The media account is free to sweep what the Lord giveth away. This was my first exposure to this gruesome kind of clean-up operation. I have distrusted newspapers and civic celebrations ever since. I have also believed, ever since, that we live among quiet heroes.

HER IDIOTS

A HALLMARK CARD MIST HUNG IN THE AIR ON THE EARLY
SPRING DAY SHE CAME TO CARETAKE THE FARM. AFTER STOW-
ING HER GEAR, RUNNING OVER THE CHORE LIST AND WAVING
THE NERVOUSLY GRINNING OWNERS ON BACK TO THE CITY,
SHE LET THE FORCED SMILE FALL FROM HER FACE, SLUMPED IN
A ROCKER AT THE WINDOW AND WATCHED HER HALLMARK
CARD SHEEP IN THE DISTANCE—GRAY CLOUD PUFFS GRAZING
THE GREEN, TRANSFORMING ROUGH PASTURE TO LAWN. THEY
WERE HER FIRST FLOCK OR HERD OF ANY KIND, HER INTRO-
DUCTION TO SHEPHERDHOOD, VENERABLE VOCATION OF NO-
MADS AND PSALMISTS. NATURALLY SHE WAS CURIOUS. SO,
LEAVING THE CABIN, SHE STROLLED TOWARD THEM, SEEKING,
AS WITH ANY NEW ACQUAINTANCE, THE EYES. AND SHE EX-

pected to see stupidity. She'd been warned. She expected lovable ignorance, perennial victimhood and a vacuous yet genuine innocence worth the costs of feed and endless vigilance. But as she strode in past the mist, squatted beside an ancient ewe and met for the first time that direct, all-uncomprehending gaze, she was astounded: nothing had prepared her for such unspeakable nonintelligence. The eyes were hideous. Two piss-colored ice cubes. They understood nothing, never had nor would. Their seeing was not perception, it was radar—a cold, bloodless means of determining locations of meaningless objects. The eyes didn't disappoint her: they appalled her. She rose to escape them and had gone a little distance when, for no reason, the entire flock started and bolted madly away. Dried balls of dung clattered on their hind legs and tails as they ran, and she laughed at the sound. That was the first day. At first it seemed funny.

WEEKS PASSED AND SHE WATCHED THEM. SOMETIMES THEY'D come to her, sometimes flee, but they came only in dumb hope of food and fled only out of causeless impulse. She thought for a while that she saw emotion in certain movements, some actual alarm or fright. But that was at a distance. Closer she'd see the unchanging eyes—yellow, insectile, mindless—and even their liveliest body movements became somehow lifeless. They were like the half-dormant houseflies on her bedroom ceiling at night that would suddenly buzz, with seeming urgency, through the blackness, only to land on an equally meaningless piece of ceiling. They might dash to their deaths, but fear did not compel them. They had two nonanatomical attributes each: hunger and stupidity. These let nothing else, not even fear, enter their lives. And always, as they ran, the adorning excrement clattered out its imbecilic music. Her laughter soon ceased.

. . .

THERE WERE TWO DOZEN. THEN ONE DAY A DOG APPEARED on a distant ridgetop, looked down at them and barked. At this they tore, turds rattling, into the bluegill pond. Thirteen drowned. Because a dog had barked. A small, fenced-out dog with a small, frustrated yap. Now she had eleven. The survivors. The best swimmers. Products of natural selection. It was weeks before their rattles dried.

AN OLD STONE WALL PROTECTED THE GARDEN FROM THE flock. Moss-covered and lichen-flecked, upright and unfailing, it had sheep-proofed flower, fruit and vegetable for a century. There were endless Achilles' heels on that farm, perennial sources of disorder—the rotting posts in the pasture fences; the weasels in the chicken house; the tansy in the cattle graze; muskrats tunneling in the pond dike. But the gray stone wall was a given: like a hill, like rain, like seasons, it served. She looked at it once. Admired it. And forgot it . . .

. . . till one dusk in late May, returning from town with a pickup load of chicken scratch, she found her flock bedded down in the garden, too glutted to stand. A mere dozen stones were tumbled from the wall, but through that fissure they'd poured like a plague of fleecy locusts, devouring the tiny corn and asparagus, the promising lettuce, broccoli, bell peppers, the ripening strawberries (leaf, blossom and fruit), the scarlet runner beans (including even their support strings), the snow peas she'd planned on for dinner. The garden was destroyed. No amount of work or money could restore the growing-time lost. Yet the sheep showed no guilt, no satiation, no satisfaction: they simply lounged, munching the last of her herb garden, the same lifeless idiocy in the mechanical yellow eyes.

Turning to the wall, she cursed it for a traitor, then ran for a shovel and beat the sheep back to their fold. Fetching barbed wire, she began stringing it in the gap, gouging her hands, feeding her fury, thinking as she worked of the grasslands of Spain turned to desert by close-cropping flocks; of grizzlies and cougars hounded and shot out of existence, eagles poisoned, vomiting their entrails in flight; wolves ripping at their own trapped feet; coyotes nibbling baits that shot cyanide into their heads; helpless welps and cubs starved or clubbed to death—all for the sake of these shit-encrusted zombies. She thought of David, and of Christ, the impossibly good shepherds. What monstrous compassion! What a waste, the love of sheep! She finished the snarl of wire in the dark. It disfigured the old wall like a rip in a painting, like a battlefield relic of the First World War. She was pleased. She hoped the sheep would try to cross it.

She had wine for dinner, and mutton—one of the drowned. A one-course meal. She gorged herself on it.

LONG BITTER DAYS OF REPLANTING FOLLOWED. BUT SLOW-burning anger lent its crooked inspiration and the work went fast. Before the garden was finished two ewes lambed. Both bore twins, though only two survived. The burying of the dead lambs, and toddling dances and cries of the survivors, finally began to cool her anger. She reminded herself that by winter their innocence would give way to the buglikeness of the full-grown. Nevertheless she'd catch herself smiling at the lambs' antics, and the thought of them caught in the barbed-wire snarl began to nag her. So one early August morning, after finishing the various feedings (sheep, chickens, cattle, fish, guineas, goose, decrepit horse), she decided to fix the breach before going inside to feed herself.

She began by removing the wire. She then lifted the largest fallen stone and dropped it into the gap. To heave this boulder into place took all her strength—and the instant it thudded down, an avalanche of smaller stones came barking down her shins. She writhed for a while and snarled out the conventional curses. Then she began again, placing the now numerous small stones in the wall's gaps and cracks. When she'd placed eight, thirteen came tumbling. These missed her shins, but she cursed just the same. Two constructive efforts and the breach was a sheep length across now. She began again, more carefully, but it only took more time for the same result: avalanche. She swore softly now, and confusedly—but then crude and clear again as a clatter of dungballs announced her flock come to watch.

She ignored them and began again. And again. And again and again, each time faster and more furious till frustration twisted in her head and empty stomach and her lumpen shins were bleeding all over her socks. When the breach was nearly three sheep lengths across, a creeping desperation put an end to her curses. She stopped heaving rocks around. She began to ponder. The idiot flock remained—even the restless lambs. Some stood, some reclined, some slobbered cud, but all eyes waited upon her. She swore she'd make them her meat in due season. Yet she felt as stupid as one of her flock.

She ogled the stones scattered round her. She ogled the wall that had supplied but now refused to readmit them. It was a Chinese puzzle—and she hated Chinese puzzles. It was an insult to her intelligence—and to her shins. "You're the same damned rocks that came from the wall," she said, wanting the reassurance of sounds more rational than those of the sheep. But her voice did not reassure her. And even the sheep had done better with the wall than she. They'd made a small hole in accord with a gastronomically sensible intention. With the intention of plugging that hole, she'd made a gulf she could now drive the tractor through.

She stood, silent, in the ruin she'd made. After an embarrassingly long time it occurred to her that neither the fallen stones nor the hole she'd created had anything to teach her about what must be done. She turned to the wall. After a second absurdly long time, it occurred to her to wonder that the wall had no mortar, no bracing, no tapering toward the top, nothing to hold it together, yet there it stood, impossibly erect and slender. At last she began to see its beauty, and her own past blindness. She'd considered it a wall-shaped stack of rocks, a wall like any other, till it had failed her. But its failure now forced her to discover that, a hundred years ago, a man endowed with nothing but hands like her own had composed this wall of nothing but rock and gravity, and that not one stone had been placed at random. Her shins cried out that no stone *could* be placed at random. She had cracked them against a work of art. She suddenly remembered, and said aloud, its name: "Drystone masonry." She realized, too, that she lived in a land of barbed wire and prefab fencing, where such masons worked no more. Were this wall to stand again, her hands must rediscover what their hands had known. She must find in each stone the center of gravity, and for each gap the stone that would not shift as the weight upon it grew. From the piecemeal rubble she'd just created, a single, cohesive thing must rise.

She began again, by simply picking up, and contemplating, a solitary errant stone. From the work of seeing alone, the sweat began to pour. Unmoving, she held that first stone long. The sun and flock bore witness. At last she began to turn, to fondle, to shift it in her stupid hands, pondering moss and weatherstains like an illiterate pondering lines in a book. She then began to try her stone in gap after gap, trying every single gap in the tumbled wall before narrowing her choices to four or five, then laying the stone in a niche it seemed to fill as it filled no other. She placed three stones in this way, placed five, spending long moments hefting and twisting each before she even turned with it to the wall. She placed nine stones, placed eleven, doubting every decision, jarring and testing each placement, trying another stone if things seemed to shift too easily. She had finally lost count—maybe her fifteenth stone, maybe her twentieth—when a piece of wall shifted as she was testing it, and five stones fell out. One struck her shin, and hurt, but this was no avalanche. Just five rebellious stones. And the rest of her work stood firm. Absently rubbing the bleeding shin, she smiled at the stones that held, her satisfaction immense.

She placed four, ten, sixteen more. She began to find pairs, then triads, then larger combinations that held in conglomerates as they couldn't hold alone. She learned to center the balance of each stone so that gravity pulled it inward and down, not simply down. And she said, later, that she began to sense, in the most nearly perfect placements, a content, a relief, almost a pleasure in the stones themselves. She said this pleasure entered her hands, her arms, her back, her head, and without thinking she began to sing. The song had no words, and she says she sings poorly. But her flock listened.

Hours flew past, and birds. The sun crossed the sky. The flock stayed on in the shade of the closest firs. Again and again stones would fall upon testing. But again and again she'd feign detachment, feign a stony patience, keep singing. Her back grew weary, her hands scuffed but cagey, her wall rose infinitesimally higher. She lifted, balanced, tested, sweated. The patience and detachment grew less feigned. Glimpsing her audience now and then, she marveled that they remained, grew grateful for their company, began to talk to them between chunks of song. They watched, chewed, made no comment, but remained close by till, at last, with aching back and bleeding hands, she placed the final stone and, unbreathing, tested it.

The wall stood strong. She turned to her flock and made obeisance. She swears both lambs bleated in reply.

SHE WALKED SLOWLY DOWN TO THE BLUEGILL POND. THE EN-tire flock followed. She said she knew they only wanted food. She said she thought she knew. But they watched as she undressed (their eyes regarding her body as if it were another stone, a shed, a tree stump), watched as she swam (regarding the pond that had killed thirteen of them as if it were another stone, another stump), watched on as she dried and dressed again, rested in the shade of the firs, gazed at the warm, green water. They had no reason for remaining there. They had no reason for being anywhere. Yet there they were, watching. And as they stayed near, she said, she began to feel something for them. Not love, she said. Love isn't that easy. Just something that made her smile and call them, "My idiots." They didn't mind.

Staring long at the pond, then turning back to the sheep, she said she saw, quite suddenly, that they were like the pond—like water. Neither wise nor stupid, really. They simply were. But, also like water, they'd been just the way they were for an immeasurably long time. And anything that old, she said, however mute, bent or idiotic, anything that unarguable—trees, weather and birds, hills, stones or sheep—could teach us, if only we'd allow it.

FROM THE DAY SHE REBUILT THE WALL—SHE'D NO IDEA WHY —her idiots never again tried to cross it. Fall came, and a good harvest from the replanted garden. Winter came, and the lambs became sheep without her ever quite noticing, teaching her, she said, that though sheep are uglier and larger they are no less innocent than lambs, "hence, at least in theory, no less lovable." Their eyes remained just as blank and yellow. They continued to run for no reason, and to rattle as they ran. They remained the most repellently buglike mammals she'd ever encountered, and to balance that buglikeness, to make it tolerable, she memorized, and loved to tell, scores of merciless jokes about sheep.

But she also learned to show them mercy. And though they never quite made a shepherd of her, they had made her a drystone mason. Though they could never return the love of shepherds, there would be no shepherds without them. And at least, she said, they'd let her glimpse the love of shepherds, with their patience like the wind. Like the wind that riffles flame, that flickers water, that caresses, coaxes, embraces—forever and perhaps for naught—even the most stolid of stones.

GIVING NORMAL
THE FINGER

for Katherine Dunn, and Artie

WHEN I WAS EIGHT I HAD A FOSTER BROTHER, ALSO EIGHT, WHO I'LL CALL EDWARD. THIS EDWARD HAD BROWN HAIR, GREEN EYES, A GRAVELLY VOICE, A MUSCULAR TORSO AND A HUGE, IRRESISTIBLE LAUGH. WHAT HE DIDN'T HAVE WERE ARMS AND LEGS. NOT EVEN STUMPS. JUST A SINGLE, BULBOUS FINGER—WITH ONE JOINT IN IT, AND A NORMAL NAIL—GROWING OUT OF HIS LEFT SHOULDER. FOR SOME REASON IT ALWAYS STRUCK ME AS AN INDEX FINGER.

THALIDOMIDE DID IT. PEOPLE SAID THIS CONFIDENTLY, AS IF THAT TOOK CARE OF THAT. BUT THE WORD *THALIDOMIDE* DID NO MORE TO CHANGE EDWARD'S EXPERIENCE OF BEING EDWARD THAN THE PLATONIC MYTH ABOUT MEN AND WOMEN HAVING ONCE BEEN EIGHT-LIMBED, SINGLE-BODIED HERMAPHrodites has done to change my experience of being a four-limbed, mono-gendered male. We've all been severed from something. The older we get the more numerous and beloved this something gets. The name for this process, I believe, is Life. And Edward's company was great early exposure, for my siblings and me, to the beautiful harsh flow of it.

The Eddie we knew had four modes of locomotion. His top speeds—which were surprisingly fast—were achieved by waddling along on his base like a penguin; he could also crawl like an inchworm, roll himself like a log, and somehow writhe along (usually when overcome by mirth) like a maggot. He was utterly tone-deaf, loved to sing at the top of his lungs, anyhow, and could select singalong records and slap 'em on the turntable with just his finger, cheek and mouth. His other great love was for what he called "wrassling," which consisted of chasing us—usually via the log or penguin gait—while we walked along in front of him begging him to give up. But he never did give up. And when we finally gave in and let him catch us by an arm with his chin and shoulder, he would —I'm not joking—either flip us hard, right over his back, or nearly jerk our arms out trying.

It was a little emasculating to hear my mother telling this limbless, two-and-a-half-foot-tall phenom not to be so rough with her able-bodied boys. But Edward, of course, loved these admonitions. And laugh if you like, he was scary: he had a full-bore heart, full-sized willpower, and no extremities to slow any part of it down. Eddie was condensed, and he cherished his greater density. It gave him greater intensity, and he knew it. In fact, the bane of his existence, in his own fierce opinion, were the physical therapists who wanted to teach him the use of artificial arms and legs, and so disperse his intensity. Adults, including my parents, were flabbergasted by his hatred of prosthetics. But put yourself in Eddie's shoes. Edward. Shoes. Get the picture? Have a friend tie your feet to your butt and your arms to your chest, stack two chairs, lift you onto the top chair, then knock you over with only one finger free to break your fall. Get the picture? We were instructed by our parents to praise Eddie when he used a steel "arm," which was actually a claw, to accidentally scratch, chip and ruin the records he could easily play without it. This industrial claw, the experts said, would help him lead a "more normal life." But Eddie wanted a life he could seize in his own two hands, both of which in his case equaled a finger. The only "normality" he therefore sought was to be self-sufficient, loved if possible and accepted by humans as being just the way God made him. And if it wasn't God—if it was industrial man and thalidomide that made him—so much the more reason why industrial humans should accept him as he was.

My family gave it a go. After a year of monthly visits we tried a straight two-week stint of Edward's company. And when it was over we decided it felt workable, that to take him in was something we were willing to do. The only gray area, for me, was a Huck and Jim–type moral quandary: the first thing Edward always did behind closed doors was swear me to secrecy, then have me unstrap the hated steel arm.

In December, a year after we'd met him, we were finally allowed to talk openly with Eddie about the possibility of adoption; to ask, for instance—though it seemed to me to go without asking—whether *he* wanted *us*. He surprised us with his response. He seemed superficially flattered yet essentially indifferent. When I thought twice about it, though, I began to understand: whereas I saw my siblings as great companions and my parents as kind and wise, Eddie saw four fleet-footed kids who'd grown increasingly sick of "wrassling" with him, and a pair of adults who believed in plastic legs and steel claws.

The adoption question was unexpectedly resolved when someone beat us to it—a "good Christian family," as the adoption people put it, with a farm in the country and a house big enough to allow Eddie a room of his own. When the good Christian wife heard about us from our near-miss brother, she sent a letter saying how blessed they were to have him, and an article and photograph from their local paper intended to illustrate that blessing. In the photo the good family, Eddie now among them, stood on the steps of the institution that had housed him for years, all of them smiling, and all "heading home." But since it was a cold December day and the kids were all in coats, hats, boots and mittens, you couldn't even tell, from the picture, which kid was wearing four prosthetics. The effect was visually tranquilizing. What thalidomide had done, a therapist, photographer and winter clothes had temporarily undone. Yet one member of the family was risking his life in order to teeter, grinning, on the brink of those concrete stairs.

WE HEARD RUMORS, DURING EDWARD'S TEENS, THAT HIS LIFE with the farm family had blown up: rumors of alcohol and drugs, of trouble with the law, of multiple disappearances—all things that could also have been said of me. We heard his adoptive family had finally refused to have anything more to do with him. Then we heard nothing.

But a decade and a half after the last time I'd seen him, I spotted a guy I knew could only be Eddie working his way along a sidewalk near the Portland State University campus. He had on a pair of gray gym shorts, some kind of padding at the base of him, and that was it. His torso was still incredibly muscular, but beyond tan or leathery: he was scraped and worn as an old punching bag. The one finger was thick and strong, like that of a construction worker; his fingernail was dirty. Since he greeted everyone who glanced, gawked or smiled at him—in other words, everyone—a lot of speech was required of him, and it seemed to have taken a toll: his voice, disarmingly rusty in childhood, now sounded like a gregarious piece of road-paving equipment. We were the same age—both twenty-two. But the longer I looked at Eddie the more certain I grew that we were no longer the same age at all. His face had an apoplectic ruddiness about it, looked easily thirty-five, and peering into his eyes I saw why: his density, his intensity, was still burning him; had been burning him all these years; would continue to burn him till he was ashes, and there was nothing I or anyone could do to change this. The heart is designed to shoot life and energy clear out to the extremities: in Eddie's eyes at age twenty-two you saw his life and energy crashing endlessly against a wall, trying to invent extremities.

I introduced myself, described our past connection, but felt very imperfectly remembered—just another long-legged guy. When I offered him a cigarette, though—a hand-rolled Three Castles—he had no objection to giving me an update on his life. So we walked over to the library lawn and sat, or I did; sitting and standing were identical postures for him. Then he talked—disjointedly but intensely, and also proudly—of obstacles he'd faced and of things he'd done. He was, I felt, perfectly honest. He'd been honest at eight; he seemed no different now. There was nothing self-aggrandizing about his stories, nothing shifty about his manner and nothing that I —having known him in childhood—found physically impossible to believe.

His whole life had been spent in frank pursuit of happiness. And his chosen means to this, he happily confessed, had been to drink, smoke, get loaded and get laid as often as possible. He'd run away from the good Christian home in his early teens by convincing a buddy to toss him into an open freight car. He was soon captured by the authorities and returned home, but he kept finding accomplices and escaping again, via the same sack-of-potatoes method. He ended up riding the rails all over the West, became a justifiable legend in dozens of train yards and skid rows, but let the air out of the legend somewhat by answering to the absurd nickname "Shorty."

His first sexual experience had been with a prostitute, but he made it clear (though I made no comment) that this had been a one-time deal. His sexual alliances now, he wanted me to know, were based on mutual attraction. He personally (he said with a jackhammer laugh) was attracted to *all* women, but to his ongoing amazement and gratitude, some women were also attracted to him. Being found desirable was clearly the surprise of his life. But I can't say that I was surprised. Predictability is, for many of us, the death of erotic feeling, and a first encounter with Eddie would certainly not be predictable. One could see at a glance how lithe and powerful his torso was. And condensed personalities exude a condensed form of attractiveness; as does courage; as does gratitude. There are advantages, as well, to a man who can't lift more than a finger to harm a woman. And so many men walk out. Eddie, at best, wobbled.

The low point of his life (and it had apparently come recently) was a stay in a mental institution. According to Edward, a trumped-up charge of attempted suicide brought on the incarceration. He said he'd been staying in a northwest Portland halfway house run by a staff that hated him. The house had a ban on alcoholic beverages—an infringement on his openly professed philosophy of life. So when a friend snuck a half-gallon jug of red wine into Eddie's room, he pinched it by the neck between his own neck and shoulder, tossed it up for a drink (I'd seen him do this, at age eight, with a half-gallon jug of apple cider). But the neck of this bottle broke, the falling glass cut his shoulder and a small vein in his throat, and when staff members ran in and found him in a sea of wine and blood, they accused him of trying to slash his throat and sent him to an asylum.

With the unpredictability I was coming to accept as his norm, Eddie told me he'd liked the asylum. It was only the falsity of the suicide accusation that outraged him. He interrupted stories all afternoon to express that outrage. He also interrupted stories to express, to their faces, his admiration for passing coeds—and sure enough, he never saw one he didn't like. "I love my life," he'd growl after both kinds of interruption, as if challenging me, or anyone, to disagree. And I'd nod, open my tobacco tin, feed his philosophy another smoke.

We went our ways after awhile; our ways have never again coincided, and our childhood friendship and chance meeting bring me to no storybook conclusion. I had an almost-brother named Edward who has faced life with a single finger. With that finger he traveled all over the West, as I have. With it he loved sex, hated liars, drank and smoked, as I have. Remembering his blunt honesty, I suspect the middle-aged face he wore in his twenties was no lie: if he's still living, he has once again surprised me. But length of life, like length of body, was an extension Eddie chose not to desire. My best hope for his life is my best hope for my own: that we remain able, to the end, to love them.

A Streetlamp

in the Netherlands

Early August, 1969. I was standing on a sidewalk outside a delftware factory in Amsterdam, smoking an English Pall Mall. The sun was bright, the morning still, the neighborhood one of shops and old, stately houses. The dullness of the delftware lecture my American traveling companions were enduring indoors added pleasure to my smoke.

The sidewalk bordered a two-lane, one-way street evenly lined with broad-leaf trees and enormous old wrought-iron streetlamps. They were the sort of lamps—we'd seen them all over Europe—that had been converted, decades ago, from gas to electricity. They'd been standing for close to a century.

They had survived two world wars. As I was staring up the empty street, my head equally empty but for a nicotine buzz, a lamp a hundred or so feet away let out a groan, then fell with a crash to the pavement.

I looked, at once, in every direction to see if anyone else witnessed its fall. The only person in sight was a silhouette in the backseat of a Fiat sedan, parked across the street from the delftware factory, and the Fiat's windows were closed; the silhouette seemed not to have noticed. I was disappointed. A fellow witness and I could have shared an amazed laugh. Alone, I was having trouble believing what I'd seen. Yet there the lamp lay, blocking half the street, its glass panes shattered, its post badly twisted. "Weird," I said aloud.

At the sound of a cartoonish buzzing I looked past the fallen lamp and saw a Vespa motor scooter far up the same street. As it came closer I made out a neatly dressed young man in front and a pair of bare knees just behind him. Closer yet the knees began to shine in the morning light. Closer yet I saw that they belonged to a pretty young woman, and that the miniskirt she was wearing had been forced, by the wind and her posture, clear up to her panties. Confused though I was by the streetlamp, I was riveted with lust by the way her beautiful bare legs embraced the young man.

They'd been using the right lane. When the man saw the fallen lamp he swerved, scarcely slowing, to the left lane. Neither he nor the woman showed any surprise at the sight of the lamp. As they passed me, doing perhaps twenty-five, I felt myself staring so carnivorously at her exposed legs that I attempted a friendly wave in hopes of softening, somewhat, my voracious staring. The young man, justifiably, ignored me. The woman didn't wave, either, but she flashed me a marvelous, and surprising, smile. Doubly smitten, I was still staring at her receding legs when the silhouette in the Fiat at the left curb suddenly opened the door. The couple on the Vespa had no time to react. The door missed the young man, but struck the woman in the center of the kneecap. Her leg snapped violently back, the scooter was thrown sideways, but the young man, using his left foot as a strut, somehow kept it upright and brought it to a stop. The woman slumped at once to the pavement and began to let out horrible, gasping groans. Her kneecap was as shattered as the lamp. The person in the Fiat remained frozen in the backseat, gaping at them both.

They were surrounded within seconds by people from the delftware factory. I tried to go help them, too. But when I got close enough to see the dent her knee had made in the metal edge of the car door, saw shattered bone knifing and blood spilling from the beautiful tan flesh for which I'd just lusted, I found myself veering like a drunk back to my original curb, the blood gone from my head. And as I hunched like a gargoyle on my curb there, trapped between the remembered gleam of her legs and animal agony of her groans, I kept looking up the street at the preposterously fallen lamp that started the chain reaction, trying, like a gargoyle, to work out a way to hate it; trying to find a way to make it stand back up and pay.

KALI'S PERSONAL

THE "PERSONALS" DEPARTMENT OF ONE OF SEATTLE'S TWO
DAILY NEWSPAPERS RECENTLY RECEIVED AN AD WILDLY BUT
LEGIBLY HANDWRITTEN IN ENGLISH AND TRANSLITERATED
SANSKRIT. THE SUBMITTER GAVE NO RETURN ADDRESS OR
PHONE NUMBER, AND ASKED THAT ALL REPLIES BE FORWARDED
TO A POST OFFICE BOX IN CALCUTTA, INDIA. THE AD ARRIVED
IN A TEN-BY-THIRTEEN-INCH ENVELOPE SO POWERFULLY
SCENTED THAT IT WAS NOTICED ALMOST IMMEDIATELY BY EV-
ERY EMPLOYEE IN THE ENORMOUS OFFICE. MOST EMPLOYEES
CAME LOOKING FOR THE SOURCE OF THE SMELL AT ONCE,
SOME DEMANDING THAT WHOEVER OR WHATEVER IT WAS BE
THROWN OUT OF THE BUILDING, SOME SIMPLY NEEDING TO
KNOW ITS SOURCE, A DAZED FEW BEGGING TO "HAVE SOME OF

it." The odor reminded various individuals—in their own words—of "musk," "bad wine," "burned fat," "carrion," "sex fluids of both genders," "singed hair," "goat cheese," "a pagan altar" and "funky underwear. *Big time* funky." Both stationery and envelope were made of the kind of grainy, inexpensive paper produced by small manufactories all over India. Both were stained—in many dime-sized and several silver-dollar-sized blotches—with a variety of fluids, including what appeared to be blood. The envelope also contained fifteen thousand extremely used, equally pungent Indian rupees (several times the amount needed to run the ad) and an apology, written in the same helter-skelter hand, for the submitter's failure to convert the currency. "It is difficult," she wrote (if in fact she was female), "for me to enter public buildings on any continent, but impossible for me to enter an American bank. I haven't the arms to carry all that they try to give me."

A scholar at an American university agreed to translate the ad's Sanskrit phrases on the condition that both he and the university remain anonymous—"especially to the writer of the ad!" He said that most, maybe all, of the Sanskrit was lifted from poetry of the Vaishnavic tradition, that the verses properly belonged to "the sublime erotic give-and-take between Radha and Krishna," and that "their appropriation by the present writer is flagrantly blasphemous and consciously, derisively obscene."

After consulting lawyers, Seattle police, the FBI and an expert on international terrorism, the editorial board of the paper converted the rupees into American dollars, mailed a cashier's check for the full amount to the Calcutta post office box, but chose not to run the ad. When they attempted to produce the ad for police lab tests, however, they discovered it had somehow been stolen from the editor-in-chief's safe. And when police tried to fetch the rupees back from the bank, the bank's manager had already paid for them, taken them home and incinerated them in his backyard barbecue "to be rid of that smell!" According to the manager and three neighbor eyewitnesses, the rupee barbecue attracted a flock of several hundred frenzied crows and caused neighborhood dogs to howl. The eyewitnesses also claim—over the manager's understandably vehement denials—that the manager stood stark naked in his backyard as he burned the rupees, that he was weeping as they burned and that he had an erection throughout this performance.

Two days after the original ad's disappearance from the safe, a single full-sized, fourteen-by-twenty-three-inch newspaper page began to appear among the rock concert posters stapled to telephone poles all over Seattle. Running down the center of this page in a single two-inch-wide column was a newsprint copy of the ad. Calcutta police now report that "lacs of letters, from all over America" are arriving at the PO box there, but that the box's owner has not been found. Seattle police have been unable to locate the people, or even the press, that printed the ad. Copies continue to appear on phone poles. No one in either city has been apprehended.

Though the handwriting, stationery and fragrance are inimitable, the ad as it reads on the phone poles—with the anonymous scholar's translations added in brackets—follows.

KALI'S PERSONAL

Single Asian female; ageless; nonprofessional; new to America; searching for virile, confident, ambitious young males of any caste, color or physical description to whom to bare my perfect breasts and shining body and give ecstasies that leave you gasping for more. I never lie. From the moment you see me you will burn for me, you will never cease burning, and you will never once satisfy me though

you'll live only to try. You will
give me your love and I'll answer
with scorn. *Prāṇavatpraṇayi-kāli!*
[Kali is more precious than life!] You
will give me your life force and
I'll turn it into a house you will
hate, make you live in it, make
you slave for it, stuff you daily
into a car in which you'll hurl to
a job that shames, flays and
damns you, and seduce a thousand others while you slave.
Naha-rehā Kāli-kāranā oṁ karuṇam
harantu vo sarasā! [Let Kali's
nailmarks remove your pain, they'll
leave you rife with emotion!] You
will give me your seed and I will
surround you with sullen incomprehensible offspring who'll worship me with the same reasonless
intensity with which they'll de-
spise you. *Kāliya suciraṁ jayanti*
gagane vandhyāh karabhrāntayah!
[Let the meaningless motions of
Kali's hands in the sky triumph for-
ever!] You will give me your
mind, heart and lingam and I will
suck, twist and torment them all,
bloating you like a mosquito
when you enter my body, laughing at your feeble love thrusts,
striking you limp before you
come, seducing our sons if you
try to flee me, remaining radiant
as you grow desperate and old

and addled. *Kāli naccāviu paṅga-naivimhai pāḍiu lou muhur muhur mohahatā babhūvuh! [When Kali danced in the courtyard the world went berserk. Frenzy wracked everyone again and again!]* I never lie. And in the end I will mount you, and with the still-perfect breasts you'll beg to mouth, then find too heavy to turn aside, I will suffocate you, growing enflamed by you at last as you thrash your life away beneath me, driving my tongue down your throat to thwart even your death-rattle, moaning and coming as your soul falls out your rectum, drinking your blood in one draught. *Dolāloladghanajaghanayā kāliya yatra bhagnāh meher krīḍangaṅganavitapino nādhunāpy ucchvasanti! [Broken by the power of Kali's hips gone wild as she writhed, the trees in Compassion's garden have not recovered!]* I'll let you lie unmourned and unburied. I'll dance in the swamp of your festering body. I'll sing at last of love as your naked soul writhes in flames that I'll journey to hell just to fan. I'll hang your charred and sightless skull on my rosary, force your shrivelled wraith to inhabit it, and make you forgive and adore me for all of this. *Emvahim Kāli-*

*paoharaham jam bhavai tam hou!
[Let the glow of Kali's breasts endure!]*

I never lie.

Yet even now you begin to
want me. And how swiftly I
moisten to your desire, how fast
my nipples rise. I feel your heat.
My hips, my cavern answer. I
writhe as I write this. I anoint
breasts and thighs with my sweat
and sex, they glisten, they shine
now, only for you. Come, my
chosen. Do not dare deny me. I
am the nightmare you long to
wake to at dawn. I am the problem to all of your answers. I am
the time of your life and the life
of your times. *Gaurī! Caṇḍī!
Devī. Ambā, Ṭhākuraṁ! Kṛpaya
parayā-visto! Rudhirapradigdhān!
Kālī! [Fair one! Fierce one! Goddess,
Mother, Mistress! Filled with infinite
pity. Smeared with blood. Kali!]*

Another
Brutal Indian
Attack

for Sherman Alexie, and Diane, with blessings

THE INDIANS LIVED IN RAILROAD BOXCARS IN THE WOODS BE-
HIND MY BOYHOOD HOME. I NEVER SAW THEM COME AND GO,
COULDN'T SAY HOW THEY TRAVELED; THEY DIDN'T SEEM TO
OWN CARS. SOME PEOPLE TOLD ME THEY WERE RESERVATION
INDIANS, THOUGH NO ONE SEEMED ABLE TO NAME THE RESER-
VATION. OTHERS SAID THEY WERE "WILD," THEN LAUGHED AS
IF THEY'D MADE SOME SORT OF JOKE. ALL I KNEW FOR CER-
TAIN WAS THAT, COME JUNE, THE SAME THREE OR FOUR FAMI-
LIES, GIVE OR TAKE A MAN OR BABY, WOULD SHOW UP IN
THOSE BOXCARS THE WAY SPRING CHINOOK USED TO SHOW UP
IN LOCAL RIVERS AND STAY ON, LIKE THE SALMON, TILL FALL.
ALL I KNEW WAS THAT FOR A THIRD OF A YEAR, YEAR IN AND

year out, eighteen or twenty Indians were my nearest neighbors to the west.

A cranky old white guy, Jake Hartwig, let them live in the boxcars for free, but not as charity. Hartwig was a commercial raspberry grower and needed the Indians to harvest his berries. He needed me, too. It makes me feel like a history book footnote—an Indian feeling, maybe—but in the western Oregon of the early sixties, white kids and Indian families worked side by side in the fields of white or Japanese berry farmers. We made four to six cents a pound, depending on the type of berry. A good day for me, eight hours of picking, I'd make three dollars. But my low income was partially explained by my high output: my scats in those days were as seedy as a bear's. I had a hard time sticking fresh berries in a box when my mouth was just as available.

The boxcars were parked on a sidetrack no longer connected to a railway: just a few lengths of double-dead-ending rails rusting in the cottonwoods there. Old Man Hartwig inherited the cars from the railroad when a sidetrack was cut off by subdivisions and the cars were left stranded. They'd been standard freight cars in their day— Burlington Northerns, Southern Pacifics. They now had a couple of windows cut in each side, no bathrooms, no electricity, a potbellied stove for unnecessary heat and necessary cooking, and whatever comforts the occupants themselves could add to the tune of four to six cents a pound. Maybe folding chairs and a card table. Curtains in the front windows. Bunk beds to consolidate kids. Wildflowers in a wine bottle. Dogs, usually with puppies, congregated under the cars; cats with kittens, too, though each fall—when the Indians disappeared as suddenly and silently as they'd arrived—the kittens remained.

Old Man Hartwig did his best to keep the cars and their contents hidden from local eyes. But if there is any topic that pioneer-stock white folks feel compelled to gossip about, it's Indians. The talk bandied about the neighborhood detailed how "they" threw their garbage in the frog ponds behind the boxcars, how the pall from "their" outhouses drifted into "our" neighborhoods in hot weather, how "their" men drank themselves crazy, mean and blind. The middle-of-the-road position in our Judeo-Suburban stronghold was "Like 'em or not, Indians can't be trusted." The hardline stance was "Get 'em outta here before somebody gets sick or robbed or killed." But I was one of those renegade white kids trying to defy friends and live down pioneer forebears by including Indians among the neighbors Christ commanded us to love.

It was not yet a popular position. Kids like me caught flack from the ruling pragmatists for romanticizing Indians. But what choice did a Bible-raised kid have? "Love thy neighbor as thyself" is an outrageously romantic notion, "Love thine enemies" even more romantic. And my feelings were not just Bible-inspired: I'd been smitten from the time I was little by the sight of Wyampum men fishing the platforms at Celilo, by Tlingit and Kwakiutl carvings in local museums, by the occasional Indian athlete who'd light up the neighborhood gym or ball field, by the Paiute points I'd find along rivers—and by TV Cochises, Tontos and Mingos, too. So though I loathed berry picking, and wasn't any too fond of Old Man Hartwig either, there were three things I did like about working in his fields. One was the four to six cents a pound. Another was the raspberries. And the other was the presence of all those Indians.

ONE OF THE FIRST THINGS I NOTICED, WORKING WITH THEM in the fields, was that only the women and girls picked. The men seemed to prefer—just as gossip predicted—to stay drunk enough to be unable to tell red people from white, which was of course too drunk to tell red raspberries from green. I tried hard to rationalize this. I didn't yet know exactly what drink did to a person, but boxcars, garbage ponds, malicious gossip and outhouses all struck me as good reasons for a person to be something other than fully alert. Indian men shouldn't have been there at all, I'd tell myself. They should have been out hunting or fishing. But there was nothing to hunt in our suburbs, it wasn't salmon season, and the salmon runs were fading fast. So they drank—with a dedication that maybe suggested they'd have been equally dedicated fishermen/hunters, if only the world was different.

This kind of thinking was a stretch, though, and I knew it. The truth was that, face-to-face and close up, the men from the boxcars scared me. They scared me not because they looked dangerous but because they looked ruined, and it's hard, face-to-face, to romanticize ruin. They seemed beyond caring what happened to them, or to anyone—hardly aware of what happened, maybe. My own Grandpa Duncan—a striking man in photos, fine singer, father of two, legendary fisherman and hunter—got the same way, over in Montana, then vanished from our lives. And he scared me, too. That grown men red or white, living fathers and grandfathers, could grow sad enough to drink enough to get that ruined; that kids like me meant so little, could assuage their sorrow so little, that they still chose ruin. It scares me still.

The boys from the boxcars didn't scare me. They worried me, though. There were five of them, all under six, and they were usually—again in accord with white gossip—dirty. What gossip failed to mention was that they had nowhere to play but a dirt berryfield, and there was no plumbing in their boxcars. It wasn't the dirt that concerned me. It was when I'd greet the boys, call them by name, try to joke and get silly with them. Because nothing would happen. They weren't unfriendly, just unresponsive. And they were this way with everyone, even their own mothers, even each other. It gradually gave me the feeling that something was way less than right—that their food must be off, their water tainted, that they'd caught something inexplicable from their ruined dads. In time I stopped trying to buddy up and we'd just stare at each other, like rabbits or fish. It was the way they seemed to want it. And giving up on words like that did make me feel more like one of them.

The girls, for some reason, were different. The girls were so different they gave me hope for the boys. There were six of them, ranging from my age (around ten) to teenaged, and they were nothing like their fathers and utterly like their mothers. That was the hope. They were dignified, physically capable, alert, animated with each other, cautiously friendly to me. They also shared some wonderfully raunchy stories now and then—if they didn't know a white kid was eavesdropping a few rows away.

Another thing about them: they were the fastest fricking raspberry pickers on earth. I noticed this in a big way—because I was the fricking slowest. Even the youngest boxcar girls made five times what I made in a day. We'd start picking at 6 A.M., we all stacked our filled crates in the same storage shed, each stack had our name on it, and by noon or so—when I'd be lugging my second crate to the DAVID stack and some Indian girl would be heaving her tenth or twelfth up onto the MARCIE or CARMINE or RITA stack—nobody could even glance at me without bursting out laughing. Which always made me laugh right back. And sometimes it would catch, like fire. Sometimes there'd be laughter all over the berryfield as I trudged back to my infernal row. And when I'd hear the whole field go off in the boredom and heat and dust, I can't say how good it sounded. It made me smile till my cheeks ached; made me eat berries till I was sick; made me fill my crates slow as ever, just to get to hear that laughter rise up again.

THE LAST WEEK I PICKED AT HARTWIG'S AN INDIAN GIRL named Mary Margaret—the girl I liked best—suggested that I could speed things up by hiding dirt clods under the berries in my crate. Rocks were too heavy, she said. They'd create suspicion and might foul up the machinery at the jam factory. But dirt clods weighed in well and would dissolve on the conveyors when the berries got washed. I just laughed when she said this—and so did Mary Margaret. I figured she was joking. But amid the interminable boredom of the next day's picking I decided that, joke or not, it was a workable idea. So I put it to use.

I made decent money for three straight days after that.

Then I got caught.

Mary Margaret happened to be passing by just when Jake Hartwig fired me. He was enraged as he did it, wanted to make an example of me—and succeeded. I was simultaneously ashamed of myself, afraid he was going to hit me (which he didn't) and afraid he'd tell my parents (which he did). Yet what I remember so clearly is not an irate old man dismantling me; it's Mary Margaret's face. She stood a couple of rows away, watching, her expression neutral as an owl's: no amusement, no visible fear, no sadness or sympathy either. Yet she remained there until the old man was finished, her eyes riveted to mine. I never saw her again after that long, strange moment, so I've wondered, I've been half-haunted, by what that stare signified. Had the dirt clod trick been honestly shared to dishonestly help me, and was she sorry that it backfired? Had we become friends? Or did she have a few clods tucked in her own crates and fear the white boy would tell where the idea came from—fear, even, that her whole family could be kicked out of their boxcar home simply because she'd joked with or pitied or trusted an outsider like me?

I don't know. And it was Indians, "like 'em or not," who I'd been told not to trust. But one thing I'm sure of, regarding those dirt clods: *I'm* the one who hid them in my berries; I'm the one who cheated Old Man Hartwig; I'm the one who put an end to the best, the most biblical, the most neighborly thing that happened between those Indians and me—which was the whole pack of us laughing because the white boy picked so slow.

. . .

A FEW WEEKS AFTER I WAS FIRED, AN INDIAN MAN STOLE THE tetherball off the pole in our backyard and hocked it for a bottle of wine. There was no evidence, no clue whatever to the thief's identity. I assumed a neighbor kid who liked to play tetherball stole it. My father, though, said it was a boxcar Indian from the start. Acting on that assumption, he drove to the only pawnshop within walking distance of our house, found my tetherball for sale on the wall there, asked who'd brought it in and, sure enough, it had been an Indian man. "A thirsty one," the pawnbroker said. Dad bought the ball back for two bucks—twice the price of the muscatel the Indian fella got for it—and returned it to me with a What-did-I-tell-you expression. I hung it back up on the pole, and that was that. Nobody stole it again, and I took up basketball anyway. Old age eventually destroyed the tetherball.

But a few days after the theft there was a heat wave, and our upstairs bedrooms were flat-roofed, like a boxcar, which made them boiling hot. So my oldest brother and I toted our sleeping bags and army surplus cots out into the backyard, set them up at the edge of the woods and were lying beneath the alders there, listening to the whispery calls of fledgling screech owls, when I heard an odd jingling sound back in the woods.

I looked up, saw nothing. But it was suddenly, unnaturally quiet. My brother didn't notice, he was telling a story, but the owls had stopped whispering. And there it was again: a quick jingling, Santa's sleigh out of season. I turned toward it—

and there was a man. The broad-shouldered, hunched silhouette of a man sneaking from tree to tree. Obviously aware that my brother and I were lying there. Obviously heard us talking. And now, obviously, stalking us. The jingling was the change in his pockets, the keys, maybe the knife.

I grabbed my brother, pointed, whispered, "There's a *man!*"

From behind his tree, invisible, the man snickered and said, "There's a *man!*" right back. He was making fun of my voice, my terror. He was teasing, as if he knew me. And drunks are that way. Drunks live in a soup that makes them think they know everybody. That was all the clue I needed: it was the Indian who stole my tetherball. Him, or another just like him. And he was plastered, crazy drunk, he didn't care what happened, hardly knew what was happening. But he was coming for us. For no reason, or crazy-drunk-pissed-off-Indian reasons, he was coming, was already too close: zipped in our bags, we'd be unable to jump out and run when he made his final lunge.

He lurched, he jingled, he sniggered his way to the next trunk. He was one tree away now. He was huge. We heard his stifled snorts, his crazed breathing. We couldn't move, couldn't think, couldn't shout.

He stepped from behind the tree. He came for us.

It was my father.

NORTHWEST PASSAGE

WHEN I WAS SIXTEEN AND HATED HIGH SCHOOL, ONE OF THE THINGS I DID TO GET THROUGH A SCHOOL DAY WAS RIP PICTURES OUT OF MAGAZINES. I DID THIS IN THE SCHOOL LIBRARY, AND THE MAGAZINES BELONGED TO THE SCHOOL: THE RIPPING WAS A DELIBERATE ACT OF VANDALISM. BUT I ONLY STOLE PHOTOS I LOVED. AND I FELT THAT, IN TAKING THEM HOME TO MY BEDROOM, I WAS STEALING THEM AWAY TO A BETTER LIFE THAN THE ONE THEY'D LED IN THE LIBRARY.

I HAD FESTOONED MY BEDROOM—FLOOR, WALLS AND CEILING—WITH BLANKETS, CHEAP IMPORTED TAPESTRIES, WOODEN CRATES AND SHEEPSKINS. IT LOOKED MORE LIKE THE INTERIOR OF A DESERT BEDOUIN'S TENT THAN THE GENERIC SHEETROCKED CUBICLE IT WAS. WHEN I'D GET MY STOLEN photos into my "tent" I'd prop them like books in front of me, light candles or kerosene lanterns before them, stare at them till they swallowed me, and virtually worship the daydreams, wanderlust and longings these makeshift icons allowed me to feel.

One such photo, plundered from a *National Geographic,* was of the confluence of the Ganges and Jumna rivers in India. It depicted a barren, boulder-strewn plateau beneath a range of mountains. You could see white water churning in the background. But the place was stripped of vegetation, desolate, and would have held no photographic interest at all if the rocky plain along the river hadn't been strewn with huts. *Hundreds* of huts. Maybe a thousand of them. Crude, leaky, diminutive hovels no red-blooded American would dream of keeping a lawnmower in. Yet in these, men were living. "Holy men," the caption called them. In any case long-bearded, huge-eyed, emaciated men, just existing on the rocks by the river there. And the reason they chose to do this, so the caption maintained, was that "the rishis of ancient India considered the confluence of two or more rivers to be a sacred place."

I couldn't have explained why I found this riverside ghetto so appealing. Trying to hone in on my feelings with the help of a dictionary, I looked up the word *holy* and in the margins of the photo wrote "1. hallowed by association with the divine, hence deserving of reverence; 2. inviolable; not to be profaned." But weeks passed and understanding did not deepen. I was still in a kind of love with the confluence-dwelling holy men and still unable to say why, when an old friend named Jered asked me to go fishing.

It was early on a school day, in mid-October. Jered's plan was to try for jack and silver salmon that very afternoon—which we'd lengthen slightly by cutting our last class. Jered and I had been fishing buddies as kids, inseparable for a season or two. In the years between I prided myself on having changed completely, while Jered prided himself on not having changed at all. I'd become a hippie; Jered still had a crew cut; I aspired (with no success) to vegetarianism; Jered was still shooting, cleaning and happily devouring scores of the indigenous mammals and birds of the Northwest; I was anti-war, Jered was ready to kill who he was told; I was trying to piece together some sort of crazy-quilt bhakti/Wishram/Buddhistic/ball-playing mysticism to live by; Jered was your basic working-class, Consciousness One, Huntin'-n'-Fishin' type guy. But I said yes for three reasons. The first was that we shared a respect, despite all differences, based on the fact that we each considered the other to be the best fisherman we knew. The second was that he had enough boraxed salmon roe for both of us, and the fishing had been, in his rudimentary but reliable diction, "hot." And the third reason, the decisive one, was that the place he proposed to fish was one the rishis of ancient India held sacred: a joining of rivers—this one in downtown Camas, Washington, where Lacamas Creek and the Washougal River both met the Columbia, and the Crown Zellerbach papermill met them all.

I knew, before going, that this confluence would be a place I would hate. I'd lived within sight and smell of the Crown Z mill, directly across the Columbia, all my life. My plan for the day, though—having read of the ancient rishis—was to see whether it might be possible to love what I also hate.

TO GET TO OUR CONFLUENCE WE DROVE HALF AN HOUR down the Oregon side of the Columbia, half an hour back up the Washington side, then parked in the Crown Z visitors' lot. Ignoring the NO TRESPASSING, HIGH VOLTAGE and DANGER signs, we passed through a hole in a cyclone fence, detoured round a gigantic mill building, crossed disused railroad tracks and bulldozed fields, reached the Washougal's last long riffle. We clambered downstream through brambles and scrub willow. We eased in alongside another huge mill wall, in front of which lay a kind of bay. The confluence proper— the exact spot where the crystal-clear Washougal blended with the complicated greens of the Columbia—turned out to be a slow, fishy-looking glide directly below the mill wall, just at the neck of the bay.

The riverbank there was interesting: it was made of hard-packed clay; bare rock; spilled oil; logging cable; shards of every kind and color of pop, beer and booze bottle; flood-crushed car and appliance parts; slabs of broken concrete with rebar sticking out of them; driftwood; drift Styrofoam; drift tires and reject mill parts— *huge* reject mill parts.

We found a rusted sprocket the size of a merry-go-round and sat on it.

Our legs fit perfectly between the teeth.

We had come, I felt in my very center, to a joining of everything that created, sustained and warped us. The question was: was it a viable home? Was it still somehow holy? Or was I, with my Bedouin bedroom and stolen Oriental photos, right to long only for escape?

We began setting up the odd tackle we'd together come to prefer: a stiff fiberglass fly rod and light spinning reel (mine open-faced, his closed); monofilament line a third the test of that used by most salmon fishermen (to increase casting distance). There wasn't a holy man in sight. There wasn't any kind of human in sight. The mill rumbled behind us like an insatiable stomach; tugs dragged log rafts up Crown Z's own private slough; a dredge worked the slough a half-mile downriver; trucks and cars whished along the jettied highway across the bay; ships and barges plowed the Columbia beyond. It was the machines you saw and heard, though, not the people inside them. Industrial men, not holy ones. Them's the kind we grew in these parts.

Yet it was still beautiful at the confluence. We could see east to the Cascade foothills, west clear to the Coast Range, and an enormous piece of Oregon lay across the river to the south. There is a Gangian majesty to the lower Columbia, and something awesome, if not holy, in knowing its currents are made of the glaciers, springs, desert seeps and dark industrial secrets of two Canadian provinces and six American states. When I kept my eyes on distant vistas, or on the two waters blending at our feet, I could even imagine some kind of "association with the divine" here. Though I'd no faith in the wisdom of the resident machine operators, I could picture Indians, the American kind, watching these same mountains while awaiting these same fish, some of them maybe knowing what the rishis knew.

But when I turned, as I had known I must, to the third waterway, things immediately began to break down. I knew, from studying maps, that a creek named Lacamas—a genuine little river— entered the Crown Zellerbach mill on the opposite side from us. I knew this creek headed in the mountains north of Camas, and that it'd had its own run of salmon once. But the mill-used fluid that shot from the flume just downstream from our sprocket bore no resemblance to water. It looked like hot pancake batter, gushing forth in a quantity so vast that part of me found it laughable. It looked like Satan's own nostril risen from hell, blowing out an infinite, scalding booger. But it was a steaming, poisonous, killing joke that shot across the Washougal's drought-shriveled mouth in a yellow-gray scythe, curved downstream and coated the Columbia's north shore with what looked like dead human skin for miles. And maybe a rishi could have pondered it and still felt equanimity. All I could feel, though, just as I'd feared, was fury and impotence and sickness. I said nothing to Jered—who'd merely pinched his nose, said, *"Pyoo!"* and set about fishing. I just squeezed my eyes shut, tried the same with my brain and waited for my friend to take us elsewhere. But I couldn't help but hear the flume's diarrheal gushing.

And then, over the gushing, a strange double splash.

The first half of the splash was a bright coho salmon. The second half was its echo, bouncing so hard off the mill wall behind us that I turned to the sound, half-expecting to see yet another river running through the rubble and broken glass.

"Look!" Jered whispered as a second bright coho leapt high in the evening light, fell back in the river—and again the loud, clean echo. Then another one leapt, and another, all amazingly high, all in the same place—a point in midriver, just upstream from the toxic scythe.

My first impulse, lip-service vegetarianism and all, was to grab my rod. A big school of silvers was clearly moving in. But Jered, the unabashed carnivore, had stopped fishing; he just stood watching and listening now. I would not have done the same if he hadn't set the example, but I too grew satisfied to watch: for those salmon leaps were language. They were the salmon people's legend, enacted before our eyes. And though we'd heard the old story a thousand times, thought we knew it by rote, there was a twist, at this confluence, that we two sons of these same troubled waters needed to sit still and hear.

The familiar part of the story, the rote chorus, told how these unlikely creatures had been born way up this mountain river, had grown strong in it, then had left it for the Pacific; yet some impression of their birthplace, some memory or scent touched them years and leagues later in that vastness, brought them schooling in off the Columbia's mouth, forced them to run the gauntlet of nets, hooks and predators, search the big river's murky greens, solve the riddle and enter again the waters of their fatal, yet life-giving, home. Then came the twist—in the shape of a scythe.

Salmon are not stupid. They grow tentative in rivers. They know when to spook, and when to wait quietly; when to leap, when to hide, when to fight for their lives. As these coho entered the confluence and tasted the scythe they must surely have tried everything—must have hesitated, sought another channel, circled back out into the Columbia, come round again and again, waiting for the pain of the thing to diminish, for rain to fall, for rivers to rise, for industries to die. But salmon have no choice: their great speed and long journeys, like ours, create an illusion of freedom, but to live as a race they must finally become as much a part of their river as its water and its stones. So in the end, they entered. With eyes that can't close and breath that can't be held they darted straight into this confounding of the vast, the pure and the insane. And the slashing leaps that now shattered the river's surface were each the coho word for their cold, primordial rage against whatever it was that maimed them—and their equally cold, primordial joy at having reached the waters of their home.

So we never did fish that day, Jered and I. We just sat like a couple of Ganges River hut-jockeys on a reject mill sprocket, watching salmon leap as the day grew dark. Yet after each leap my breath caught as the splash resounded, impossibly loud, against the walls of the mill, and the surface rings tripled, at least for an instant, the two dimensions of the killing scythe. Feeling a frail hope welling, feeling a need to memorize, for life, this same wild leap and passage, I suddenly began to dread my old fishing partner—or to dread, at least, the Consciousness One, Huntin'-n'-Fishin' type summary I expected him to make at any moment, thus crew-cutting the beauty off of all that we were seeing.

But when I finally did turn to my stick-in-the-mud friend, he didn't even notice me, and in his eyes, which were brimming, I saw nothing but that same cold anger, and that same wild joy. Jered was not watching fish jump. He was raging and exulting with the coho as if they were *our* people; as if ours were the ancient instincts that had sorted the Columbia's countless strands, ours the unclosing eyes the scythe betrayed and blinded, ours the bright bodies leaping and falling back into the home waters—falling just to burst them apart; just to force them to receive, even now, our gleaming silver sides.

THE GARBAGE MAN'S DAUGHTER

Day creeps down. The moon is creeping up . . .
Ho ho . . . The dump is full of images . . .
Is it peace,
Is it a Philosopher's honeymoon, one finds
On the dump? Is it to sit among mattresses of the dead,
Bottles, pots, shoes and grass and murmur aptest eve;
Is it to hear the blatter of grackles and say
Invisible priest; is it to eject, to pull
the day to pieces and cry stanza my stone?
Where was it one first heard the truth? The the.

—Wallace Stevens, from "The Man on the Dump"

1. The Happy Ending

My parents' life before me, to hear them tell of it, was a fairy tale. My unlikely birth, to hear them tell of it, was the happy ending to that tale. They are trying to be kind when they say this—trying to express gratitude for my entry into their world. But what I hear loudest when they call me their "happy ending" is the word "ending."

The fairy tale of my parents' married life before me (allowing for the slightly specious tone of an outsider) goes like this:

Once upon a time in a Pacific Northwest city there lived a fat, friendly schoolbus driver named Esther Jones who, oddly enough, enjoyed her work.

Once upon the same time, and once a week or so upon the same schoolbus driver, there lived a sad-faced but good-hearted Safeway cashier named William Jones who, not at all oddly, did not enjoy his work, but who was too disinterested to bulldoze his way into a managership, too proud to brown-nose his way into an assistant managership, too lazy to seek work elsewhere and too confused to know what work he'd have sought anyhow, since all he'd ever really wanted to be was a ship's captain—a nineteenth-century clipper ship, no less, with three towering rows of white sails.

Esther the schoolbus driver had once entertained a similarly lofty and unworkable desire. Ever since her days as a white-bloused, wool-skirted and knee-socked student at Our Lady of Bitter Sorrows School for Girls, she'd wanted to become a nun, provided the nun she became was a perfect replica of Saint Teresa of Avila. After meeting William, however, she decided that nunhood might be superfluous to sanctity, and set her sights on an urbanized, schoolbus-driving sainthood, the details of which she'd work out as she went along.

William and Esther met at a high school homecoming dance, fell in love at fourth or fifth sight, went steady for a year, were engaged for another, had a small family wedding, made a down payment on a tract house in a rowdy, mixed-race neighborhood and proceeded to transport young scholars, bag grocks, pay off the domicile and suffer a horrendous string of DES-inflicted miscarriages for the next two decades. But despite twenty years of insipid work, insipid health, an insipid house and a future spared from insipidity by little more than Presbyterian promises of an insipid-sounding heaven, William and Esther still loved each other—or so they redundantly maintained. And even according to friends and neighbors, an eccentric mutual regard did indeed seem to be in operation.

Everywhere the Joneses went they went together, engaging along the way in such superannuated activities as hand-holding, out-loud-reading and sweet-nothing-whispering. And week after week, year in and year out, they kept buying each other the kind of trinkets, bouquets and surprises we associate with the very first stages of romance. They also did dishes together, weeded flowerbeds together, scrubbed toilet bowls and bathroom tiles and went shopping together, bowled, Putt-Putt golfed, shot snooker together. And the vintage Lincoln Continental in which they traveled—"The Honky Clipper," William had christened it—lent a ponderous mystique to all these comings and goings.

Enviers and ill-wishers used to hope that since William was a Republican and Esther a Democrat, politics might pop their tenacious romantic bubble. But William was the most radical of Republicans, Esther the most spiritual of Democrats, and every election season "The Honky" captain and his lady-love struggled through the *entire* voter's pamphlet together, discussing each impenetrable issue and tedious candidate till they were in complete agreement—and not out of civic-mindedness, but simply because they couldn't bear the thought of canceling out each other's votes.

Religion was, of course, another subject with bubble-popping potential: Esther, as her adoration of Teresa implied, was a devout closet Catholic; William was a befuddled agnostic loudly devoted, like most agnostics, to his befuddlement. But every Sunday the agnostic and Catholic navigated the Lincoln to a whitewashed, wishy-washy Presbyterian church, entered hand in hand and found the anemic sermons and milk-toast hymns to be the perfect spiritual compromise.

Once upon a time, then, an aspiring saint and Continental captain were muddling along rather nicely when, shortly after their fortieth birthdays, Esther became pregnant for the sixth time in her life. Ever true to their respective visions, Esther proceeded for the sixth time to look forward to the birth of a first child, while William battened down the hatches in expectation of a sixth financial, physical and emotional disaster. But this time, for the first time, the third month of pregnancy passed without mishap, then the fourth, then the fifth. Esther's belly continued to swell. When, during the sixth month, tiny knees and elbows began making odd, oceanic ripples upon that swell, Esther quit driving schoolbuses and made ready the new family member's room. But not till the tenth month, not till the very moment the doctor thrust my slippery body into his disbelieving hands, would William admit that I indeed appeared to have been born. Like a good closet Catholic, Esther laughed and thanked God. Like a good agnostic, William cried, "I don't believe it!" and thanked Esther. Then, in keeping with the laws of their tandem paradise, they compromised yet again, naming me after Esther's improbable Spanish heroine, but also after the only "ship" William had ever actually owned—a small salmon-fishing dory, bought on a whim, beloved but never used, and sold for a song after it sank in its moorage: Dory Teresa Jones.

THAT, MORE OR LESS, IS THE FAIRY TALE. MY PARENTS, ACcording to that tale, lived in a wonderland built of their love for each other, my birth was the culmination of that love and we all lived happily ever after. What this happy-ever-after leaves out is that I was soon to become the assassin of their love. My arrival, happy or not, eventually blasted William and Esther out of their fragile wonderland into the late twentieth century, with all the tension, horror and nonsense that implies. I have long since fled the nest, and they have long since rearranged their lives accordingly. But that rearrangement is not the original fairy tale. They're old now, and tired, and sometimes tired of each other. Sometimes, now, they tell each other so—in very un-fairy-tale-like ways.

For this change, this loss, my father blames me. He doesn't come right out and say it—in fact he still insists that he loves me, still sends Xmas and birthday gifts, still telephones now and then to chat, still plays Father. But there is a resentment-tinged perfunctoriness to his performance, and we both know it. My existence brought unromantic complications to a marriage that had been the joy of his life. I can't undo those complications. I can't give him his fairy tale back. So what *can* I do?

It's an option, I suppose, to resent him in return. But resentment strikes me as a boomerang emotion—the carcinogenic form of forgiveness, maybe. The way my parents and I believed and disbelieved in each other when I was little, the way we created and confused, encouraged and thwarted, loved and misloved each other, is a sad story. But it could also be seen as a *good* story. The only ingredient missing, in my opinion, is forgiveness.

So I'm heading back to the time of our trouble. I'm heading back to who we were to begin with, and who we coerced each other into becoming. I'm heading all the way back—and this time, William and Esther, I hope to bring you with me—to The Dump.

2. THE BUDDHA OF FACTS

William and Esther imagined, during my infancy, that they had incorporated me into their sweet, private wonderland. But from the moment I began developing a self to express, that self proved to be fairy-tale-resistant. My earliest memories aren't early enough to help diagnose this resistance, but if I were to guess where it came from, I'd say that the romantic bubble in which William and Esther thrived might, from my perspective, have felt more like a cellophane bag I needed to poke a hole in, to avoid suffocation.

In any case, from as far back as I can remember I was a little girl with a mission in life. That mission was to deal in facts. No levitating saints or dream clipper ships for this kid. The facts were contemporary; the facts were inanimate and uncaring; above all, the facts were *real*. And no matter how dull, grisly or difficult to countenance they might be, the facts were to be faced, then responded to as logically as possible.

My first complete sentence was a statement of fact, uttered while sailing the city asphalt in The Honky Clipper. It was "See the dead doggie."

Being the sort of father who found everything his daughter did astounding, William was too amazed by the sentence to do anything but gawk. Esther, however, provided me with an additional fact: "Yes, poor thing," she said. "Hit by a car."

As parental legend has it, I scowled with concentration as I processed this reply, then responded with impeccable one-and-a-half-year-old logic. A car had killed the dog. We were ourselves riding in a car. I therefore began to howl, *"No kill doggie! No kill doggie!"* and refused to be consoled till William had curbed The Clipper. From that day forward I proved impossible to coax into any internally combusting conveyance without first exacting from its driver a life-threatening vow to mangle no animals of any kind.

Further examples of my fact-facing mission:

—For my third birthday I requested a subscription to *National Geographic*.

—A half year or so later I abruptly stopped calling my parents

"Mom" and "Dad" because I considered their actual names more factual.

—At my fourth birthday party, William's sister, Helen, presented me with one of the vacuous-visaged, intricately-plumbed, TV-advertised dolls of the day. After listening carefully to her claim that "Dollie cries real tears and makes real peepee," I picked the thing up, squeezed a bit of fluid from its "peepee" hole directly into my mouth, tasted it, swallowed it, handed the doll back to its appalled purchaser and replied, "It's just water, Auntie H. Dollies are fake. I only play with animals and peoples. Animals and peoples are *real.*"

—Shortly before my fifth Xmas I told William and Esther: "Please don't sign my presents 'From Santa' this year. There is no Santa, and I don't need presents. If you really want to give me something, I wouldn't mind a gyroscope. But don't sign it 'From Santa,' please."

—When I received a gyroscope (appropriately unsigned), I instituted a ritual of spinning the thing for thirty minutes a day while watching "The CBS Evening News."

—One evening, during the CBS News & Gyroscope Rite, Aunt Helen stopped by, studied me for a moment, then thought to ask (due to the infamous Peepee-hole Incident) why I was playing with a gyroscope, it being neither an animal nor a person. Keeping a perfectly straight face as I stared at the equally straight face of Dan Rather, I replied, "I'm not playing, Auntie H. I'm studying. Animals and peoples live on a planet. I'm studying how a planet spins." Helen had no further questions.

BY THIS TIME, WILLIAM AND ESTHER HAD NO HOPE OF EVER incorporating me into their own or any other kind of fairy tale. On the contrary, they were scrambling to show how much they loved me by incorporating *themselves* into my obsession with facts. By nature, though, they were as uninterested in my obsession as I had been in their marital fairy tale. It's funny how bored we can be with the interests of those we love. And how blind to the long-term effects of those interests. William and Esther never asked what I hoped to achieve with my increasingly vast heap of facts. They never seemed to wonder what satisfactions, what dreams, what terrors my facts were giving me. For the most part they just adored me, and fed me what facts they had at their disposal as if they were the fuel upon which I ran.

They found my CBS News & Gyroscope Rite so adorable that they took many snapshots of it. I've got a faded Kodachrome in front of me now. It shows a skinny five-year-old girl dressed like a boy; oversized brown eyes; grave little hyphen of a mouth; pale skin with a definite blue cast, thanks to the TV. Her posture is that of a Buddha statue. Her expressionless face is glued to the face of a youthful, equally expressionless Dan Rather. Her gyroscope is spinning where Buddha's upturned palms would be. It is a serious pose, despite a superfluous cuteness. There is something almost iconographic about it. I can see why my parents were beguiled, and felt that the rite expressed something essential about me. But I can also see in the snapshot, far more clearly than I can remember feeling, how lonely and sad the little girl looks. Determined though I was to become the Buddha of Televised Facts, it is obviously not one of the happier incarnations.

As I BECAME AWARE THAT WILLIAM AND ESTHER HAD BEGUN to find my obsession with facts adorable, I tried my damnedest to become even more obsessed. Soon I was not just watching the CBS news, I was memorizing big chunks of it and quoting it back to anyone who'd listen. Soon I was playing not just with a gyroscope but with science kits, microscopes, chemistry sets, power tools, at the same time spurning stuffed animals, dolls, playhouses, commercial toys and every kid in the neighborhood who would not spurn the same—which was, before long, every kid in the neighborhood. Noticing my solitariness, my parents helped me fill it not by encouraging new friendships, but by buying me an aquarium and an endless supply of fish; a terrarium and an endless supply of snakes, lizards, turtles; cages full of hamsters, white and brown rats, guinea pigs, mice, and so on. I thanked them (with the most blandly matter-of-fact thank you imaginable), then concealed my desperate affection for my pets by giving them numbers instead of names, by breeding them and by working scientific experiments on them.

I set out to memorize facts by the thousand, to make as many arcane, fact-based pronouncements as possible, to speak in robotically even tones no matter what my emotional state. I set out to erase all signs of childhood from my mind, my bedroom and my behavior. And—except for a few crucial vestiges that I was utterly unaware of—I pretty well succeeded. By the time I was six, William, Esther and every other adult friend of the family believed that I was a genuine genius/nerd/prodigy pursuing a bizarre solo dharma. By the time I was six I neither asked for nor was ever again offered a stuffed animal or doll. By the time I was six, the CBS news, gyroscopes, lab rats, facts and physics were all I would allow myself to combat every misery, mystery and fear that life on earth had to offer. By the time I was six I had no friends my own age, had become virtually non-befriendable and believed with all my might that this was exactly the way I wanted it.

And William and Esther—wanting nothing but my happiness—aided and abetted me in every way. They had no idea what my life felt like. And I, believing my feelings to be irrelevant to the fact of me, never told them. On the evening, for instance, that a bathtub experiment ran amok and I accidentally drowned Hamster #4, I hid in the dark of our basement for hours so that they wouldn't see me crying, and told them, when I finally emerged, that I'd been working on an experiment involving darkness and the speed of dilation of the pupils.

3. PROPHECIES

Every child's daily desire is basically the same: what kids want from their day is the maximum number of opportunities to exercise their imaginations and bodies via the myriad activities known as "play." In America's vast, cloned suburbs the toys of choice in my day were things like G.I. Joes, Kermit the Frogs and Barbies. In the war zones of the same era the toys of choice were spent cartridges, military insignia and broken guns. The play urge in children is so strong that they will indulge it no matter what imaginary fodder, what play-grounds or what toy materials fate may offer them. That is how the toys, in my mirthless, self-imposed world of facts, became the wars, famines, serial killings, environmental debacles, hate crimes, sex crimes and congressional and presidential lies I watched nightly on the news.

The strangeness of these toys is the only explanation I have for the strangeness of a second ritual I introduced to the family routine: the Suppertime Doom Prophecy.

MY FIRST PROPHECY WAS MADE ONE EVENING WHEN I WAS seven and toying with a plateful of Chinese take-out. The words were born of sheer impulse—a sudden desire to play, in company, with one of the news-toys I carried around constantly in my head. What I suddenly said to my parents, without premeditation, was "I think I'll die soon, probably of cancer, a car crash or sniper fire."

Needless to say, they were not prepared. As had by then become his habit, William bestowed the Incredulous Gawk. Meanwhile Esther, with a look of shock that rapidly melted into deep concern, gasped, "Why on earth do you say *that*, Dory dear?"

My reply—"I don't want to talk about it"—was again sheer impulse: Dan Rather never discussed his shocking statements, so why should I? But I could see that this reticence upset them even more deeply. And I was intrigued by the consternation I'd so effortlessly evoked.

"If you don't want to talk about it," William had asked, "why did you mention it?"

"I just thought I should tell you," I said—another impulsive remark, "so you wouldn't feel too bad if anything happened."

They both paled. William then launched a garbled, fear-tinged monologue on the irrefutability of statistics, the consolation of probability and the long life expectancy of American women. Esther mumbled something about the side-effects of MSG, made an outloud mental note to avoid Chinese take-out, and let William yammer on. But watching their troubled faces, I felt in awe of my own power. When a lifelong emotionless little fact-facer suddenly blurts some random ghastliness, it has the factual *umph* of counterfeit money. I had no idea what I wanted to purchase with my fake money, but I sure did want to see whether my parents would mistake it for the real thing again.

So the following night—over a bowl of homemade potato soup that nixed Esther's MSG theory—I suddenly remarked, "I'm not exactly sure what rape is, but I think before long I'm going to have to find out."

Once again I'd bowled a strike. My parents looked flattened. William repeated the previous night's Gawk, and Esther again gasped, "Why on earth do you say *that*, Dory dear?" So I again said, "I don't want to talk about it." But this time we *did* talk about it. And what my counterfeit prophesy turned out to have purchased was weapons: weapons that wounded—in a way that neither politics, religion nor miscarriages had ever done before—my parents' marriage.

"Has anyone threatened or frightened you?" Esther asked first.

I shook my head. (And I should confess that my fear of rape in those days was nil: I was just playing with another news-toy.)

"You're just warning us again," Esther asked, her voice trembling, "so we won't feel too bad if something happens?"

I nodded.

Then William said, "Hey! What's that knocking?"

But Esther and I didn't hear anything.

"There's someone at the door," he insisted—with a deranged smile. Then, in a perfectly convivial tone, he called out, "Ah! Mr. Rapist. Come in. Dory told us you'd be coming, so we don't feel too bad that you're here. Would you like to rape her right in front of us, or up in one of the bedrooms?"

"Stop!" Esther shrieked.

William and I gaped at her. The shriek was unprecedented—Esther's loudest and angriest husband-directed sound in nearly thirty years of marriage. True, William's chat with "Mr. Rapist" had been more or less depraved. But in William's defense, he was trying to "make a point." And he'd *always* had a tendency to wax caustic, or grandiosely ironic, when he was scared. He used to tease Esther, for instance, by calling her breasts (which are very large) "hooters," yet the year his own beloved mother died (an event that left him a wreck for months), he had informed us of the fatal diagnosis by saying, in a voice breaking with genuine grief and fear, "Mom's got hooter cancer." His rapist-at-the-door outburst was the same kind of thing: grossly inappropriate words born of real concern. And Esther would normally have corrected him with a mere look. But because she, too, was terrified by my topic, she'd shrieked. And William's feelings were doubly hurt when, after this watershed outburst, she didn't even allow him to apologize: she paid him no heed at all.

"Dory dear, listen," she said with the same look of huge compassion she'd shown me the night before. "I know you're interested in facts. But you realize, don't you, that the future is *never* an established fact?"

"Yes," I replied in my most Dan Ratherish manner. "But, as William reported last night, you can predict bits of the future by studying facts from the past. We're all going to die, for instance. And some day the sun's going to burn out, or else the earth's going to get sucked into it and burn up. We know this. We can't fight it. We also know about the increase in rape in cities all across America. So before I get much older, it's a pretty sure thing that—"

"No need to elaborate!" William interrupted, again looking deranged. "I *have* seen a lot of raped kids limpin' around the neighborhood lately. And a fair number dead of cancer and sniper fire, too. Given the stats on folks choking to death at supper, we'll be lucky to live out the evening at this table, by the way. And then once we're in bed, of course, the Break-in Murder Stats kick in. It'll be a miracle if we all three make it as far as morning. But if we do, the A.M. Rush Hour Fatal Collision Stats'll just be waitin' to send our faces smashin' through the—"

"*William!*" Esther's second shriek in thirty years. "You're talking to a *seven-year-old child!*"

"You mean I'm talking *like* our seven-year-old child!" he roared back.

"Please," I said, stunned by the chaos I'd created—but still straight-faced. "Don't fight, you guys. It's no big deal. Let's just forget the whole thing."

"Easier said than done!" William muttered.

At which point Esther excused them both and dragged William off to their bedroom, where they spent the better part of an hour debating the propriety of sarcasm in dealing with a child. And —another ominous first in their marriage—the debate went unresolved.

I wasn't finished with them, either. The following night, after William and I waited, as we always did, for Esther to recite her silent premeal prayer, I said: "Esther? Do you believe a real God actually *hears* you when you do that?"

"I most certainly do!" she said fervently.

"Could you send a message to Him for me, then?" I asked.

"I'd be happy to, dear!" she cried, delighted by my uncharacteristic interest.

Her delight was premature. "Please tell Him that I don't understand Him," I said, "and that I don't like Him, and that I think He might be sick, mentally, if He even has a mind."

William turned on The Gawk. Esther blurted, "Dory! Why would you want me to tell God *that?*"

"Because of the world," I said. "God made it, right? And *look* at it."

"But the world is a *beautiful* thing!" Esther argued.

"You're just saying that," I told her. "It's a horrible thing and you know it."

"The world is both terrible *and* beautiful, isn't it?" William said, desperate to impress his lady-love by transcending the caustic tone of the night before.

"Maybe it is," I told him, "but this is none of your business."

"Dory!" Esther cried. "God is *everybody's* business!"

"But *you* talk to God," I calmly replied. "William doesn't. Asking William to send God a message is like picking up the toaster to make a phone call."

"She's got a point!" William laughed.

"She may have a point," Esther said, "but I'll relay no such message. You can be perfectly honest with God, Dory, no matter how unhappy you are with Him. Even the saints, even Teresa herself, complained to Him at times. You're welcome to criticize Him, question Him, you can discuss *anything* with God, honey. And if you listen close enough, don't be surprised if you get a *wonderful* reply!"

"And don't be surprised if you don't," William added.

"Don't worry," I said. "I won't."

During the following, and final, night's message of doom, I experimented with the strangest news-toy yet: the nightmares the news gave me. I'd had recurring nightmares ever since my CBS News & Gyroscope Rite began, but had said nothing about them to my parents for the simple reason that nightmares aren't facts. After the last few nights' prophecies, though, I'd come to suspect that my nightmares, expressed in broad daylight, might scare William and Esther even more than they scared me. Having never seen anybody that scared, I was curious: so curious that I convinced myself that I was working a legitimate scientific experiment. Of course there *was* no scientific legitimacy to my Suppertime Doom Prophecies. But I believe, in retrospect, that they possessed spiritual legitimacy. I'd begun to sense—in an instinctual, childish way belied by my Dan Ratherish manner—that my role as a Facer of Facts had become a prison cell. I wanted, in my inarticulate way, either to blast my way out of that prison or to yank my parents into it to keep me company. So blast and yank I did. And once again, my childish blast hit my parents with the force of sheer fact. But once again, what I ended up blasting was not my prison of facts, but my parents' love for each other.

My opening statement—made over a dessert of raspberry Jell-O that would eventually become a prop in our discussion—was this: "I'm pretty sure our deaths will all be violent. I'm pretty sure that Esther is going to die first, then me, then—"

"Oh for *Christ's sake!*" my father shouted.

"William!" Esther shouted. "Don't shout at Dory! And don't swear!"

"What makes you think I wasn't praying?" he retorted.

"You don't pray and you know it!" Esther snapped.

"Well, Dory's enough to make me start!" he snapped back. "Dory honey, for Christ's sake! We *all* have morbid fantasies. I sometimes dream I open the front door and a stranger is standing there. He smiles a perfectly pleasant smile. He says, 'Do you know what day it is?' He then whips out a shotgun and blasts me in the stomach. But I don't drag that kind of crap out over dinner every night!"

"Oh my *God!*" I cried, with uncharacteristic emotion—not because I felt any such emotion, but because I'd just thought of a ruthlessly good scare tactic. "I'm so sorry!"

"You are?" William was surprised. "Well, that's all right. It's just a little hard on the ol' digestion when you keep bringing up your deepest, darkest—"

"I don't mean about that!" I cut in. "I mean about the guy with the shotgun. Because I've had the same dream! *I've* seen him blast you, too!"

"Oh for Christ's sake!"

"William!" Esther shouted.

"I'm *sorry!*" he shouted back. "But damn it, Dory! The mind has an endless supply of garbage in it, and most of that garbage is best left lying in there to rot!"

"I disagree completely!" Esther hollered. "It's *not* garbage, Dory! We *need* to face our dreams and fears. They're not facts, of course, they're not real. But we need to face them! And I'd like you to start now, by telling me why you think any of us are going to die violently."

"It's just these dreams I keep having," I said—and this time I spoke the truth. "Like, in the one where you die, you're in your schoolbus, which is lying on its side in an intersection. Hit by a truck. A big blue truck. The same one every time. And every time, at first, you think you're lucky, because the kids climb out the emergency exits, the seats empty, everybody seems okay. But a couple of kids sneak out the rear emergency exit and end up on the wrong side of the bus from the rest of you. And when you don't see 'em, you think they're missing. So you go back inside. You start crawlin' over the sideways seats, trying to find 'em. But you can't find 'em, of course. They're not there. And just when you hear 'em shouting, and see 'em waving at you, safe outside the window, you notice the smell of gasoline. And that's when there's a terrible—"

"*Ahhhhhgh!*" William cried, picking up his raspberry Jell-O. "Look at *this!*" He squeezed it, sending it dripping down through his fingers. "It's like a *brain* being pulverized in a head-on car wreck! But not like *my* brain! Oh no! *My* brain looks more like that *burnt hamburger* we just ate, because it's shot full of *cancer!* Right, Dory? Picture the festering black *rot* in there! Think how fast it's growing! What a *relief* it'll be when the *sniper* on the Safeway roof blows my burnt hamburger all over the pavement as I'm walking in to work tomorrow!"

"You *disgust* me!" Esther said with terrible sincerity.

"Oh, come on!" William said cajolingly. "Dory's playing the kids' game of Gross-Out, and you're taking it seriously. But the object of the game, Esther, is just to make us chunder up the ol' groceries! So come on. Your turn now, Big Mean Mama! Really make us spill the ol' cargo!"

The kids' game of Gross-Out . . . Though my nightmares were genuine nightmares, and though my dream of Esther in the flaming bus was a real dream, I felt that William had hit some sort of nail on the head. Maybe my nightmares were just my own brain playing Gross-Out with me. Maybe I had no reason to be frightened by them. I felt grateful to William. I felt much less afraid. I wanted time to think this Gross-Out possibility over.

But Esther was livid. "You should be *ashamed!*" she told William. "And that hamburger was *not* burnt! Tomorrow you can cook your own damn dinner!"

This, for my mother, was horrifically strong language. And

William knew it. And was crushed by it. I saw that my experiment was a bust, saw that I'd scared my parents so bad they had taken up arms and started shooting at each other. I was ready to call a halt. "This is *my* fault," I said firmly. "And I'm sorry. It won't happen again."

"But we *want* you to talk to us!" Esther cried, shooting William a lethal glance. "Your father's just in a *disgusting* mood."

"I'm in a *great* mood," he said, weakly but defiantly. "Dory predicts I'll outlive you both!"

"You make me *ill,*" Esther told him.

"It's *my* fault," I said again. "I *should* keep this stuff to myself. I *was* playin' Gross-Out. What William said helped me."

"See what you've done?" Esther hissed at William. "She's afraid of things! She needs to talk to us *desperately*. And you've slammed her shut!"

"I'll still talk!" I promised. "Just not at dinnertime. I'm not afraid of bad dreams, either. Don't worry!"

"You poor thing!" Esther gushed, tears filling her eyes. Then she turned to William—and rage filled her tears. "You should be *ashamed,*" she said again, her voice tinged with something frighteningly close to hatred.

"Excuse me," William rasped, looking like a half-crushed insect. "The news is starting." He slid back his chair and literally staggered from the room.

Appalled by the pain I'd caused, I shot out of there after him and tried to make amends by watching the news from his lap. But, like so many scientists before me, I found it's incomparably easier to work the experiment than to repair the damage afterward: when Esther saw me slumped in William's lap, she only took it as further proof of the severity of my fears, and felt a whole fresh wave of fury at her husband.

. . .

THAT WAS THE LAST OF THE SUPPERTIME DOOM PROPHECIES. But a once-steady facer of facts had shot far beyond science, a once-charmed marriage had crashed down out of the clouds, and neither William, Esther, nor I had any idea what to do about it. To try to help me or the marriage with Catholic doctrine would, Esther felt, have been unfair to her religious truce with her husband. And to repair anything or anyone with his nebulous agnosticism was, William knew, impossible. As befit our respective systems of belief, Esther tried prayer, William tried wringing his hands and feeling all fuddledy-duddledy and I continued to sit in the living room for half an hour each evening, spinning a gyroscope and facing the facts of human and animal life on Earth—as interpreted by "The CBS Evening News." And at Xmas that year we again proved how much we confused and sabotaged and fooled each other, when my parents' only gift to me—at my own endless insistence—was a two-year subscription to *U.S. News & World Report*.

4. OVERSHOOTING THE MARK

By the time I turned seven I had long since exposed and debunked Santa, the Tooth Fairy and the Easter Bunny. Noting that the Fairy only came on nights when I'd told my parents I'd lost a tooth, that the Bunny's candy was sold at William's Safeway and that Santa's handwriting was identical to Esther's, I felt no need to catch anyone red-handed. There was no room for doubt: the fat man in red, the egg-strewing rabbit and the tooth-hoarding fairy were all, in fact, William and Esther Jones. What continued to mystify me was why parents chose to invent these fraudulent creatures at all. If they wanted to substitute money for teeth or stash colored eggs under the couch, why not just do it and admit they'd done it? Why the covertness? Why the fake wee fairies and red-suited fatsos?

I could think of just one logical explanation: *embarrassment*.

Certain activities must embarrass grown-ups into inventing fantasy lackeys to do the activities for them. The weird thing, though, was that apart from a certain childishness there was nothing very embarrassing about the things "Santa" and Company did. On the contrary, they were rather sweet. If parents had any sense, I thought, they'd take full credit for Easter eggs and North Pole products and let the imaginary lackeys take the rap for the *truly* embarrassing things they did. Like when Esther had the bladder infection that resulted in a bout of enuresis, instead of all the blushing and weeping and pained public apologies, she could have said, "Guess what? That dang Bed-Wetter Fairy snuck under the covers again last night and peed all over me!" Or like when William forgot Esther's birthday, or their anniversary, or any of the other things he was always forgetting, he could've just hollered, "Blast! That damned Memory Vampire sucked my brain dry again!" Esther could have cooked up Theological Pettifogger Fleas whose bites inspired her ridiculous doctrinal debates with her Baptist sister, Kristin. William could have concocted a Santa Sot who perched on his shoulder at dinner parties, voodooing him into crapulation as he struggled to fill its vast ectoplasmic belly. They both could have used a Poop Elf to blame when they stank up the bathroom and forgot to light a match. But they did nothing of the sort. Instead they blamed *themselves* for all the tacky, petty or humiliating things they did, then insisted, when they did something nice, that "No. *We* didn't do that. *Santa Claus* did that."

I considered myself, at seven, to be a consummate judge of these make-believe beings. I judged Santa mildly absurd, the Easter Bunny utterly pathetic, and the last time my parents suggested I place a lost molar under my pillow for the Tooth Fairy, William woke me up, screaming, in the middle of the night, a mousetrap dangling from his index finger. Yet there was one make-believe person who gave me some faith in adults' imaginative abilities. This was the Garbage Man. I know I must have seen garbage trucks, and at school we actually *used* Dumpster bins. But when my allegiance to hard facts collided with my condescension toward make-believe beings, I somehow overshot the mark and created a little make-believe myself: I truly believed that once a week my father or my mother, and *all* American fathers or mothers, snuck out of the house, made off with their family's loaded garbage can, emptied it somewhere (I didn't much care where: it was just garbage), snuck the empty can back home and afterward claimed the entire operation had been affected by a grubby but otherwise Santa-like personage known as the Garbage Man.

What's more, I actually *liked* this particular sham. In the first place, he was a *man,* not some obese, sleigh-driving elf or anthropomorphized rodent. In the second place, he charged cold hard cash for his services. Nobody ever stopped to think of the billions of dollars, rupees, pesos, francs, lira or shekels that Santa and the like would need to practice their preposterous vocations. In the third place, all my parents ever did was *complain* about the G-Man—stuff like: *"Boy,* did that Garbage Man make a racket this morning! I thought I'd *never* get back to sleep!" Or "Can you *believe* it! The Garbage Man raised his prices *again!"* Or "When will that big bearded oaf learn not to throw the lid right on top of our daffodils?" Though it was all, I believed, sheer bunkum, I found the negative-campaign tactics wonderfully convincing. My parents' endless carping actually caused me to conjure an illusory person I grew fond of: I pictured the Garbage Man as a big, heavy-bearded, robust, dirty lout who greeted all criticism with an ear-splitting guffaw, then roared, "You don't *like* my noise? You don't *like* my prices? *Fine!* Haul your *own* goddamn garbage!"

It struck me as odd that such keen attention to detail would be squandered on this one insignificant being. Esther's Holy Trinity seemed more important to her, and all three of It sure could have used a similar fleshing out. America's Xmas and Easter "magic" were also dying for some Garbage Man–type ploys. Why didn't people think to strew a little rabbit crap across a favorite couch or carpet while stashing the colored eggs? Why didn't they save a bundle some Xmas by having "that damn Santa" go on strike? Why didn't they put the Tooth Fairy out of its pillow-plundering misery by letting it start a mail-order cash-for-teeth service, adding believability to the scam by leaking rumors of some priceless by-product—hand-carved baby-tooth chess sets; exquisite baby-tooth scrimshaw; maybe a crushed-baby-tooth ointment that cured herpes or impotence or crabs—that was making the little Scrooge fabulously rich?

Even at their best, America's parents struck me as B-minus conjurers. But at least, I figured, their work-jaded, sitcom-shriveled imaginations had come up with the Garbage Man. Of course there was nothing truly embarrassing about hauling off trash. But garbage *did* stink, and hauling it away would have to be a thankless, menial chore. So why not concoct some big daffodil-crushing dolt to do it for you, but pretend that he charged you through the nose in revenge? It was a slick little ruse. I was glad the Oldies had it in them.

BUT IN THE SPRING OF MY SEVENTH YEAR I MOVED FROM A little downstairs bedroom in the back of our house to a larger upstairs bedroom in the front of the house. And one warm April night I went to sleep, for the first time ever, with that bedroom's street-facing window wide open. And very early the next morning—I'll never forget: it was a Tuesday—I woke to the sound of singing robins, followed by the barking of dogs, followed by the roar of an engine and a loud, metallic clatter, so I sprang from my bed to see what was the matter.

And what to my wondering eyes should appear but a huge filthy truck full of trash in the rear, and a burly young driver with a thick earth-brown beard, a can on his shoulder and a gait that appeared to be taking him swiftly, for such a large man, straight toward our very own garbage-filled can!

I raced downstairs and round to the back door, fumbled with

the double lock and deadbolt, and by the time I'd poked my head out he had already emptied our little can into his big one and was striding away, humming some unrecognizable, garbagey tune. Afraid to call to him, afraid to let him know he'd been spied, I tore back up to my new bedroom, watched him empty our trash into the back of his truck, stalk off across the street, steal the neighbors' garbage just as he'd stolen ours, return to the truck, hop up behind the wheel and roar off down the block in a rank blue cloud.

I collapsed on the bed, my fact-facing brain wobbling like a gyroscope fast losing momentum. Had it really been him? Was that *the* Garbage Man? Who else could it have been? What other big, jolly, dirty bearded guy would be crazy enough to roam the city before the sun even rose, happily gathering up all the trash? A blizzard of unraveling facts began to blow through my brain: because if one big bearded guy gathered up the garbage, why couldn't *another* big bearded guy pull on a silly red suit and break into houses, leaving gifts for kids under gaudy dead trees? Why, for that matter, couldn't some semi-deranged rabbit with birdlike nesting instincts hide stolen eggs in houses at Easter time? And why couldn't some furtive, nocturnal creature thus far unknown to science sneak into houses to indulge a pack-rat-like fetish for kid-teeth, leaving coins found in gutters in the tooth's place? Sure, adults also did these things. I'd caught William, his finger anyway, red-handed. But that didn't mean the original creatures didn't exist! Maybe adults started stealing various magical duties when their kids became such butts or unbelievers that the magical beings refused to serve them. Maybe Santa *hated* the paunchy jerks who imitated him! Maybe there was an outright war going on between real Magic and human fraud. I didn't know. All I knew was that the repercussions of this thing were overwhelming: *the world just might be a more mysterious place than Dan Rather had ever led me to believe!*

I felt a sudden fear. What if the Garbage Man was William in some brilliant disguise? I snuck down the hallway to peek into my parents' bedroom. They were both there, sound asleep and snoring so grotesquely I knew it couldn't possibly be faked. I ran downstairs, double-checked our garbage can: *still empty!* I'd seen the Garbage Man, all right. And the implications were limitless.

But the place to begin, I figured, was where I'd always begun: with cool, verifiable facts. Vowing to keep what I'd seen secret—lest I be scoffed by skeptics (especially myself)—I vowed to look into the Garbage Man facts and face them. To face them even if they proved, for once, to be not grim, but wonderful.

5 . HE COMES IN GLORY

All my life, up until that first encounter with the Garbage Man, I'd expected the world to present itself to me as an endless series of facts —and that was exactly how it *had* presented itself. (As Esther liked to say, "Ask and ye shall receive.") That many of these facts turned out to be dark was, of course, depressing. But it was a dependable depression. In turning on the CBS news, I always knew where I stood: facts would pour in; terrible things would once again have happened; I'd snuggle, helpless in the face of those things, down under a blanket of gloom; the commercials would feel like a kind of compensatory, psychological thumb-sucking: I'd spin my gyroscope. And the whole arrangement—gloom blanket, thumb-sucking ads, gyroscope and all—felt muzzy and familiar, even cozy.

The instant I laid eyes on the Garbage Man, that coziness vanished. I was thrown into a state of wonder—and you don't experience wonder the way you experience facts. Most facts tend to just sit there, inert, like objects on a shelf, until you decide to reach up and grab one. With wonder, *you're* the object on the shelf. Wonder reaches up and grabs *you*. I have learned, as an adult, that only by experiencing ignorance can I be opened up to fresh knowledge— and wonder is, I believe, simply the experience of that good ignorance. But as a little genius/nerd/prodigy I shunned ignorance, or at least camouflaged my own by smothering it in facts. In so doing, I'd managed to screen wonder out of a time of life that was supposed to be filled with the stuff. That first glimpse of the Garbage Man was my first really powerful jolt of good ignorance. And the experience itself was "wonderful."

But the aftershocks were not. In the days following that first G-Man sighting, I became a wreck. I had trouble eating, had a terrible time sleeping—my parents thought I'd come down with some kind of bug. But it was more serious than any bug. My world of gloomy but solid statements had been torn into a big open question. My muzzy prison of facts had become a wide-open door. The girl I'd always been had been cracked open like a nut. Someone new was sprouting from the crack. And I didn't know her. I didn't know me anymore.

And I was afraid.

ON THE SIXTH NIGHT FOLLOWING THE GARBAGE MAN SIGHT-ing, I set my alarm clock for 4 A.M., slipped it under my pillow and went to bed with my clothes on, hoping that my parents' old grumblings about him coming once a week were true. I again had a terrible time falling asleep, thrashing and spinning in both brain and body till the sheets, thoughts and blankets were all twisted round me like the wrappings round a mummy. Then there was a whole room-ful of mummies, just like me—long, helpless rows of us, and some dumb, beautiful, girly-looking fairy hovering in the front of the room, giving us all a lecture. The whole idea of fairies had always annoyed me—and this damned fairy looked like a flying Barbie doll. Her lecture was in fairy talk, an incomprehensible series of high-pitched, piercing, effeminate beeps. It was endless. It was insuffer-able. *If I could get out of these sheets,* I thought, *I'd swat you like a fly!*

But she was a fairy: she heard my thought. And went berserk.

She shot toward me, letting out even shriller beeps. She began to circle me, wings buzzing like the giant housefly I wanted to swat. She had long red fingernails that suddenly looked poisonous. She had matching red lipstick and sharp fairy teeth. Her lipstick began to run down her chin like blood. She laughed when I saw this. I writhed in my wrappings, shouted for help; she circled closer and closer, laughed harder, shrank herself suddenly—and shot straight into my ear! I gasped, lurched . . .

And found myself lying in the dark, the little fairy bitch somehow trapped beneath my pillow, still beeping with all her might.

My first impulse was to smother her.

My second was to peek: 3:59, said my beeping alarm clock. Then I remembered: the Garbage Man!

Instantly awake, I jumped out of bed, opened my window wide as it would go, pulled up a chair, left all the lights off and began to wait.

For a long time I stared avidly at the corner where I expected his truck to appear. But when the city stayed quiet, the street empty, and my straining eyes began to burn, I allowed them to leave the corner and look around at this least familiar time of night. *The Wee Hours,* William called them. I didn't know why. But at once they felt different to me from the other dark hours I knew, the hours of evening or early night. Not a car, not a soul, not a dog, cat or possum stirring. No wind, no breeze at all, yet the night air poured in like water and ran cold, thick and quiet down my back. A few sickly stars pierced the downtown glare, but I recognized no planet or constellation, and I knew the night sky well. The lit windows that gave our neighborhood life were all black now, bombed-out looking. The few streetlights turned everything an unfamiliar sepia tone. Favorite trees, neighbors' houses, even my own yard seemed alien in that light. The air, though heavy, had a fathomlessness to it, as if the usual atmospheric barriers between city and sky had dissolved; the wastes of space seemed to be reaching, undiluted, all the way down to the asphalt and lawns. And it seemed plausible, in that fathomlessness, that any sort of being, from anywhere, could ride the watery air down, alight unobserved, have its way with the sleeping world. *No wonder he chooses this hour,* I thought.

Then, quite suddenly, I began to shiver. The cold, I thought at first, drawing back into the room, wrapping the bedspread round my shoulders. But the same alien air had been gathering in my room, turning things chill, turning them foreign. Even the clock was in its grip, for despite the steady ticking, time had nearly ceased: 4:01, said the glowing green numbers.

"It's the same old room, same old house, same old city," I whispered aloud.

But now my voice was not the same. There was a hollowness to it that seemed to come from the unnatural air. *Who were the Wee whose hours these were, anyway?*

I looked again at the clock: 4:01, it still said, redundant as a depraved fairy. I leaned—too quickly, too much like someone fleeing fear—back out the open window. Distant sirens mourned fires or crimes. The few dull stars were the wrong color. There was no wind, no breeze at all, yet the night breathed into my face, slid down my spine, slid into the black behind me, congealing, listening, taking shape, till I heard a slow suction. A steady inhalation that was not my own. Coming from across the room. From the closet behind me. From the pitch-black nothingness behind the hanging clothes. "There's nothing there," I said, in the voice no longer mine. *Nothing there,* yet I felt that nothing chilling me, sucking the night in past me, pulling the entire sky down into a lung so vast it could never be satiated, could never fill.

I realized I couldn't move. I was frozen. Couldn't cry out for my parents, couldn't reach for the light, couldn't turn to face the nothing. And if I didn't cry out or turn, it would acquire a mouth and hollow eyes, its breathing would rise to a moan, and it would slide from the closet and slowly up behind me. Terror suffused me, erased me, began to lift me from my body as I waited for it to come. Then, through the window, a sound:

Dogs. Far up the street, dogs barking.

Then, close by, a robin sang.

The breathing stopped, listened with me. A second robin answered, then a third, fourth, fifth. The barking too became a choir. I looked up at the sky—and saw that all but one of the sickly stars had faded, and that the one had been Mars all along. I turned to the closet—and in the dusky light saw nothing but my own shoes and clothes. Then, over the din of dogs and birds: a faint metallic clatter! A distant roar! He was coming! He was coming! And I was ready.

DASHING DOWNSTAIRS, I UNLOCKED THE BACK DOOR, STEPPED outside, then seated myself as casually as possible, for one in whom casualness is impossible, on the steps beside our can. The truck, and the man, banged and roared their way toward me. My heart banged and head roared in response.

Not till his machine idled at our curb, not till I heard the very thudding of his boots, did it occur to me that if the Garbage Man was like Santa and the Tooth Fairy and so on, he might run, or simply vanish, if he saw me. Jumping up, I sprinted in blind panic for the camellia bushes at the near corner of the house. But just before reaching them I bounced off a dirty pair of coveralls striding round the same corner.

Snorting like a rodeo bull, the Garbage Man glared down at me.

Undersized and overmatched as a bucked bullrider, I stared back up.

He lowered a gloved hand, pulled me to my feet, brushed the grass off my backside and, in the colossal voice I'd dreamed he would have, hollered, "Holy *moly* you scared me! What's a squirt like you doin' outta bed s' early!"

Clutching a camellia for balance, I managed a speechless shrug. It was true! He was real! He was standing right next to me! I could *smell* him! *A cigar stump stuck out where his mouth met his cheek and its blue smoke encircled his head with a reek. He had a broad face and a gut like a pillow that shook, when he laughed, like a bowl full of Jell-O. Though smiling, he showed neither manners nor grace as he asked, "Why ya got that dumb look on your face?"*

I shrugged, and again failed to return his smile. Rich, rank garbage and body smells wafted from his beard and clothes, overwhelming me with the raw fact of him. He looked just like Santa's grubby younger brother or nephew or something. *"Well?"* he bellowed again. "Don't just *stand* there! *Say* somethin'. Let's hear ya say guh-mornin' kind sir!' "

"Good . . . morning, kind sir!" I peeped.

"Guh-mornin' yerself!" he roared. Then he strode over to our can, slung the lid off (right down onto the daffodils!), upended its contents into his own massive receptacle, heaved the load easily up onto his shoulder, gave me a parting wink and sauntered off singing a version of "Ol' Man River" so low and gravelly and hopelessly out of key that the banging of metal and growling of engine seemed the best possible harmonies.

Still clutching the camellia, I watched him toss our trash aboard his outlandish truck, cross the street to raid the neighbors' trash, toss it too aboard his rig, hop up behind the wheel and drive away with a wave and a bellow. A blue cloud of diesel smoke rose like Christ Himself up over our yard as, far down the street, a fresh choir of dogs sang out their greeting. I slapped my face in disbelief, staggered to the steps, plunked down in a stupor, thought: *This is it. There you have it. Santa, the Easter Bunny, the Tooth Fairy—they must all be real . . .*

I pictured again the big, florid face. He seemed almost human, really. You'd never guess he maybe lived forever and all that magical sort of thing. But he *had* been jolly. Maybe not so jolly as Santa, but no wonder. Santa worked one night a year in a flying sleigh, hauling nice things to good people. The Garbage Man, though, worked in that smelly old truck, hauling *rotten* things away from *all* people. And I bet once a week didn't do it. Because imagine how much garbage there must be! He must have to work every night of his life!

But where did he take it all? I'd heard people refer to a place called The Dump, but figured it was one of these Santa-lives-at-the-North-Pole, The-moon-is-made-of-green-cheese, Jesus-lives-in-Heaven type deals. Since the G-Man was real, though, The Dump must be, too. It must be where he took all the garbage in America! It must be where he *lived!* I pictured a tarpaper shack perched on a vast, reeking mountain; pictured a whole Garbage Family jammed into his shack with him; pictured them roaming the fetid slopes every day of their lives, saving the usable, eating the edible, eking out their garbagey existence . . .

Then I noticed the rotten-fish stench billowing from my own garbage can—and felt sick. Those poor people! Living off all the most unwanted putrescence and tripe on earth! Clothes the Salvation Army wouldn't take. Food nobody's dog would eat. Junk no 'Nam vet or fireman or Christian could even fix. I pictured the Garbage Wife—a chain-smoker, I guessed, curler-headed and care-worn, trying to feed and clothe a houseful of kids on nothing but refuse. I pictured the Garbage Children learning to crawl and walk and play in the rat-infested offal, the shattered glass, the festering slops of entire cities. I grew furious with myself, with my parents, with the whole smug populace for our inconsideration. I stood up, leaned over the garbage can and forced myself to inhale its stench until I gagged.

THAT MORNING AT BREAKFAST I HAD AN ANNOUNCEMENT TO make: "William, Esther, please listen!" I said. "I have three things to tell you. One, I have met, and actually *spoken* with, the Garbage Man!"

I paused to let the full weight of this hit home. William and Esther exchanged bamboozled glances.

"Two, I want you to know that I'm completely rethinking this whole Santa Claus/Easter Bunny/Tooth Fairy business . . ."

I paused again, shooting each parent a grave look. William sent a hand up to arrange the hairs on the top of his head, forgetting that, like his God, they had long since ceased to exist. Esther cleared her throat and managed to say, "That's interesting, Dory dear."

"Three," I continued, "from now on I want you both to stay out of the garbage can. Let me handle *all* the garbage. Every last bit of it! Understood?"

They exchanged another flummoxed glance. "If you like," Esther finally said. "But you don't have to."

"I *want* to!" I said vehemently.

"All right, then," said Esther, while William went on playing with the memory of his hair.

Thus began my brief but utter worship of a cigar-chewing, Dump-dwelling god.

6. "HO-HO . . . THE DUMP IS FULL OF IMAGES"

Till the end of June and throughout July, I waited till my parents were either distracted, asleep or at work, then virtually gift-wrapped every morsel of family garbage. Anything offensive to the nose I shrouded in plastic or newspaper, taped tightly shut and labeled WORTHLESS. Anything remotely suitable for use or repair—worn-out shoes, empty jars, rags, wrecked clothing—I wrapped in clean white butcher paper, sealed in double plastic bags and labeled COULD BE OK. Edible table scraps I placed in cottage cheese or yogurt con-

tainers, labeled, refrigerated and placed on top of the can the morning the G-Man was due. Unsatisfied with these offerings, I also rose
at four every Tuesday, snuck into the kitchen, made an opulent sack
lunch, wrapped it, sealed it in Ziploc plastic bags, labeled it FRESH
THIS MORNING! and placed it on the very top of the entire can.

Every time the G-Man came, I was waiting on the back steps,
worshipful of his every word and move. Well, *fairly* worshipful. I was
a bit confused that he invariably upended our trash can into his,
since that meant his lunch got mashed on the bottom of the heap. I
was also a little distressed by the way he blithely tossed his big can's
contents into the back of the truck with all the unsorted, unlabeled
stinko stuff. And I was downright horrified the first time he pushed
a button on the back of the truck, activating some kind of hydraulic
crusher that rammed his lunch and all my other neat packages right
up into the bowels of the whole runny truckload. But *he* was the
Garbage Man. He must know what he was doing. Maybe he was so
accustomed to sorting through guck at The Dump that he didn't
mind having to pick his lunch out of it. Or maybe he liked to let his
wife and kids discover the surprise packages (I'd learned he *did* have
a wife, and three kids—one a girl, just my age). Maybe he had
supernatural techniques for rejuvenating mangled trash; maybe he
could transform one mashed sandwich into a whole week's worth of
food, like Jesus had supposedly done with some loaves and fishes;
maybe his rough treatment of my packages was a test of some kind,
and if I passed it, he'd let me in on deeper secrets.

Or maybe he wouldn't. It didn't matter. My efforts and packages were a gift gratefully offered to the miracle of his existence.
What he did with that gift was entirely up to him.

FOR HIS PART, I SUPPOSE, THE G-MAN GOT USED TO THE
skinny, lank-haired, brown-eyed girl who so reverently awaited him

on the Jones's back steps each week. Of course he'd no idea why I was always there, and no idea what he meant to me. Maybe he thought I was an insomniac. Maybe he thought I had such rotten parents that I cherished a little company with an adult who wouldn't belt me. Maybe he thought I'd blown a head gasket. It didn't matter. He accepted my company as he accepted everything else on his garbage routes. Goggle-eyed or not, I was a pleasant enough switch from vicious dogs and stinking Dumpsters. In time he even began to take a breather at our house, shutting off his engine, turning his empty can upside down near our back steps, plunking down on it, pulling a cigar from his overalls, lighting up and chatting with me— or *to* me, really. I hardly said a word, though the intensity of my listening usually made him stay longer than he intended. "You listen to me the way a sponge listens to water," he once said with a nervous laugh.

"And one other weird thing, while I'm at it," he added. "You've got the neatest, cleanest garbage I ever saw in my life! 'Cleaner'n our goddamned *house!*' I told the woman the other evenin'."

Naturally, I thought, my belief unscathed. *It's hard for her to keep your house clean when you live on The Dump.*

DURING OUR CAN-SIDE CHATS I DISCOVERED THAT THE GAR-bage Man's name was not just "Garbage Man." It was Wally. This seemed logical to me, since Santa's name was also Saint Nick and Father Christmas, the Easter Bunny's was also Peter Cottontail, Jesus' was also Christ, the Messiah and so on. Apparently all these eternal types required a number of aliases. I also learned that Wally wasn't the only Garbage Man in the world. There were lots of others, he said. Hundreds, maybe, even right in our own city. This threw me at first. But then I saw that it, too, was logical, since if there were lots of Garbage Men there must also be lots of Santas, Easter Bunnies and Tooth Fairies, which explained how they achieved national or even global coverage.

I became especially obsessed with the Garbage Man's daughter, whose name, Wally once said, was Becky. Was she beautiful, I wondered, like a Snow White among a bunch of garbage-hauling dwarves? Or was she burly, dirty and cigar-smoking like her dad? And how did she like life on The Dump? Did their shack have just one room or did she have a room of her own? What could she see out her window, what did she eat, wear, say, think? What did she do for fun? Above all, was Becky magic, like Wally, Santa and them, or just normal, like me? And could she marry out of the magic if she wanted? If so, could I marry *in?*

I longed to ask a thousand questions. But for weeks the G-Man's presence so overwhelmed me that I did nothing but stare and listen. As our meetings grew somewhat routine, though, and he seemed perfectly amiable and not about to disappear, I reached a point where my curiosity burned hotter than my awe. Rising extra early one Tuesday in August, I packed Wally an enormous lunch, sat down on the back steps, thought long and hard about what question I most wanted to ask, chose one, worded it carefully, memorized it and waited.

But the Garbage Man was running late that morning. By the time he'd arrived, emptied and flipped our can, sat down, produced a cigar, licked it, bit its end and lit it, the question had affected my brain the way a bottle of beer affects an already-full bladder. Unable to slow it or guide it, unable to remember how I'd worded it, I just blushed up at the Garbage Man and let fly with: "Will Buh-Becky be a Guh-Garbage Woman when she guh-guh-grows up?"

And he flinched as if I'd slapped him! His face turned red, then grayish. His eyes glazed, then turned hard and cold. He jumped to his feet, spat out his cigar and snarled, "Not if *I* can help it, Miss Hotshot! And if you think you been *slummin'* with me, if you think you're *better'n* my daughter, if you think you're even half as good, *you got another fuckin' think comin'!''*

And he turned and was gone.

The truck was out of earshot before I could even move. When I did move, it was to the bottom step, where I had to sit with my head between my knees to keep from being sick. I'd never been so confused in my life. All I could see, over and over, was his face twisting from pain to hate to fury. As if I'd somehow *betrayed* him. As if it were an *insult* to think Becky might follow in his footsteps. As if he was *ashamed* of what he was! Why? He was the Garbage Man! The best thing that had ever happened to me! And he was ashamed. I had to know why my words hurt him. But how?

Raising my head, I noticed his cigar on the lawn. Fetching it, I sat back down on the steps, sniffed it. It stung my nose and brought tears to my eyes. I flung off the tears with a fierce snap of the head. The cigar was still wet with his saliva, and still, barely, burning. If it went out, I felt suddenly, he'd never speak to me, he'd never like me again.

Hoping that spit-to-spit contact might build some kind of bridge between us, I fought down my disgust, stuck the cigar in my mouth and began to puff. My tongue, nose and eyes were instantly streaming. My stomach began to heave. Defying nausea, defying my entire body, I sucked his wet, rancid stogie till my head began spinning, became a dying top or gyroscope, spun slower, spun wobblier, no chance to right itself, yet taking forever to fall. I know, now, that no matter what the world offers them, children will believe in something: God; the UN food truck; the garbage man; crack cocaine if they can afford it; if not, the high they get sniffing leaded gas. But a child's soul *is* going to worship. It longs to bow down. The intense imaginings, the play of children *is* worship. It was not my body, it was my soul that held that cigar between my teeth: held and believed in it till I sank to my knees, as if to pray . . .

and threw up, violently, on the sidewalk.

. . .

I WAS SO SICK THAT DAY THAT I COULD ONLY DREAM, AND regret, and dream again of what had happened. But when I went to bed that night my head finally cleared, and a harrowing series of insights began clicking into place:

When garbage smells even worse than a cigar that made me vomit, how could collecting the stuff be anything but loathsome work? It couldn't. The G-Man must hate his job and find it shameful. This was my first thought.

Why, then, did he do it? I felt there could be just one answer: he *had* to. Something or someone must force him to. Insight number two.

Then all hell broke loose: if something forced the Garbage Man to do work he hated, then maybe *all* the magic beings were forced to do what they did. And maybe they *all* hated it! Was it possible? Could it be that Santa, Wally, the Easter Rabbit, perhaps even Christ only did their wonderful work because they *had to?* Was all the jollity and peace-be-unto-you's and ho-ho-ho's just part of the job, like the painted smile on a clown, the demeaning uniform of a fast-foods waitress, the fake politeness of a chain-store lackey like William? Were these powerful beings, at bottom, just as miserable as everyone else in the world? And if so, what or who was making them that way? Who possessed the ability to force big, strong, magical guys like Santa and Wally to do, forever, work they *hated* doing?

Again, I saw just one possible answer: God. My God, yes! *God* must be wrecking Santa's and Wally's lives, just the way He'd wrecked His own Son's life! So these wonderful beings were just glamorous slaves, really. Like genies who must answer to any fool that rubs their lantern, these beings had to kowtow to humans simply because of the Almighty's insane preference for our species! So of course they hated their slavery! Imagine spending eternity serving kids who grew up to be the maniacs, war-mongers, murderers and politicians that inundated the evening news! Imagine an eternity spent delivering plastic claptrap and sugared eggs to brats so greedy they couldn't revere Christmas or Easter for any other reason! Imagine an eternity spent gathering our worthless teeth—or hauling off our garbage! Poor Wally! He *hated* his life. And hearing my question again in light of what I now understood, I felt I had in effect snarled, "Will Becky be my garbage-hauling *slave* when she grows up?" It was a wonder he hadn't crushed me on the spot with his steel can!

"Not if I can help it!" Wally had growled, knowing that to save his daughter from his own awful fate he must defy God Himself. But Dory Teresa Jones would help him, by God!—or by golly, anyhow. And I would start *now!* I'd start by giving Becky some of the things that made my own life bearable—things that Garbage People, in their poverty and degradation, could never afford. Dashing round my room, I collected my favorite shirt (a night-blue flannel), three favorite books *(The World Almanac, The Guinness Book of World Records, The Complete Adventures of Sherlock Holmes)* and my very favorite possession (the gyroscope), took them downstairs to my garbage-wrapping station, placed them in a large box, wrapped the box in butcher paper and plastic, labeled it FOR BECKY! FROM YOUR SECRET FRIEND! and placed the package lovingly down upon the scoured and disinfected bottom of our can.

7. CATCHIN' THE FEELIN'

The following week I debated hard about whether to go out and watch the Garbage Man at all: much as I loved to study him, I believed now that what I'd been studying was his bondage and his shame. I finally decided to at least briefly greet him, though, and to try to give him some subtle sign of my new understanding.

He looked sullen, and a little frightening, as he came trudging across our lawn. With all my heart, I called out, "Good morning, kind sir!" He scowled and walked right by me, kept scowling as he emptied our can, and did not sit down for the usual long smoke and chat. But on his way back to the truck, just as he brushed past me, he winked, right through his scowl. It thrilled me to my socks! Had he read my mind and heart? Could it be some secret wink that he and Santa shared with a whole network of anti-slave conspirators? I couldn't be sure, but I was giddy with hope.

Dashing up to my room, I grabbed my best pair of jeans, my favorite sweater and my brand-new bright red Converse sneakers, ran downstairs and wrapped them, labeled the package TO THE GAR-BAGE MAN'S DAUGHTER! FROM A FRIEND OF GARBAGE FAMILIES AND OPPRESSED PEOPLES EVERYWHERE! and placed it tenderly in the bottom of the can.

But I'd overlooked something. Any good mother, and not a few fathers, are aware of most of the self-purchased materials that enter and exit their homes. And Esther was an excellent mother. For weeks she'd been silently replenishing our tape and plastic-bag and Ziploc bag and butcher-paper supplies as I'd gift-wrapped package after exquisite package—which she knew I then dumped in the garbage can. She'd noticed food disappearing from her pantry and refrigerator. She'd risen early and nervously eavesdropped through the kitchen window as Wally and I conversed by the back steps. And now she saw me limping round the house in a worn-out, too-small pair of Taiwanese tennis shoes just days after William had bought me a coveted pair of red Converse. Piecing a theory together, she stepped out to the garbage can, and in a neatly wrapped package found not only my shoes, sweater, jeans and note from the "op-pressed peoples' friend," but a mind-boggling explanation for a mo-rass of small mysteries.

Esther waited till late morning, when I left the house to catch and catalog insects in the vacant lot next door, then went straight to my room and took inventory.

WHEN WILLIAM GOT HOME THAT NIGHT, ESTHER PULLED HIM aside for a briefing, followed by a discussion of what ought to be done. True to their respective religions and politics, William favored further surveillance, Esther immediate confrontation. When the discussion turned into an argument they stopped at once, hugged each other (albeit mechanically) and pulled out their automatic argument ender: a quarter. William flipped. Esther called tails and won. Esther then marched, and William slumped, into the living room.

They found me in an armchair, the CBS news under way. Esther stared meaningfully at William. William stared meaningfully at me. I glanced at them briefly, suspected trouble, turned back to Dan Rather, and Dan introduced the White House correspondent. The correspondent stood in a drizzle in front of the president's mansion, squinting at the camera as if the drizzle were vile filth. I suppose some of it may have been. William cleared his throat, but I ignored him, so he turned to watch the correspondent, too. Esther, however, stepped in front of the TV, turned off the sound, glared at William and said, "Well?"

"Uh, Dory honey," William began, still watching the tiny piece of correspondent visible between Esther's legs. "Uh, Esther, or, we both were, uh, wondering. Where are your new red sneakers?"

The screen flashed. The correspondent's left arm became Rather's left ear. I murmured, "Gave 'em away."

William nodded as if he too had given away several pairs of new shoes lately. Rather's ear turned into a gleaming cap on a tube of toothpaste. "And, uh, how about your new jeans?" William asked.

"Them too," I said.

Disconcerted by the way her family kept peering between her legs, Esther moved away from the screen, giving us full view of a brunette baring creamy white teeth at a tall man who ignored her because creamy white wasn't white enough. "William, *please,*" Esther said.

Tearing his gaze from the now foamy-mouthed brunette before the magic whiteners in her new toothpaste could devastate the tall man, William turned to me—and realized something was missing. "Where's your gyroscope, honey?"

"Gave it away, too," I whispered.

"Dory dear," Esther said impatiently. "Just *who* are you giving your things *to?*"

"Becky," I confessed.

"And who is Becky?" she asked.

A mother and daughter as similar as Esther and I were different flashed onto the screen: they were the same height and hue, had the same short, sopping-wet hair and wore smiles that seemed identically unnecessary since all they were doing was discussing a bottle of shampoo. Then the screen flashed and *zam!*—they were aerobicizing side by side, their near-identical bodies swathed in skin-tight red and white outfits, the near-identical haircuts gleaming in the same wall-sized mirror, leaving millions of viewers with the indelible impression that Mom was not a whit less shapely or bouncy than Daughter, because of a shared brand of shampoo.

"Becky," I replied, with no smile but enormous pride, "is the *Garbage* Man's daughter!"

Hearing the emphasis I placed on the third-to-last word, Esther shot a questioning glance at William—but he was watching a bright red Japanese pickup truck fly over a ridge, splash through a river, fishtail round several sharp curves, then speed toward a huge paper hoop confusingly reminiscent, in its taut red and whiteness, of skin-tight aerobics outfits. A crowd of people from many walks of life were gathered, hands joined, round the hoop. "LET'S GO, AMER-ICA!" said the words on the hoop. Then, in majestic slow motion, the Japanese pickup smashed triumphantly through the words as the people all laughed and leapt high in the air.

William smiled. Esther scowled. I remained expressionless. The TV flashed like a deck of tarot cards from the leaping people to a stern Dan Rather to a foreign correspondent to a pile of bloodied bodies strewn along a desert road. At the sight of the bodies William rushed over, gave the volume a twist, heard the word *Palestine,* and in another outburst of the same weird malady that once resulted in his coining the term "hooter cancer," muttered, "I didn't know those Middle Eastern countries got so green!"

Slowly recognizing—thanks to Esther's face—how awful this sounded, he added, "Poor devils." He was not a callous man, just an exhausted one. The Safeway had been horrendously busy all day. It hardly mattered anyway, since the tarot screen had long since turned the Palestinian bodies back into Rather, into a correspondent in a crowd of dying African women and children, into Rather, into a listing oil tanker, into a writhing, blackened sea bird, into Rather, into a man-made canyon between skyscrapers, into a vast room full of almost epileptic-looking men in white shirts and ties, into a seven-point drop in the Dow.

"Where did you meet Becky?" Esther asked, seeing that William had gone blotto.

"I never met her, exactly," I admitted cautiously. But then a dam burst inside me. Exasperated by their suspicion, I began to make what I considered a defiant confession—though why it was defiant, or just what I was confessing to, remained mysterious to my parents. "I never met Becky, no!" I began angrily. "But Wally's told me all about her. She's exactly my age, but I'm taller, so the clothes will fit in a while. And she'll like the other stuff too, I'll bet, since she's desperate not to be a—you *know,* like Wally, when she's older. And I *know* you're religious, Esther, I know you love *God,* and all that. But I've got to tell you, I'm with Becky and Wally on this one! 'Cause remember when Jesus said, 'Father, remove this cup,' and God didn't? Remember 'Father, why hast thou forsaken me?' right on the cross? Okay, then! It's the same old song and dance with Wally and Becky! And *I* for one have had enough! Because what's so special about humans? Why should *we* get all the breaks and slaves and saviors? Wally and Becky are special too, you know! And it's not *fair* of God to shove 'em around! How would *you* like to be a Garbage Lady all your life? How'd you like *me* to have to be one? See? So Wally wants Becky to make the big break, the great escape. And I apologize to you, I'll even apologize to God, if you make me, but *I'm helpin'* '*em*. I won't stop! And that's all there is to it."

Hearing this from his heretofore scientific daughter, William gave me one brief Gawk, then virtually dove back into the boob tube. Esther, though, stuck to the single aspect of the issue she felt she understood. "Dory honey," she said. "If you haven't even *met* Becky, how are you able to give her all these things?"

It was a simple, fact-seeking question. And it was deadly. I felt my glare of defiance melt into a scowl of worry. "I . . . I just put them in the garbage can."

Now Esther's eyes narrowed. "Be honest, please, Dory. This is important. Does the trash collector *ask* you to put your things in the can for his daughter?"

I began to blink, and to have trouble breathing. It wasn't so much the question that stunned me as the way my mother tossed off the words *trash collector*. I felt as if she'd called a black man a nigger or an Asian a gook. I also knew that such language was unthinkable in Esther. I realized at last that a very big mistake had been made somewhere—and that this mistake had almost certainly been mine.

"What a face you're making, pumpkin!" William chuckled. "All Esther wants to know is whether the trashman *asks* you to give things to his little girl."

"I'm not a *pumpkin!*" I snapped, but my defenses were collapsing. "And the *Garbage* Man is not a . . . he's never asked me for *anything,* ever! I just do it."

"But Dory honey," Esther persisted. "Does he even *know* you put your things in the garbage for his daughter?"

Picturing, suddenly, the careless way that Wally tossed my packages into the back of his truck, picturing the hydraulic crusher that rammed his lunch and every other gift I'd given them right into the stinking center of his loads, I cried, "He *must* know, mustn't he? He's the *Garbage* Man, isn't he? So they *must* find the stuff sooner or later. They must find it at home—on The Dump!"

Hearing this, William and Esther turned to each other and saw, as if in a mirror, amazement, giving way to amusement, giving way to sorrow: though the details remained unclear, they realized their fact-facing daughter had built some kind of clipper ship or patron saint out of a garbage man—and their questions were a broadside cannon volley smashing that ship or saint to pieces.

I turned back to the television. It showed the aluminum shed on the bankrupt Dakota farm into which the farmer drove his truck, wife and baby so that they could all be together while the carbon monoxide killed them. It showed the schnauzer the farmer chose to leave behind. It showed the high school class pictures of the most recent three girls killed by the ice-pick stabber in Florida. It showed Dan Rather scowling like a Garbage Man himself, his expression sternly implying that these suicidal farmers and ice-pick murderers would never do. "Have you ever *seen* a garbage dump, honey?" William asked.

I shook my head.

"Would you like to?"

The exaggerated gentleness, the sympathy oozing from his voice, filled me with sick dread. But the facts. "I guess I better," I murmured.

An amiable horse kissed the president's wife on the mouth; the wife turned to the president and pooched out her lips; the president

winced, and only kissed her on the cheek; then everyone, even the
horse, laughed. Dan Rather smiled wanly and said, "Good night."
Then a dolphin slapped a girl in a bikini, Gordie Howe slapped a
goal, Joan Collins slapped a man who slapped her right back, Chris
Evert swung at a tennis ball and missed, Larry Holmes swung at a
white man and didn't, Lee Iacocca looked inflated, inhaled a helium
balloon, squeaked, "Buy American!" and a zeppelin exploded, an
old hotel imploded, a mountain exploded, Dr. J. swished a sixty-
foot jumper, the crowd exploded, and with a sound like jet-fighters
the strobed words CBS! CATCH THE FEELIN'! strafed the screen.

"We'll drive to the dump first thing in the morning," said
William.

I nodded. But for the first time since giving it away, I wished I
had my gyroscope.

8. MOUNT DUMP

*We drove fast, dead away from the city, sped past the last housing tracts, past
farms, into dark forest and up into mountains. We shot through a rocky
pass, saw snow and a few black ravens, wound back down into trees. Firs
gave way to pines, then the forest abruptly ended, and on a road straight as a
yardstick and empty as sky we drove out onto a desolate plain. The mountains turned blue and sank like ships behind us. The air grew smoky in front
of us, or clouds began to gather, or both. The pavement ended, the road
turned to washboard gravel, and the straightaway before us ran clear up into
the clouds. We entered them. The car began to shake; its engine began to
roar; the sound grew louder and louder, and when I turned to William to
voice concern, I found him bearded, overalled and puffing a huge stogie.
Rolling down my window to keep from being sick, I saw The Honky
Clipper had become a big, battered garbage truck. Then, in Wally's voice,
my father growled, "There she is!" And I turned to the source of all the*

smoke: a huge, smoldering mountain. "The Dump!" my father, or Wally, said.

It was even more massive than I'd expected: big as Baker, Hood or Adams, big as Mount Rainier. Crude roads spiraled round its sides, with scores of motley garbage trucks snaking slowly up and down them. Whole towns of tar-paper shanties clung at preposterous angles to the mounds and crags. There wasn't a tree, a shrub, a living plant in sight. There wasn't a stone or mound of soil in sight. The mountain was solid garbage. But which shack was Wally's? Which sallow-faced woman peering out from inside was his wife? And hey! Where was William? Where had the truck gone? Why was I on foot? And where were my shoes?

Oh yeah. Back home in the trash, waiting for Becky. But I couldn't be far from the summit. I'd make it. Even barefoot I'd maybe make it.

I wandered past the last high shanties, avoiding the furious stares of the Garbage Wives. The summit was lost in clouds, and the clouds had thickened: it began to rain—and by the time the drops reached me they made gray blotches on my skin and clothes, so that soon I'd turned the color of the Garbage People myself. A sound like screaming seagulls drifted down from the hidden summit. I walked faster, beginning not to care when the broken glass or shredded metal gashed my feet. Then, through the mist and smoke, I saw them—the hundreds, the thousands, the tens of thousands of Garbage Children. And on a steep little mound just above them, Santa, the Easter Bunny, the Tooth Fairy. Everybody was on The Dump!

Even Jesus was up there. His cross lay on its side near the summit, a bald whitewall tire hanging from one of its arms. But Christ wasn't on it. He was poking in a fresh truckload of refuse, looking for a loaf and a fish. Santa was picking through the same heap. And it must have been one of Wally's loads, because the packages they were ripping apart were my own.

Santa worked with joyless, nervous speed, tossing everything aside but food, which he threw, without looking, into the vast throng of kids down behind him. The kids swooped down on the scraps like frenzied gulls, tearing at the child who first caught it, shrieking with rage as he or she tried to eat and fend them off and run all at once—and when a runner tripped or stumbled, the pursuers piled on like rioting soccer fans. I watched till it no longer mattered who caught or ate what, who got clubbed or slashed by whom, or which ragged girl might be Becky. I watched till it didn't matter that some of them were toddlers for whom no one fended, and that when the piled bodies untangled, broken kids crawled bleeding down the slope, or just lay there convulsing, or perfectly quiet, never to rise again.

Turning back to the mound, I saw that Christ's and Santa's beards and hair were identically gray and stringy, that their once white robe and red suit were in filthy tatters, that their faces were blotched with the same rain, pale with the same exhaustion, their eyes bloodshot and half wild with the same despair.

The Tooth Fairy and Easter Bunny were both nearby, but no one paid them any heed. The Bunny's fur was matted in places, gone in others. There were open sores and clustered white nodules on its head and back. It was limping furtively from place to place, trying to hide the single dirty blue egg it held in its mouth. But whenever it found a likely recess a rat would dart forward, squealing and tearing at its fur, driving it away. The Tooth Fairy turned out to be some kind of oversized, mechanized insect, its thorax a huge yellow molar, its eyes and mouth three oozing black cavities, its legs six long, jointed dentist's tools that clattered as it scuttled, roachlike, from place to place. It was still looking for teeth, even there on the mountain, and finding them, too, in the mouths of dead or dying kids. It made a sickening, wet, sucking sound as it squatted over a fallen child, but the kid would just lie there, watching. When the Fairy detected a loose tooth—by smell, it seemed, to judge by its phlegmy snuffling—it sent a leg tipped by a metal forceps into the child's mouth, ripped out the tooth as the child briefly writhed, and stuffed it into one of its oozing eyes while its black mouth gurgled, then spat a piece of silver. None of the other kids looked twice at this money. There was nothing to buy on The Dump. They needed food.

The mob of Garbage Kids sporadically screamed; the sound was exactly like that of gulls; and when I looked back down to the base of the mountain, I saw that the road I'd come on had vanished underwater, and *that we were ringed in forever now by sea. Santa had lost his hat and seemed never to have had sleigh or reindeer, but he had a cough that racked his shriveled body as laughter had once shaken his fat. The nail holes in Christ's hands and feet were festering—I could smell them as I drew closer—but He went ceaselessly on with His search. He found eyeless heads and clean-picked spines of fishes. He found bright plastic polka-dot wrappers from long-gone loaves of Wonder Bread. Neither He nor Santa spoke. The only sounds were the sporadic screams of children, the soft soughing of the rain and Santa's tubercular hacking. On bleeding feet I limped over, and began to try, somehow, to help.*

They did not look up.

A robin sang.

I woke in a sweat, wiped my face on the cool sheet, groped my way to the bathroom, turned on the cold water and dashed it against my face over and over and over again.

9. THE BRIDGE

Sitting alone in the Lincoln, waiting for William to take me to the genuine dump, I felt my life's mission was irrevocably gone. It had seemed so simple once. I faced the facts ("See the dead doggie"), then rationally responded. And the grown-ups, if they weren't appalled, were delighted and amazed. But how could I rationally respond to anything when I no longer even knew what a fact was? I had *longings*. This was a fact. I had fears, yearnings and dreams that were ruining my sleep and ruling my waking mind. Yet fear, yearning and dreams were none of them facts. What should I make of this?

What should I make of the fact that right at that moment, when I closed my eyes there in the Lincoln, I felt as if I were sitting in an empty, dismal alley between two doors in two huge buildings? What should I make of my feeling that inside one door was the

Mount Dump of my nightmare, and inside the other was the unknown but undoubtedly dreadful place to which my father was
about to take me? What should I make of my unwillingness to enter
either door, even if it meant hunching in this dismal alley forever?
What should I make of the fact that, in spite of these distinct, intense
feelings, there were no such doors, buildings or alley?

Opening my eyes, I tried to quell my growing panic by focus-
ing on the visible situation alone—the "sitting in a parked car facts."
This impulse was a godsend. It allowed me to discover, in an instant,
that the fake leather seat upon which I slumped was actually roomy
and comfortable, nothing like an alley. It allowed me to see that the
wooden dashboard in front of me had once been part of a tree, and
that its deep, grainy brown still exuded the tree's soothing presence.
It allowed me to slip off my thongs, place my bare feet on the wood,
feel its coolness and smoothness, note that my feet were brown from
summer sun, compare their brownness with that of the wood and
conclude, with inexplicably deep satisfaction, that the dashboard's
brown was ever so slightly browner.

I sighed. Why was I feeling better? Why were the simple "sitting in a parked car" facts so soothing? I had no idea. But I kept
looking for more. I noticed that my left big toenail was half black
where I'd stubbed it on a brick a month or so ago, and that the
blackened toe was pointing at a strand of spider's silk hanging from
the sun visor. I saw that morning sunlight was making a tiny prism
in the strand, and that this prism was moving in a breeze so gentle
that not even my bare feet could feel it. Seeking the source of the
breeze, I realized that the window nearest me was maybe a fifth of
the way down, and that the car was filled with an unusually fresh and
fragrant air. Breathing deeply, I realized what was different about the
air: *autumn.* That was the fragrance. Fall was coming. And somehow
this was the most soothing thing yet. Something about the fact that
no matter what the world's armies or politicians or lunatics had been

doing all summer, and no matter what Wally, Becky or The Dump turned out to be, the planet was still going about the slow, stately business of tilting, as it gyred round the sun, causing solar rays to strike me at a different enough angle that I recognized, at just that moment, the whole symphony of facts called "a change of season." I nearly laughed at the simple beauty of this—which was very unlike me. Then I nearly cried at it—which was unlike me as well. I had no words, then, for any of these feelings. But I felt again that sense of sitting in an in-between place. Not an alley, this time. Just a hiatus between seasons. A calm little pool in the steady stream of the Present. Yet to sit so completely in the pool *felt* like a "present," like a gift. It was so serene and cool and sunlit. And The Honky Clipper, parked though it was, really did seem to be gliding like a ship. Summer was slipping away behind her, autumn sliding toward her prow, and a little cobweb hung over her helm, bowed, like a spinnaker, by a breeze imperceptible even to bare brown feet. I felt a rush of trust—felt that life might be not just tolerable but beautiful, if I could only remember to find the bare Present. The panic, the disappointment, the fears that had just filled me were no real part of this Present. Again, I had no words to express this. But I'd begun to feel that there was *always* a simple Present, and that this might be the one "fact" that ever needed facing . . .

Then, two additional facts came trundling out of the house.

William's shirt was half untucked. His zipper was partway down. The hair below his bald spot was mashed like a meadow after a hailstorm. His face, when the soft sunlight struck it, went into an apple-doll squint. He was probably trying—without coffee, it looked like—to recall what on earth had made him promise to visit a dump at this ungodly hour. Some craziness about a garbage girl, or woman? Something about Jesus telling Dory to give her shoes to the trash collector's kids? His squint unshrivelled some when he caught sight of The Honky Clipper. What a steed. What a scow. Not a scratch on her. But what a dinosaur, too. And what a gas hog! He wondered how badly he'd get skinned if he traded her in on one of those snazzy little Nipponese pickups.

Esther followed, in bathrobe and curlers, carrying a cup of coffee in both hands like an acolyte bearing a chalice. Except the bathrobe had purple and green starfish on it. And her curlers were bright orange. And folds from her pillow had stenciled creases in her soft pink cheeks. I tried not to notice, but there also seemed to be some smut on her nose. Not "morning people," my parents.

William climbed into the car, put on his sunglasses and started the engine. Esther handed him the cup. While he sipped at it she mentioned, to my relief, both the shirttail and the zipper. William made the necessary repairs, then said, "One good deed deserves another, Mama. There's somethin' grim on your nose."

They cackled like laying hens while Esther took care of it, then exchanged one of the compulsory little kisses they exchange whenever one of them leaves the property without the other. Esther then waddled round the car, obviously intending to bestow a similar kiss on me—but I hit a button, zipping my window, then another, locking my door. She settled for kissing her own index finger, touching it to the glass by my face and proclaiming, as if it solved all problems, "I'll have breakfast waiting."

I watched her finger smudge slowly vanish. Then William belched, muttered, "Sorry!" said, "Let's go, America!" reached for the gearshift—

—and gasped, jerking his hand away.

A spider was crouched on the gear lever. A brown orb weaver. The same one that hung the little spinnaker over the dash, most likely. "Let me catch it," I said, but William was scared of spiders and instantly took a swipe at it. It jumped to the floor and headed for cover. He tried to crush it with his foot, pinned some legs, but the spider tore the trapped legs out of their sockets and scuttled back under the seat.

"Damn!" my father said.

I leaned down and looked. The orb weaver was squatting by a rag directly beneath William. It had six legs left. A tiny bead of fluid shone where one of the legs was missing. "See it?" William asked.

I closed my eyes, then said, "Nope." Stating a fact. I loved orb weavers. The patterned backs, myriad eyes, mathematical minds, ascetic patience; the little gray mummies that collected beneath their webs. I even loved the coma-inducing bites—so much more merciful than the crude methods by which humans dispatched one another day and night round the globe. The only thing I *didn't* like was when I'd catch one by the silk to get it out of the house (to save it from William or Esther), and it would lower and lower and lower itself as I rushed for the door, yard after yard of silk spilling from the bellies of even the littlest ones, till I feared they'd use up their insides before I ever set them free.

I wanted to free this one now, but had to pretend it didn't exist to save it from William. Looking right at it, I aimed my mind at its mind, and thought, *Hold still. I'll free you later.*

"Oh well," said William. "On to the dump!"

EXPECTING A LONG DRIVE, I SLUMPED DOWN IN MY SEAT, closed my eyes, forgot all about seasons and prisms, lost all track of the simple Present and hunched, half-terrified, in my grim little mental alley again. But we hadn't driven more than five or six miles, all of them in the city, when my father said, "Snap to, matey!"

I loathed his nautical terminology, but did sit up, looking for what I guessed would be a modest mountain. What I saw instead was an interminable peek-proof cyclone fence, then a broad asphalt driveway. HAUTON & LEE LANDFILL, said a huge sign. And under the names was a complicated list of hours, rates and rules. I'd half-expected something like this, but still my stomach knotted. We drove through the open gate—

—and where last night there'd been a mountain there was now only sky. My gaze fell lower and lower and lower still, till it entered a pit as square as a tombstone, deep as a canyon, big as a small town and roaring like Niagara.

William pulled up beside an aluminum trailer, the entire outer wall of which proclaimed: PAY HERE. There was one window in the wall. A woman in a red wig slid the window open. There was a cash register to her right, a tray full of lipstick-smeared cigarette butts to her left. Her fingernails were those of the Barbie fairy. Her bored eyes were caked in blue eyeshadow. Her mouth was twisted into a permanent smirk. Except for the fact that her face was clean, she looked like the Garbage Wives in my dream.

Cowed by her scowl, William blurted, "We've, er, only come to look!"

"This ain't no national park," the woman said. "You get in people's way. Wear 'n' tear on driveways. A look'll cost a buck."

William paid her the money. We then drove down a graded gravel drive wide as a freeway, and William parked the car at the edge of the vast pit. I stayed slouched in the seat, holding my stomach. William studied me a moment, then climbed out, circled round, and tried to open my door. "Come on," he called through the window.

I didn't move. He used his key. The door swung open. The roar hit me like a sonic boom. "Come on," he repeated, patting my bare knee. "Hop out. It's really kind of a fascinating place!"

It was his excruciatingly forced good cheer that spurred me into action. I brushed past his extended hand, circled the car, stepped up on the front bumper, sat on the hood, crossed my arms over my abdomen and at long last beheld The Dump:

No families, no shacks, no ragged scavengers. Just a steady stream of trucks, all identical to Wally's, all driven by tired- or sad- or sour-looking men. Truck after truck bearing load after load of reeking, runny, unsalvageable refuse, backing up to the brink, disgorging their dredge, then back to the city for more. And the instant they were gone a bulldozer the size of a house tore into the load, ramming it off the edge and down into Jurassic depths where more 'dozers, dump trucks and spike-wheeled steamrollers mashed it flat, covered it with fill, buried it under layer upon layer of detritus and dirt.

"They'll be closing this place soon," William shouted over the roar. "Big as it is, it's not big enough! There's a new system going in east of the mountains. A *huge* one! It'll handle every city in the Northwest. Enormous plastic-lined pits. Double walls. Very sanitary. The trucks'll just empty at the railroad depots in every town. They'll haul it all east by train."

He was stating the facts. He was trying to be helpful. But when he again laid a hand on my knee I felt like a pinned spider. I threw off his hand, jumped down from the hood and stepped alone to the brink.

"All right," I told myself, trying to face it all down at once. "Okay. No mountain, no Becky, no Dump, no magic people. And my gyroscope and stuff is under there. Lots of layers down, by now. That's the way it is. That's the way it is . . ."

But as I watched the machinery roar back and forth, crushing my gifts to nonexistent wonders, my useless love for Wally, crushing the first hope I'd ever held that the world might contain some mystery or hidden power potent enough to counteract the chaos I studied every night on TV, I began to tremble. William noticed and moved up behind me. Afraid, I suppose, of how close I stood to the edge, but just as afraid to have his hand again rejected, he hunched behind me, fretting with his shirt buttons and hair.

"I didn't get the facts," I said quietly. But then my voice cracked and my face gave way. "I wanted it to be *true!*" I sobbed. "I wanted them to be *real!*" And now he took my shoulders, tried to give me a hug. But again I broke free, angrily swiped at my tears, took a deep, determined breath and in a low, dull monotone said, "I got carried away."

Said: "Stupid."

Said: "Forget it. Thanks for bringing me."

And turned back to the car.

William stepped back, letting me walk to the Lincoln alone. And for a long time he stayed at the brink there, watching the big machines work, terrified, I suppose, to follow me and find himself again rejected.

So, alone in the Lincoln, I went on striving to face the new facts.

The world is dying, I was thinking. I know I was young, but that's exactly what I felt. *The world is dying, and people and animals, too. And there's no secret, there's no magic, there's nothing powerful or good enough to save it.*

If William were me, I was thinking, *he'd get a library book about landfills and read it.*

If Esther were me, I was thinking, *she'd pray.*

"But I'm *me!*" I said aloud. "And it's dying, and there's *no one!*" And the sense of helplessness so overwhelmed me that the blood pumped from my heart in a jet too strong for my body. I doubled a fist, started beating my thigh. My heart was dying to worship, my soul begging to bow down. I felt my life, my very life, depended upon me finding, at that very moment, some secret or escape clause or being that could lead me to an unknown source of light.

And that's when I saw, first, just a tiny prism. Then a single strand of spider's silk, trembling in the dusty, sunlit air. Impossibly frail. Built by a cripple. Yet it stretched from the driver's seat, to the steering wheel, to my father's open window—

—and no brown orb weaver anywhere in sight.

. . .

WHEN WILLIAM OPENED HIS DOOR I QUICKLY TURNED AWAY to my window. And I know, now, that my turning filled him with sadness and fear. Such a simple thing, my turning. Yet that was the day and moment when my father's eyes began darting away whenever I'd try to meet his gaze. And fifteen years later, they still dart away.

There is a formative period in the life of families during which parents and kids don't just live with each other, they *create* each other. At that moment in the car, my father's and my ability to create each other ended. Things froze between us. At the moment I turned away, William decided that he'd failed me, that I was hopelessly wounded, that Esther would blame him for it, that the joy had somehow vanished from their marriage, that life was unanswerably unfair and unanswerably hard. He had brought me to the landfill to help me—had brought me face to face with my supposedly beloved facts. And I'd rejected his help, rejected his touch, rejected his hug. He had nothing more to offer. For him to meet my eyes, from that moment forward, was to meet, head-on, that rejection.

This, I believe, is very close to what he felt.

So William, Dad, Father, *please,* listen. It's all been a mistake, this freeze between us. And I have written these many pages almost solely to come to this:

I was *smiling* as I turned away. Smiling, and sitting again in the Present as if in the ship you've always longed for, with autumn sliding toward me, and summer slipping away behind. I can't explain it, I can't possibly say why, but *all hope,* for me, had just hung from a diaphanous one-strand bridge. And in the nick of time I'd found that bridge, and crossed it. I began, at that strange moment, to find my way. I continue to seek the bare Present, because of that moment. I doubt you'll understand this, but I eventually became a

Buddhist (half agnostic, half closet-Catholic!) because of that moment. My life's effort, my life's prayer, began in that landfill. *So how
can you think you failed me by taking me there?*

I can, and do, ask your forgiveness for this long misunder-
standing. But I can't ask it for what happened at that moment. For I
swear I turned—still smiling—not from you, but from your opening
door, simply to keep from seeing my beautiful bridge snap.

POSTSCRIPT: THE GARBAGE MAN'S DAUGHTER

Dear Dory,

 I read your story. I cherished it. I thank you for
it. But it isn't quite finished. I find I understand a
few things I saw fifteen years ago. Things as unknown
to you as your bridge and smile were to me. Hoping
you won't mind, I'm going to try to make those
things into a last chapter here.

 This chapter happens in our yard, very early in
the morning, exactly six days after I took you to that
landfill, over a decade and a half ago. I play no part
in the story. I'm just the observer. There are just two
characters here, and one of them stays invisible. Yet
thanks to you, your story, I understand my visible
character so well I might make like a fancy author
and climb right inside his head a time or two.

 According to the Stevens' poem you started
with, I guess I should start by saying "day was
creeping down." Except it wasn't. It was dark, the
hours still felt "Wee," and the lawn was still an
"unfamiliar sepia tone" beneath the streetlights when
the dogs started barking, the big truck drove up to

our curb, the engine shut off, and the visible one of my two characters came trudging across our lawn.

Now here are my first fancy author's assumptions: I think this character noticed, as he was crossing our lawn, that the days were growing shorter and that fall was coming fast. I think this was the first time he'd noticed it all year. And I don't think he noticed it because he was a budding Buddhist or had slipped into a Simple Present or anything like that. I think he noticed it because, in the dim light and shadows, he would barely be able to make out a certain solemn, wide-eyed little face he wanted very much to see.

I got a good look at my character's face, through our open kitchen window. In fact, as he was coming round the corner of the house I saw his face conducting an out-and-out battle with itself. First he wore a great big philosophical sort of scowl. Then he started grinning. Then he seemed to feel his grin, and started struggling to get his scowl back. Then he just shrugged and went back to grinning. I had no idea what this was about, fifteen years ago. But now (thanks to you) I'm sure he was thinking something like: "So what if she knows I like her? She might be nuts, but she don't bite."

When he reached the back steps and found them empty, he turned to the camellias back at the corner. He was still grinning while he did that, obviously hoping our second character would come jumping out. But then—remembering, I think, the unchanging dash of a mouth and dead-earnest brown eyes—his grin faded, and I figure he thought something like, "Nope. Not the playful sort. She just ain't here . . ."

I don't believe this surprised him much. He knew she couldn't always be there. Another two weeks and school would be starting. The weather would be turning cold. What did surprise him, though, when he pulled the lid from our can, was the stench that came billowing out. And his reaction to this was something! Jamming the lid back down, he stepped quickly back from the can and looked up at our unlit second story. I had to duck fast, since I was watching him out the window directly below. But even while ducking I heard him growl, in a voice, as you say, like Santa's grubby nephew's voice, "Hope ya ain't sick!"

You must know, Dory, that it was mostly ugly suspicions that had me up so early, spying on this man. But seeing his losing struggle with the scowl, I'd felt inclined to like him. And now this "Hope ya ain't sick!" clinched it. I knew you had a friend there, not some child-cheating conniver, so I raised my face back up to the kitchen window, not caring now whether he saw me; figuring if he did, we could just talk.

He was busy, though, pulling out the stogie he'd saved to smoke in your company. And watching his face—I mean seeing it all over again, as I write this, in light of your story—I believe, pretentious as it may sound, that I know exactly what went on in him for the next minute or two:

I believe that first, just as he was tearing off the cigar's cellophane, he somehow knew that my second character—you—would never be there waiting for

him. Not ever again. And I don't believe this
surprised him too much. What _did_ surprise him,
though, what I saw right through that window was a
grief that blew into him like a cold wind, twisting his
face up, bending that big overfed body, leaving him,
for a while there, so weak and full of sorrow that it
was as if he'd lost his own daughter. As if he'd lost
Becky. I know this about him, Dory. I don't know
how, but I know.

He flipped over his can after a while, and
half-collapsed onto it. Then he licked the cigar, bit it,
lit it and had himself a long, slow smoke, all the
while muttering this and that to the steps, as if our
second character was still there. (And I may as well
admit it: at this point I outright _loved_ the guy.) His
chat with the empty steps seemed to soothe him. I
guess the worship of emptiness has that effect on
some people, huh? (I guess maybe I'm wrong. Maybe
he _was_ a Buddhist.) At any rate he finally sighed,
stood up, emptied our stinky can into his big one,
tossed his cigar in after it, shouldered his load, told
the empty steps, "Gotta scoot" and trudged away.

I was so damned fond of him by then that I
shot up to your bedroom—where you lay sound
asleep—just so I could watch him a little more. And I
got your window open and the lace curtains pulled
shut before he could have seen or heard me. Yet
when he reached his truck he did another strange
thing. Quick as a cat he spun, loaded can and all,
toward the house and stared right _at_ your window.
And he kept on staring, Dory, though the curtains
lay still and I never once moved. Forgetting the load
digging into his shoulder, scowling to see through the

distance and dark, he stared so long the dogs forgot all about him, and quit barking. It was into that quiet that the first robin sang.

"Shadow, must've been," I heard him finally mutter. Then he did a last strange thing. Still watching your window, he gave it, gave <u>you,</u> a slow, garbage-can-hampered, yet surprisingly deep bow. Then in that voice that made you wish he'd clear the googy from his throat but at the same time reminded you of elves or angels or something, he said, "Good-bye, little daughter."

And I found myself blinking back tears.

When he started toward the next house the barking started up. He joined the dogs, and the singing robins, with "Ol' Man River," the little bit he knew.

Day crept down. The sky turned a lighter gray. It began to rain.

Forgiveness is ours, Dory.

Love,

William,

Dad,

Father.

THE MICKEY MANTLE
KOAN

for my mother

ON APRIL 6, 1965, MY BROTHER NICHOLAS JOHN DUNCAN DIED OF WHAT HIS SURGEONS CALLED "COMPLICATIONS" AFTER THREE UNSUCCESSFUL OPEN-HEART OPERATIONS. HE WAS SEVENTEEN AT THE TIME—FOUR YEARS MY ELDER TO THE VERY DAY. HE'D BEEN THE FASTEST SPRINTER IN HIS HIGH SCHOOL CLASS TILL THE VALVE IN HIS HEART BEGAN TO CLOSE, BUT HE WAS SO BONKERS ABOUT BASEBALL THAT HE'D PREFERRED PLAYING A MEDIOCRE JV SHORTSTOP TO STARRING AT VARSITY TRACK. AS A BALLPLAYER HE WAS A COMPETENT FIELDER, HAD A STRONG AND FAIRLY ACCURATE ARM AND STOLE BASES WITH EASE—WHEN HE REACHED THEM. BUT NO MATTER HOW MUCH HE PRACTICED OR WHAT STANCES, GRIPS OR SELF-HYPNOTIC TRICKS HE TRIED, HE LACKED THE HAND-eye magic that consistently lays bat-fat against ball, and remained one of the weakest hitters on his team.

John lived his entire life on the outskirts of Portland, Oregon —650 miles from the nearest Major League team—and in franchise-less cities in the fifties and early sixties there were really just two types of fans: those who thought the Yankees stood for everything right with America, and those who thought they stood for every-thing wrong with it. My brother was an extreme manifestation of the former type. He conducted a one-man campaign to notify the world that Roger Maris's sixty-one homers in '61 came in three fewer at-bats than Babe Ruth's sixty in '27. He maintained—all statistical evidence to the contrary—that Clete Boyer was a better third baseman than his brother, Ken, simply because Clete was a Yankee. He combed the high school every October for fools willing to bet against Whitey Ford in the World Series, and if he couldn't find one there he knew he'd find one at home: me. He tried to enhance our games of catch by portraying the first two-thirds of Kubek to Richardson to Skowron double plays, but the intensity of his Kubek for some reason caused his Richardson to imagine my "Moose" to be the genuine six-four article—so off the ball would sail into the neighbor's apple orchard. He may not have been the only kid on the block who considered Casey Stengel the greatest sage since Solomon, but I'm sure he was the only one who consid-ered Yogi Berra the second greatest. And though he would concede that Ted Williams, and later Willie Mays, had slightly more produc-tive careers than Mickey Mantle, even this was for a pro-Yankee reason: Mantle was his absolute hero, but his tragic hero. The Mick, my brother maintained, was the greatest raw talent of all time. He was one to whom great gifts were given, from whom great gifts had been ripped away, and the more scarred his knees became, the more frequently he fanned, the more flagrant his limp and apologetic his smile, the more John revered him. And toward this single Yankee I too was able to feel a touch of reverence, if only because, on the subject of scars, I considered my brother an unimpeachable authority: he'd worn one from the time he was eight, compliments of the Mayo Clinic, that wrapped clear around his chest in a wavy line, like stitching round a clean white baseball.

Yankees aside, John and I had more in common than a birthday. We bickered regularly with our middle brother and little sister but almost never with each other. We were both bored, occasionally to insurrection, by school-going, church-going and any game or sport that didn't involve a ball. We both preferred, as a mere matter of style, Indians to cowboys, knights of the road to Knights of Columbus, Buster Keaton to Charlie Chaplin, Gary Cooper to John Wayne, deadbeats to brown-nosers, and even brown-nosers to Elvis Presley. We shared a single devil's food chocolate cake on our joint birthday, invariably annihilating the candle flames with a tandem blowing effort, only to realize that we'd once again forgotten to make a wish. And whenever the parties were over or the house was stuffy, the parents cranky or the TV insufferably dumb, whenever we were restless, punchy or just feeling the "nuthin' to do" feeling, catch—with a hardball—was the nuthin' John and I chose to do.

We were not exclusive, or not by intention: our father and middle brother and an occasional cousin or friend would join us now and then. But something in most people's brains or bloodstreams sent them bustling off to more industrious endeavors before the real rhythm of the thing ever took hold. Genuine catch-playing occurs in a double-limbo between busyness and idleness, and between the imaginary and the real. As with any contemplative pursuit, it takes time, and the ability to forget time, to slip into this dual limbo, and to discover (i.e. lose) oneself in the music of the game.

It helps to have a special spot to play. Ours was a shaded, ninety-foot corridor between one neighbor's apple orchard and the other's stand of old-growth Douglas firs, on a stretch of lawn so lush and mossy it sucked the heat out of even the hottest grounders. I always stood in the north, John in the south. When I had to chase his wild throws into the orchard I'd sometimes hide the ball in my shirt and fire back a Gravenstein, leaving him to judge, while it was in the air, whether it was fit to catch and eat or an overripe rotter about to splatter in his mitt. When he chased my dud pegs into the firs, he'd give me an innocent, uncomplaining smile as he trotted back into position—then rifle a cone, dirt clod or stone at my head.

But these antics were the exception. The deep shade, the two-hundred-foot firs, the mossy footing and fragrance of apples all made it a setting more conducive to mental-vacationing than to any kind of disciplined effort, so a vigorous serenity was the rule. We might call balls and strikes for an imaginary inning or two, throw each other a few pop-ups or grounders or maybe count the number of errorless catches and throws we could make (three-hundreds were common, and our record was high in the eight-hundreds). But as our movements became fluid and the throws brisk and accurate, the pretense of practice would inevitably fade, and we'd just aim for the chest and fire, *hisssss pop! hisssss pop!* till a meal, a duty or total darkness forced us to recall that this is the world in which even timeless pursuits come to an end.

Our talk must have seemed strange to eavesdroppers. We lived in our bodies during catch, and our minds and mouths, though still operative, were just along for the ride. Most of the noise I made was with the four or five pieces of Bazooka I was invariably working over, though once the gum lost its sugar I'd sometimes narrate our efforts in a stream-of-doggerel play-by-play. My brother's speech was a bit more coherent, but of no greater didactic intent: he poured out idle litanies of Yankee worship or even idler braggadocio à la Dizzy Dean, all of it artfully spiced with spat sunflower-seed husks.

Dan Jenkins defined the catch-player perfectly when he spoke of athletes who "mostly like to stand around, chew things, spit and scratch their nuts." Not too complimentary a definition, perhaps, yet from the catch-playing point of view, what are the alternatives? Why run around wrecking the world for pay when you could be standing in one place transcending time? Why chew Rolaids, swallow your spit and feel too inhibited to scratch where it itches when you could be chewing Day's Work or Double Bubble, thooting out end-over-enders, easing the itch and firing off hisses and pops? Whatever he really meant, Yogi Berra defended catch-players best. He said: "If you can't copy 'em, don't imitate 'em."

BUT ONE DAY, WHEN WE WERE SIXTEEN AND TWELVE RESPEC-tively, my big brother surprised me out there in our corridor. Snagging a low throw, he closed his mitt round the ball, stuck it under his arm, stared off into the trees and got serious for a minute. All his life, he said, he'd struggled to be a shortstop and a hitter, but he was older now, had a clearer notion of what he could and couldn't do, and it was time to get practical. Time to start developing obvious strengths and evading flagrant weaknesses. "So I've decided," he concluded, "to become a junk pitcher."

I didn't believe a word of this. My brother had been a slugger worshiper from birth. He went on embellishing his idea, though, and even made it sound rather poetic: to foil some muscle-bound fence-buster with an off-speed piece of crap that blupped off his bat like a cow custard—this, he maintained, was the pluperfect pith of an attribute he called "Solid Cool." What was neither poetic nor cool was the errant garbage he began winging my way, or the whining I did as I took so many ball-hunting excursions back into the apples that I was finally moved to stage a sit-down strike and tell him to go hunt his own junk.

But to my surprise, he did go hunt it. And to my regret, I didn't recognize till months later just how carefully considered this new junk-pitching jag had been. That John's throwing arm was better than his batting eye had always been obvious, and it made sense to exploit that. But there were other factors he didn't mention: like the sharp pains in his chest every time he took a full swing, or the new ache that half-blinded and sickened him whenever he ran full speed. Finding the high arts of slugging and base-stealing physically impossible, he'd simply lowered his sights enough to keep his baseball dreams alive. No longer able to emulate his heroes, he set out to bamboozle those who thought they could. To that end he'd learned a feeble knuckler, a roundhouse curve, a submarine fastball formidable solely for its lack of accuracy, and was trashing his arm and my patience with his would-be screwball, when his doctors informed our family that a valve in his heart was rapidly closing. He might live as long as five years if we let it go, they said, but immediate surgery was best, since his recuperative powers were greatest now. John said nothing to any of this. He just waited till the day he was due at the hospital, snuck down to the stable where he kept his horse, saddled her up and galloped away. He rode about twenty miles, to the farm of a friend, and stayed there in hiding for nearly two weeks. But when he stole home one morning for clean clothes and money, my father caught him, and first tried to force him, but finally convinced him, to have the operation and be done with it.

Once in the hospital he was cooperative, cheerful and unrelentingly courageous. He survived second, third and fourth operations, several stoppings of the heart and a nineteen-day coma. He recovered enough at one point, even after the coma, to come home for a week or so. But the overriding "complication" to which his principal surgeon kept making oblique references turned out to be a heart so ravaged by scalpel wounds that an artificial valve had nothing but shreds to be sutured to. Bleeding internally, pissing blood, he was moved into an oxygen tent in an isolated room, where he remained fully conscious, and fully determined to heal, for two months after his surgeons had abandoned him. And, against all odds, his condition stabilized, then began to improve. The doctors reappeared and began to discuss the feasibility of a fifth operation.

Then came a second complication: staph. We were reduced overnight from genuine hope to awkward pleas for divine intervention. We invoked no miracles. Two weeks after contracting the infection, my brother died.

AT HIS FUNERAL, A PREACHER WHO DIDN'T KNOW JOHN FROM Judge Kenesaw Mountain Landis eulogized him so lavishly and inaccurately that I was moved to a state of tearlessness that lasted for years. It's an unenviable task, certainly, trying to make public sense of a private catastrophe you know little about. But had I been in that preacher's shoes I think I might have mentioned one or two of my brother's actual attributes, if only to assure late-arriving mourners that they hadn't wandered into the wrong funeral. The person we were endeavoring to miss had, for instance, been a C student but an excellent horseman, had smothered every kind of meat he ate, including chicken and fish, with ketchup, and had often gone so far as to wear sunglasses indoors in the relentless quest for Solid Cool. He'd had the disconcerting habit of sound-testing his pleasant baritone by bellowing *Beeee-Ooooooooooo!* down any alley or hall that looked like it might contain an echo. He'd had an interesting, slangy obliviousness to proportion: any altercation from a fistfight to a world war was "a rack," any authority from our mother to the head of the UN was "the Brass," any pest from the neighbor kid to Khrushchev was "a butt wipe," and any kind of ball from a BB to the sun was "the orb." He was brave: whenever anyone his age harassed me, John warned them once and punched them out the second time, or got punched trying. He was also unabashedly, majestically vain. He referred to his person, with obvious pride and in spite of his teen acne, as "the Bod." He was an immaculate dresser.

And he loved to stare at himself, publicly or privately, in mirrors, windows, puddles, chrome car fenders, upside down in teaspoons, and to solemnly comb his long auburn hair over and over, like his hero, "Kookie" Kookson, on "77 Sunset Strip."

His most astonishing attribute, to me at least, was his never-ending skein of girlfriends. What struck me when I was small was that he wanted them around at all; what impressed me later was that he was able to be so relaxed and natural around them. He had a simple but apparently efficient rating system for all female acquaintances: he called it "percentage of Cool versus percentage of Crud." A steady girlfriend usually weighed in at around 95 percent Cool, 5 percent Crud, and if the Crud level reached 10 percent it was time to start quietly looking elsewhere. Only two girls ever made his 100 percent Cool List, and I was struck by the fact that neither was a girlfriend, and one wasn't even pretty: whatever 100 percent Cool was, it was not skin deep. No girl ever came close to a 100 percent Crud rating, by the way: my brother was chivalrous.

He was not religious. The devout wing of our family believed in resurrection of the body, provided a preacher had at some point immersed the whole sinful thing, so my brothers and I were baptized en masse in the winter of '62, in a frigid outdoor swimming pool. The only revelatory moment for John and me, however, occurred in the shower room afterward, when we simultaneously noticed—then noticed each other noticing—that the icy immersion had caused the privates of our NFL-tackle-sized pastor to shrivel into an object a hungry rodent could have mistaken for a peanut, shelled no less, and clearly in no kind of shape for sin. John believed in God, but passively, with nothing like the passion he had for the Yankees. He seemed a little more friendly with Jesus. "Christ is cool," he'd say, if forced to show his hand. But I don't recall him speaking of any sort of goings-on between them till he casually mentioned, a day or two before he died, a conversation they'd just had there in the oxygen tent. And even then John was John: what impressed him more than the fact of Christ's presence or the consoling words He spoke were the natty suit and tie He was wearing.

John had a girlfriend right up to the end—a tall, pretty blonde with the highest rating yet: only 1.5 percent Crud. He was my most intimate friend, but a hero to me even so. In fact my faith in his heroism was so complete that when my mother woke me one spring morning by saying he'd just died, I was unable to feel grief. What my orthodox, baseball-worshiping brain fixed upon instead was the top-of-the-line Wilson outfielder's glove I would now be inheriting, and the dreams and courage I believed I'd keep alive by simply sliding it onto my left hand.

BUT ON THE MORNING AFTER HIS DEATH, APRIL 7, 1965, a small brown-paper package arrived at our house, special delivery from New York City, addressed to John. I brought it to my mother, and leaned over her shoulder as she sat down to open it. Catching a whiff of antiseptic, I thought at first that it came from her hair: she'd spent the last four months of her life in a straight-back chair by my brother's bed, and hospital odors had permeated her. But the smell grew stronger as she began unwrapping the brown paper, till I realized it came from the object inside.

It was a small, white, cylindrical cardboard bandage box. "Johnson & Johnson," it said in red letters. "12 inches × 10 yards," it added in blue. Strange. Then I saw that it had been slit in half by a knife or scalpel and bound back together with adhesive tape: there was another layer, something hiding inside. My mother smiled as she began to rip the tape away. At the same time, tears were landing in her lap. Then the tape was gone, the little cylinder fell in two, and inside, nested in tissue, was a baseball. Immaculate white leather.

Perfect red stitching. On one cheek, in faint green ink, the signature of Joseph Cronin and the trademark, REACH, THE SIGN OF QUALITY. And on the opposite cheek, with a bright blue ballpoint, a tidy but flowing hand had written,

To John—
My Best Wishes
Your Pal
Mickey Mantle
April 6, 1965.

THE BALL PROCEEDED TO PERCH UPON OUR FIREPLACE MAN-tel—an unintentional pun on my mother's part. We used half the Johnson & Johnson box as a pedestal for it, and for years saved the other half, figuring that the bandage it once contained held Mantle's storied knee together for a game. Even after my mother explained that the ball came not out of the blue but in response to a letter, I considered it a treasure, told all my friends about it, invited the closest to stop by and gawk at it. But gradually I began to see that the public reaction to the ball was disconcertingly predictable. The first response was usually "Wow! Mickey Mantle!" But then they'd get the full story: "Mantle signed it the day he died? Your brother never even *saw* it?" And that made them uncomfortable. This was not at all the way an autographed baseball was supposed to behave. How could an immortal call himself your pal, how could you be the recipient of the Mick's best wishes and still just lie back and die?

I began to share the discomfort. Over the last three of my thirteen years I'd devoured scores of baseball books, fiction and nonfiction, all of which agreed that a bat, program, mitt or ball signed by a Big League hero is a sacred relic, that we *should* expect such relics to have magical properties, and that they *would* prove pivotal in a young protagonist's life. Yet here I was, the young protagonist. Here was my relic. And all the damned thing did before long was depress and confuse me. I stopped showing the ball to people, tried ignoring it, found this impossible, tried instead to pretend that the blue ink was an illegible scribble and that the ball was just a ball. But the ink *wasn't* illegible: it never stopped saying what it said. So finally I tried picking the ball up and studying it, *hard,* hoping to discover exactly why it haunted me so. But it was far too easy to come up with reasons. The hospital reek of the entire package. The date of its arrival. The even crueler date of the inscription. The way the box, like my brother, had been sliced in half, then bound clumsily back together. Severed white skin. Brilliant red stitches.

   Best Wishes . . . Pal . . .

   A lot of us strive, in a crisis, to fall back on reason. But when our dreams come false and our prayers become unanswerable questions, the reason we fall back on has a tendency to turn caustic, and so, in trying to explain our crisis, merely explains it away. Applying my reason to the ball, I told myself that a standard sports hero had received a letter from a standard distraught mother, had signed, packaged and mailed off the standard, soporifically heroic response, had failed to realize that the boy he inscribed the ball to might be dead when it arrived, and so had mailed us a blackly comic non sequitur. "That's all there is to it," reason told me. Which left me no option but to pretend that I wasn't hurting, that I hadn't expected or wanted any more from the ball than I got, that I'd harbored no desire for any sort of sign, any imprimatur, any flicker of recognition from an Above or a Beyond.

   I then began falling to pieces, for lack of that sign.

   The bad thing about falling to pieces is that it hurts. The good thing about it is that once you're lying there in shards you've got nothing left to protect, and so have no reason not to be honest. I finally got honest with Mantle's baseball: I finally picked the thing up, read it once more and admitted for the first time that I was *pissed*. As is always the case with arriving baseballs, timing is the key—and this cheery orb was inscribed on the day its recipient lay dying and arrived on the day he was being embalmed! This was *not* a "harmless coincidence." It was the shabbiest, most embittering joke that Providence had ever played on me. My best friend and brother was dead, dead, dead, Mantle's damned ball and best wishes made that loss far less tolerable, and *that,* I told myself, really *was* all there was to it.

I hardened my heart, quit the baseball team, went out for golf. I practiced like a zealot, cheated like hell, kicked my innocuous, naive little opponents all over the course. I sold my beautiful inherited mitt for a pittance.

BUT, AS IS USUAL IN BASEBALL STORIES, THAT WASN'T ALL there was to it.

I'd never heard of Zen koans at the time, and Mickey Mantle is certainly no *roshi*. But baseball and Zen are two things that Americans and Japanese have each imported without embargo; and *roshis* are men famous for hitting things hard with a big wooden stick; and a koan is a perfectly nonsensical or nonsequacious statement given by an old pro *(roshi)* to a rookie (layman or monk); and the stress of living with and meditating upon one of these mind-numbing pieces of nonsense is said to eventually prove illuminating. So I know of no better way to describe what the message on the ball became for me than to call it a koan.

In the first place, the damned thing's batteries just wouldn't run down. For weeks, months, *years,* every time I saw those ten blithe, blue-inked words they knocked me off balance like a sudden shove from behind. They were an emblem of all the false assurances of surgeons, all the futile prayers of preachers, all the hollowness of good-guys-can't-lose baseball stories I'd ever heard or read. They were graffiti scrawled across my brother's ruined chest. They were a throw I'd never catch. And yet—REACH, the ball said, THE SIGN OF QUALITY. So year after year I kept trying, kept struggling to somehow answer the koan.

I hit adolescence, enrolled in the school of pain-without-dignity called "puberty," nearly flunked, then graduated almost without noticing. In the process I discovered that there was life after baseball, that America was not the Good Guy, that Jesus was not a Christian and that some girls, contrary to boyhood certainty, were nothing like 95 percent Crud; I discovered Europe and metaphysics, high lakes and wilderness, black tea, rock, Bach, trout streams, the Orient, my life's work and a hundred other grown-up tools and toys. But amid these maturations and transformations there was an unwanted constant: in the presence of that confounded ball, I remained thirteen years old. One peek at the "Your Pal" koan and whatever maturity or equanimity I possessed was repossessed, leaving me irked as any stumped monk or slumping slugger.

IT TOOK FOUR YEARS TO SOLVE THE RIDDLE ON THE BALL. IT was autumn when it happened—the same autumn during which I'd grown a little older than my big brother would ever be. As often happens with koan solutions, I wasn't even thinking about the ball when it came. As is also the case with koans, I can't possibly paint in words the impact of the response, the instantaneous healing that took place or the ensuing sense of lightness and release. But I'll say what I can.

The solution came during a fit of restlessness brought on by a warm Indian summer evening. I'd just finished watching the Miracle Mets blitz the Orioles in the World Series and was standing alone in the living room, just staring out at the yard and fading sunlight, feeling a little stale and fidgety, when I realized that these were just the sort of fidgets I'd never had to suffer when John was alive—

because we'd always work our way through them with a long game of catch. With that thought, and at that moment, I simply saw my brother catch, then throw a baseball. It occurred in neither an indoors nor an outdoors. It lasted a couple of seconds, no more. But I saw him so clearly, and he then vanished so completely, that my eyes blurred, my throat and chest ached, and I didn't need to see Mantle's baseball to realize exactly what I'd wanted from it all along:

From the moment I'd first laid eyes on it, all I'd wanted was to take that immaculate ball out to our corridor on an evening just like this one, to take my place near the apples in the north and to find my brother waiting beneath the immense firs to the south. All I'd wanted was to pluck that too-perfect ball off its pedestal and proceed, without speaking, to play catch so long and hard that the grass stains and nicks and the sweat of our palms would finally obliterate every last trace of Mantle's blue ink, till all he would have sent us was a grass-green, earth-brown, beat-up old baseball. Beat-up old balls were all we'd ever had anyhow. They were all we'd ever needed. The dirtier they were, the more frayed the skin and stitching, the louder they'd hissed and the better they'd curved. And remembering this—recovering in an instant the knowledge of how little we'd needed in order to be happy—my grief for my brother became palpable, took on shape and weight, color and texture, even an odor: the measure of my loss was precisely the difference between one of the beat-up, earth-colored, grass-scented balls that had given us such happiness, and this antiseptic-smelling, sad-making icon ball on its bandage-box pedestal. And as I felt this—as I stood there palpating my grief, shifting it round like a throwing stone in my hand—I suddenly fell through a floor inside myself, landing in a deeper, brighter chamber just in time to feel something or someone tell me, *But who's to say we need even an old ball to be happy? Who's to say we couldn't do with less? Who's to say we couldn't still be happy—with no ball at all?*

And with that, the koan was solved.

I can't explain why this felt like a complete solution. Reading the bare words, decades later, they don't look like much of a solution. But a koan answer is not a verbal or a literary or even a personal experience. It's a spiritual experience. And a boy, a man, a "me," does not have spiritual experiences: only the spirit has spiritual experiences. That's why churches so soon become bandage boxes propping up antiseptic icons that lost all value the instant they were removed from the greens and browns of grass and dirt and life. It's also why a good Zen monk always states a koan solution in the barest possible terms. "No ball at all!" is, perhaps, all I should have written about this thing—because then no one would have an inkling of what was meant, and so could form no misconceptions, and the immediacy and integrity and authority of the experience would be safely locked away. ("If you can't copy 'em, don't imitate 'em.") But it's a time-honored tradition, in baseball, to interview the bubbling, burbling athlete when the game is done. So I've bubbled and burbled.

THIS HAS GOTTEN A BIT IFFY FOR A SPORTS STORY. BUT JOCKS die, and then what? The brother I played a thousand games of catch with is dead, and so will I be, and unless you're one hell of an athlete, so will you be. In the face of this fact I find it more than a little consoling to recall my encounter, one October day, with an unspeakable spark in me that needs *nothing*—not even a dog-eared ball—to be happy. From that day forward the relic on the mantel lost its irksome overtones and became an autographed ball—nothing more, nothing less. It lives in my study now, beside an old beater ball my brother and I wore out, and it gives me a satisfaction I can't explain to sit back now and then and compare the two—though I'd still gladly trash the white one for a good game of catch.

As for the ticklish timing of its arrival, I only recently learned a couple of facts that shed some light. First I discovered—in a copy of the old letter my mother wrote to Mantle—that she'd made it clear that my brother was dying. So the Mick had signed the ball knowing perfectly well what the situation might be when it arrived. Second, I found out that my mother actually went ahead and showed the ball to my brother. True, he was embalmed when she did this. But what was embalmed, the koan taught me, wasn't all of him. And I've no reason to assume that the unembalmed part had changed much, so far. It should be remembered, then, that while he lived my brother was more than a little vain, that he'd been compelled by his death to leave a handsome head of auburn hair behind, and that when my mother and Mantle's baseball arrived at the funeral parlor, that hair was being prepared for an open-casket funeral by a couple of cadaverous-looking yahoos whose oily manners, hair and clothes made it plain they didn't know Kookie Kookson from Roger Maris or Solid Cool from Kool-Aid. What if this pair took it into their heads to spruce John up for the Hereafter with a Bible Camp cut? Worse yet, what if they tried to show what sensitive, accommodating artists they were and decked him out like a damned Elvis the Pelvis *greaser?* I'm not trying to be morbid here. I'm trying to state the facts. "The Bod" my brother had so delighted in grooming was about to be seen for the last time by all his buddies, his family and a girlfriend who was only 1.5 percent Crud, and the part of the whole ensemble he'd been most fastidious about—the coiffure—was completely out of his control! He *needed* "Best Wishes." He needed a "Pal." Preferably one with a comb.

Enter my mother—who took one look at what the two rouge-and-casket-wallahs were doing to the hair, said "No no no!" produced a snapshot, told them, "He wants it *exactly* like this," sat down to critique their efforts and kept on critiquing till in the end you'd have thought John had dropped in to groom himself.

Only then did she ask them to leave. Only then did she pull

the autographed ball from her purse, share it with her son, read him the inscription.

As is always the case with arriving baseballs, timing is the key. Thanks to the timing that has made the Mick a legend, my brother, the last time we all saw him, looked completely himself.

I return those best wishes to my brother's pal.

Yellowjacket

for Frank Boyden, river brother, on his 600th moon

WHAT THEY'VE DONE TO ME HAS HURT.

WHAT I'VE DONE TO THEM, WITHOUT WAITING FOR AGGRES-
SION ON THEIR PART, IS STALK THEIR UNDERGROUND
STRONGHOLDS BY NIGHT, POUR GASOLINE DOWN THROUGH
THE ARCHITECTONIC HALLS AND NURSERY CHAMBERS, BURN
THEIR SLEEPING BODIES TO CINDERS, DIG EVERY LAST CHAM-
BER OUT WITH A SHOVEL, GRIND THE PALE BLIND YOUNG
(STILL, SOMEHOW, WRITHING) INTO THE DIRT WITH MY HEEL
AND MUTTER, "WHAT ELSE CAN I DO TO YOU?" I HAVE
MASHED JUST HALF THEIR BODIES AGAINST THE WINDSHIELD
WITH A STAB OF A PENCIL, WATCHED THEM DROP DOWN INTO
THE DEFROSTER, AND SHRUGGED AT THE SOUND OF THE

other body-half still crawling down below. I have crushed them by the hundreds against the grill of my speeding truck, shotgunned their paper palaces unprovoked, smashed them out of the air, when all they sought was escape from the bewilderment of my windows, with spoons, spatulas, newspapers, books, whatever weapon lay at hand, maybe bhakti poems, Buddhist sutras, biographies of Gandhi, maybe bibles flopped open to Matthew 5:44 . . .

I've always known, without hesitation, how to hate this enemy. It's taken forty years and most of an autumn to show me how, without hesitation, to love it.

CONTEXT IS EVERYTHING.

After six slow-fading weeks of the second summer named Indian, perhaps for the way its glory grew a little cooler, a little more pallid, a little more mulched by the day, then the week of hard frosts, midnight blasts of the jacklighters' rifles ringing down the valley, the deer not dead vanished, the last swifts and swallows gone, even the slowest cricketsongs ended; after the geese again broke the human monopoly on stupidity by setting south in laborious, windwarped scribbles that never once spelled V the very morning the first storm came howling up out of the south; after eight straight days of squalls and sheetrain, the faces of jack-o'-lanterns carved too soon imploding, sky in tiers, layer on layer of gray scudding in off an ocean now everything but pacific, even the leaves that refused to turn torn away to wash, green, down rivers thick as something a man of faith might walk across; then all this morning, no rain, strangely, but fast, grayblack skies, gale warnings on every band, and an eerie-warm wind rammed inland by the biggest front yet—

only then
did it come to a place in the air a body's length beyond
my second story window. But in that seadriven gray
as the whole house drummed to the storm's first pelting

drops, the sudden stillness of a drop of broken yellow
stopped my mind, leaving an emptiness that could make
no distinction between me and this lifelong enemy blown
from its search for a summer that will not fade
into the lee of a thirty-foot noble fir that twelve
years ago made the christmas of a boy
now grown and gone—
a lone
yellowjacket,
hovering like an ornament
of the immaculate
heat of mid-july
fiery weapon useless
solar fury fast fading
yet so beautifully
black
and brightest yellow
and so furiously struggling
the struggle to be
nothing
but a yellowjacket
as the next
oceanborn
gust
dashed it away.

Molting

To turn, turn, will be our delight
till by turning, turning, we come round right.
—Shaker hymn

Mid-November, Tamanawis County, Oregon. The annual autumn storm has been blowing in off the Pacific for more than a week. The storm snuck up, as it most always does, when a mist we mistook for morning fog slid into the Indian summer woods. By increments the grains of mist kept thickening, till at sundown they'd become the first raindrops in months. The winds came on in the wee hours, giving me strange, insistent dreams of travel, first by train, then by ship. In the hold of one such ship was a vast room full of nothing but school desks, with a sad, pale child at each desk. They were dressed like Pilgrims, or Puritans, all of them. And having nothing to do, no school supplies, no teacher, they sat drumming their fingers on the tops of their desks, faces wan and morose, hundreds of little fingers drumming, drumming, till I woke to the sheetrain drumming the walls of the house and the sound of my three-year-old, Tucker, coughing.

In the eight days since that dream the rain has not stopped. Waterfalls fly from the roof. The swallows' mud igloos hang empty in the eaves. Jays and thrushes appear now and then at the feeder, but dart away without eating when the wind blows their feathers inside out. For three days and nights a lone flicker has been clinging to the leeward eave. When Tuck opens the window just beneath it, the flicker, rather than fly, merely turns its head away, like a toddler who thinks that by closing its eyes it becomes invisible. The bird reminds me of myself this time last year—at the tail end of my dying marriage. The driveway is a matched pair of unnavigable creeks. The actual creek is a wide, brown river. Sometimes everything reminds me of my dead marriage. When the rain falls approximately downward instead of streaming by in sheets, I call it a lull and do what needs doing. During such a lull I slip on boots and slicker, grab the wood-carrier and step outside.

The air is surprisingly warm. It smells of salmon and deer carcasses, distant mudflats and a whole dead summer's worth of leaves. The kitchen clock just showed twelve, so somewhere a sun is at its zenith. But it's hard to imagine suns in this valley. The hills across the river have been buried so long under cloud that I no longer remember their contours. The grayness is complete, layer after layer of cloud-mass skulking in off the ocean, staining the landscape, staining the sense of sight, staining even what's imaginable to the mind. The dreams of train and boat travel now feel literally true: the glowing October beaches and golden meadows are so irrevocably gone it's as if we've been blown from our moorings into a different region, a gray-aired, cave-dark forest. And for six sodden months, this dark forest is where we'll remain. I lift the tarp from the cordwood. Gallons of pooled water crash down into the grass. The wind rises, howls at the house corners; the rain swings from vertical back to horizontal. But I don't rush. And when the rain strikes my face I don't wince or squint. In a region where half one's life takes place in rain, it's crucial to pretend it's the air's normal condition.

The wood-tote in my hand was old but in perfect shape when my grandfather gave it to me fourteen years ago. He said it was an "antique" and "worth money"—his notion of the greatest good. Its canvas was jet black, its handles lathed and polished, and an anthropomorphic silver moon glowered from the blackness on one side. I hung it on a wall, endured its silver glower, heard it called "folk art," heard "That's an antique!" heard "That thing's worth money!" for one full winter. Then it occurred to me that a greater good for a wood-tote might be to tote wood. There are canvas patches and cross-stitched repairs on the key seams now, and a crack, covered with fiber tape, in one handle. The moon's face is chipped away in places, and everywhere smudged with mud and alder stains. But in hauling four cords up two flights for thirteen winters, it has earned its glower. And the immaculate folk art that annoyed me has become a doomed tool that I love.

I load the tote full to bursting to avoid taking two trips—"a lazy man's load," my grandfather would have called it. But I have many times tried what my family called "sensible loads," and not once did they fail to fill me with something close to grief. I am one whose arms demand not just one but two full bags of groceries, one who finds it better to stagger up stairs than to defy the strange demands of my arms.

As I grunt my way up the porch steps to the door I forgot to leave open, the cat minces, meowing, from under the house. I brace my load against the wall and grope for the knob while she weaves in and out my ankles. Lifting her aside with my boot tip, keeping my load braced, I kick the door open, then call her. She sits down on the top step and watches me. I call her once more, wait, call again. She looks away, starts washing a paw. Knowing very well what the problem is, I sigh, take a breath and deploy my ludicrous falsetto imitation of my ex-wife's deft soprano: *"Kittykittykittykittykitty."* The cat scoots instantly into the house. I follow, kicking the door shut behind me.

INSIDE AND UP ANOTHER FLIGHT OF STAIRS, IT'S A GRIM molting season for Tucker and me—a time of forced transition from the flagrant glories of Indian summer to the initially hard-to-find fascinations of the winter indoors. The air smells of alder smoke, chicken stock and the compost bucket I forgot to empty. My huge load and I reach the living room just in time to see the cat hop onto the stereo, sit down on one of Bob Dylan's *Biograph* disks and start cleaning off clots of filth and fur. The dog, Zeke, is curled on the slate behind the woodstove, already lost in his winter-long hobby: making dismal snorfling sounds as he ferrets in his hind end for vermin. Running out of strength, I rush to the woodbox, let the load crash down, shove two fat chunks in the stove, slam the cast-iron door shut.

"Good job!" squeaks Tucker, who admires slams and crashes. They remind him of his new hero, Jerry the Mouse, who at this very moment is slamming and crashing Tom the Cat all over the TV screen. Tucker doesn't normally squeak, or watch videos by day. But thanks to a recent refusal to associate with raincoats, rubber boots or anything else that implied summer was over, he's caught a nasty cold, thus limiting his entertainment options. I had repeatedly explained that the seasons turn, that winter was here, that raincoats and rubber boots were now necessary evils, that nature is cyclic, that cycles are wonderful, that the sun would shine gloriously on the rain-washed beaches in December. All this did was inspire him to shift his loss-of-summer anger from my despot buddy, God, to me. With three-year-olds, cycles of nature are best discussed in June.

I sit down at the kitchen table—the farthest point from the TV

—and open a book. Tucker calls in, begging me to partake in the joys of Tom and Jerry. Knowing he'll badger me if I don't, knowing he'll be back at his mom's tomorrow, I cave in, but lobby for absolute control of the TV volume, and for uninterrupted reading. Tuck says okay. He adds, "I promise." And the instant I join him on the living room couch he jumps up, throws both arms round my head and starts yanking on it, yelling, "You're Tom! I'm Jerry!" I explain that I am not Tom, that mine is not a cartoon head and that if it came off, like Tom's sometimes does, he would be out a dad. He retorts that it *is* a cartoon head, that he *is* going to pull it off and that he *wants* to be out a dad. It occurs to me to say, "Freud would be pleased to hear it." But I manage to say nothing, remove his arms, grab his ankles and hold him upside down for a while. There's a rule I've discovered as a single parent: a wrestling match is worth a thousand words. Today, though, it does not help Tuck's congestion, nor is the view of his clogged nostrils appetizing. "Put me up-side-up!" he demands. I say I will if he lets me read. He says he promises. I tell him he already promised. He hollers, *"THIS TIME I PROMISE LOUDER!"* I set him down. He turns to Tom and Jerry. I pick up my book.

It's a loaner—a fragile old British hardcover with the eminently forgettable title *Twelve Whom Fame Forgot*. Its equally forgettable topic is a dozen nineteenth-century scientists whom the author feels were undeservedly short-changed by fame. The book was foisted on me at a party last week by an ex-archaeology/anthropology-double-major-turned-whitewater-guide who acted as if the party were a Class V rapid, his book was a life preserver and I was his underaged client. I dutifully toted the thing home, found it far removed from any subject I am aware of caring about and contemplated merely pretending to have read it. The instant I did so I began to feel that I might drown.

The chapter my dried-lupine bookmark and I are presently paddling through concerns a British archaeologist, Kendall Burke by name, who would dig up artifacts on other continents, take them home to scientific colleagues in London and get so embroiled in controversies over just what the artifacts were or what they signified that he would eventually fly into a rage, pack his toothbrush and shovel, sail away to another continent and start digging again. It's a disappointment to me, though no surprise, that even Kendall Burke somehow reminds me of my dead marriage. But the words of the book, even the calm ones, have begun to shake. "Watch!" my son is saying, yanking again on my arm.

Forgetting his "louder promise," I do:

Jerry Mouse has jumped up in an open window and is sticking his tongue out at Tom Cat. Tom tries to slam the window down on Jerry, but somehow crushes his own fingers instead. Giggling, Jerry locks the window with Tom's fingers still in it, and as Tom stares in dismay the crushed fingertips bulge bigger and bigger, till finally they pop like balloons. Though he speaks no English, Tom yowls like a human: *Hoohoohoohoo!* Thrilled silly, Tucker tries to imitate the sound—and gives himself a coughing fit.

I fetch him some orange juice.

I fetch myself a cup of tea.

I reopen the book.

A distinguished Oxford linguist has just blasted my archaeologist's, Burke's, monograph claiming that the Old French sentences on a tile he unearthed in Spain should be attributed to "a scribe of Charlemagne." When the experts all side with the linguist, our archaeologist takes a train up to Oxford and challenges his debunker to a duel. When this challenge is rejected, Burke breaks the man's nose. As a result he is thrown, in one fell paragraph, out of every important scientific society in England, thus losing all sources of funding for future shoveling expeditions. Fortunately (or so avers the author), Burke is independently wealthy. Procuring passage to Northern Africa, he is soon busy as a gopher again, digging holes.

A gust of wind shakes the house. I turn to the window. The

alders outside are dull gray and naked; the spruces, in this light, nearly black. The meadow is a yellow-gray unwelcome mat mouldering round the house, even its late-blooming yarrow just a stand of stiff brown stalks now, their blossoms all rotten or gone to seed. The world has molted. Grays, greens and browns are the only colors left. No shine, no brightness anywhere. And four solid months till the skunk cabbage blossoms, five till the salmonberry, six till the buttercups and bird's-foot lotus. Turning a page, I notice the color of my hand has slipped south as well, leaving me the pale white hand of a damned Puritan. The woodstove hisses. The cat, still on the stereo, starts gagging on her own fur. Zeke, the demented canine archaeologist, keeps digging in his butt. Phlegm rattles in Tucker's throat and chest. Tom Cat, driving a steamroller, guffaws mercilessly as he runs Jerry Mouse down, leaving him flat as the page my Puritan hand just turned. Fortunately (or so the manipulative music implies), Jerry's sidekick, Nibbles, has a bicycle pump, which he uses to blow Jerry back up. Half-panicked suddenly, desperate for a few paragraphs with no cartoon accompaniment, I plan a cartoon escape:

"Knock knock," I tell Tuck.

"Who's there?" he answers, grinning.

"I gotta take a humongous."

"I'g, ugh! otta tug! mongoose who!?" he laughs through his phlegm. And I'm up and on my lying way to the bathroom, in need of nothing more humongous than a moment's peace.

Closing the door, then the toilet lid, I lean against the cold porcelain, set my tea on the sink edge, reopen the book and read,

> But in 1887, at the second excavation site, Burke unearthed the seven Coptic fragments that remade his reputation after J. W. Wiles and other authorities ascribed certain utterances among them to Jesus Christ. Though Burke himself called the discovery "a stroke of im-

becilic luck," he reveled in the vindication it gave him. In his infamous "readmission speech" to the Royal Society, he joked that he had renounced his outspoken Atheism and founded a Protestant sect that used the Nile Sentences as its sole Scripture. Lord Groton and the other Christian members were, needless to say, far from amused . . .

Keeping a finger in my place, I skip ahead, looking for the Coptic fragments. Can't find them. I check the footnotes, but find no reference to them, page through the index, find nothing there. I skip to the end of the Burke chapter:

Though almost unanimously considered to be apocryphal today (the two common objections being simply the tenuousness of the anonymous scribe's assignation, and the stylistic incompatibilities with Christ's canonical statements) the Nile Sentences created controversy from the day of their discovery till the day of Burke's death. And what part did Burke play in this controversy? We ought by now to be able to guess! Despite an utter lack of exegetical training; despite having referred to himself, in his epistolary warfare with Lord Groton, as "a biblical nonauthority, a theological nonentity, and a better man because of it"; despite countless references to Jesus as "an historical figment," "the pious man's Baron Munchhausen," and so on, no one fought harder to prove the authenticity of the Nile Sentences than Kendall Burke himself. Shortly before his death in late February, 1894, Burke remarked to his acerbic and somewhat treacherous biographer, Derek Parsons, that he considered the Coptic fragments his most important find. "Even on his death-bed," Parsons writes, "Burke is said to have mentioned the by-now-discredited Nile

Sentences, saying that he felt himself to be 'basking in their glow.' A peculiar sentiment indeed in a self-described 'champion of the empirical'!"

Perhaps so. But a fitting enough climax to a career remarkable for its unmatched pugnacity, its theatricality, and also for its unresolvable inconsistencies.

End of chapter. End of Kendall Burke. And no Nile Sentences, no footnotes, no references, nothing. Damn it. If they aren't in the book somewhere I'm going to toss it in the stove.

The phone rings. I leave the bathroom and grab it before Tuck can reach it. He has the habit of answering politely, saying "I'll get him" when it's for me, then hanging up when he comes to find me. It's my next-meadow neighbor, Gretchen. She says the roof blew off their wood rick while she and her husband were away in the city, that it rained on their firewood for three days, that they're going to pick up cedar-mill scraps for kindling tomorrow, but can she borrow some of my kindling today? I tell her all I've got is alder cordwood, which makes dumb kindling and doesn't split worth a damn, but she's welcome to it. "Is it dry and does it burn?" Gretchen asks. Yes and yes, I tell her. She'll be right over. *Click.*

I return to the kitchen, freshen my tea, pretend not to hear Tucker begging me to sit by him. But I find, when he adds, "I'm lonely," that I've no desire not to give in.

Ignoring my son's squirming, ignoring the TV, intent on finding the elusive Nile Sentences, I am soon so absorbed in the search that when Tucker yells, "Look!" I have no parental persona with which to defy him and automatically do look.

Tom Cat has snatched Jerry's friend, Nibbles, and stuck him in the toaster. Tom pushes down the lever, ties a napkin round his neck, dips a knife into butter, licks his chops, waits for the toasty aroma, drums his fingers, waits some more—then sees that Jerry

Mouse has pulled the toaster's plug. Furious, Tom grabs Jerry instead, butters him and starts to swallow him raw. But Jerry props Tom's jaws open with a knife, jumps in his mouth, grabs his tongue, pulls it out about three feet, dives into the toaster with it and ties it in a knot in there. While Tom struggles desperately to untie his tongue, Nibbles plugs in the cord, Jerry pushes down the toaster lever and *Fwam!* the toaster slams down over Tom's head, covering it clear to the shoulders. Tom paws frantically at the air. Smoke pours from the toaster. *Hoohoohoohoo!* Tom cries. Nibbles and Jerry hold their little tummies and laugh. When the toaster finally pops up, Tom's head looks exactly like a piece of burnt toast—with a pair of huge, blinking eyeballs in it. And the toaster is *still* hanging from his knotted tongue.

But watching my son's stuffy-headed, mesmerized laugh, I am suddenly drowning in recognition: the congested head, the cartoon stupefaction, the eyeballs staring from the toast—I've lived exactly what Tucker is living. And what strikes me, what makes the recognition hurt, is that I know, now, that it's a *battle* he's experiencing. For all the innocuous music, calculated cuteness and adorable tummies, war is breaking out in my three-year-old son. Innocent as he feels, innocent as he *is,* Tucker wants Tom and Jerry to slip through the TV screen, enter this world and fill it with slapstick impossibilities, painless tortures and humanoid *hoohoohoos.* But there is no world, outside the screen, where torture is painless. And I grew up with boys, lots of them, who never learned this—boys not much older than Tuck who in cartoon moods dropped real Fourth of July sparklers on live garter snakes trapped in Coke bottles, who saw no boundary there, felt no guilt and graduated to flinging real "Tom Cats" from cars doing ninety, shooting real sheep and cattle when they were out hunting deer, crushing real human beings with *hoohoo* pumpkins tossed from speeding pickups, jumping real girls who wanted no part of them, cruising real streets in my hometown to find and beat up the black strangers they called "spear chuckers" and

Arabs they called "dune coons," who still hit no boundary, felt nothing in them say no, and so enlisted in armies, went to cartoonish boot camps, learned to bark "Yes, *sir!*" at officers and were freed at last to unleash genuine, knotted-tongued, toast-headed, government-approved mercilessness upon real bomb targets, real schools and hamlets, real fleeing refugees, real flesh and blood . . .

And God damn it: those two big eyes in the smoking piece of toast! I laughed, too.

Using *Twelve Whom Fame Forgot* as a shield to ward off the screen's blue light, I open it at random, find myself looking at an appendice, and there they are: the sentences translated from the Coptic—including words ascribed to Christ. Skipping the scholarly explanations, knowing cartoonishness could intervene at any moment, I dive into the first sentence. It reads,

Jesus said unto them, *Smite the rock and thou shalt find me; cleave the wood and there am I.*

And I see a round of alder as the ax comes down; see the fresh white opening as the wood leaps apart; see, standing on the block as the halves fall like bodies to each side, the nothing, the everything, *there am I* . . . Chills fly up and down my spine. Tears fill my eyes. Then the dog, Zeke, bursts with a roar from behind the stove, scratches the floor with spinning claws; Tucker lurches, spills the dregs of his orange juice; I grab his glass to save it and spill my entire cup of tea.

Zeke keeps barking. The door. Someone is knocking.

My wet-wooded neighbor.

I shout "Come in!" run for a sponge, wipe up the spills and pull on my boots, trying all along to feel the sentence. I look for Christ in the couch stains. Christ in the sponge, Christ in the empty cups, Christ in my boots, but Gretchen just keeps knocking, Zeke

just keeps roaring, Tucker jumps on my back, yells, "Jerry's getting
Tom!" and I can't even tie my laces, let alone smite or cleave or find.

"Shuttup!" I finally bellow at the dog.

But it's Tucker who goes limp with shock and fear.

"I meant the hound," I say, giving him a pat. But the truth
doesn't help. Hoping to pull him back from tears, I tell him,
"Look!" and we turn to watch Tom Cat sneaking down a row of
garbage cans, lifting lids, looking for the one with Jerry inside *(there
am I . . .).* Tom lifts lid after lid, pokes his hungry head deep into
each can. Meanwhile Jerry is walking right along behind Tom's
back, covering his little mouth to silence his gleeful snickers. And
under the lid of the last can we see the huge, glowering eyes of
Jerry's pal, Spike the Bulldog.

"Uh-oh," whispers Tucker.

Tom reaches the fatal can, lifts the lid, sticks his head and upper
body clear down the dog's enormous throat, withdraws, sees the
huge teeth, realizes what he's done. But Gretchen is *still* knocking
and yelling unneighborly things at Zeke, who is still roaring as if
he'd like to open her throat. I set Tucker on the couch, run downstairs, hear the snarls, chomps and crashes, behind me, of bulldog
fangs and garbage cans, followed by Tom's weirdly human
Hoohoohoohoo! But this world is still, thank God, the world: when I
let my real dog out he throws his front paws into Gretchen's hands,
grins and growls ecstatically and licks her face while she hugs him
and says, "Pipe down, Dogbrain!" They're old friends. They always
treat each other this way.

The rain has stopped for the first time in eight days, but the
sky to the west is a slate-colored fist recoiling for another blow. We
hurry to the woodpile, pull up the tarp; a fresh gallon of water
crashes to the ground. Gretchen says she doesn't need much, she'll
have the mill scraps tomorrow. I pick out five straight, dry rounds of
alder. She says that's *way* too much—which is exactly what I have to
say whenever I borrow things from her—so I ignore her.

She pulls my ax from the spruce chopping block. I get an ugly premonition but feel trapped, by our genders, from asking her to give the ax to me. Gretchen is an accomplished carpenter, gardener and handywoman, far more skilled with tools than I. But my ax is rickety, and alder tends to shear off unpredictably when you try to split it small, and sometimes people who do things right, like Gretchen, have trouble doing things wrong, like make kindling out of alder with a rickety ax. I mention some of this, hoping she'll invite me to chop. Instead she nods, spits in her palms, swings away, hits the first round straight down and dead center—and for no rational reason the wood defies its own grain, shears off, the ax-head flies sideways and barely misses her shin.

Gretchen slowly straightens. She clears her throat. She hands me the ax. "Tell you what," she says. "You chop. I'll pick up."

Extending my arms to keep the ax from my legs, I split the alder thin as I can and to hell with the shearing. (I have long arms.) Gretchen totes the result, shards and all, to her decrepit Volkswagen. Zeke follows, smiles up at her, then takes a long, very yellow pee on one of her tires. She calls him terrible names. He smiles again. And sprays another tire.

"Nostalgia," I tell her, and she knows what I mean: in the city where Zeke spent his puppyhood I mowed lawns for a living while he pursued a satellite career as a free-lance olfactory detective, peeing on thousands of car tires, then trying to find them again, on later jobs, in distant parts of town. It was his heyday.

I look west, see the rain curtain flying toward us, work faster, finish chopping, then help Gretchen pick up. She thanks me two or three times too many. Then we chat a little bit and toss sticks for the dog, reluctant to go back inside our houses before the approaching wall compels us.

Not yet three in the afternoon, but the day is turning dusky. And when I spin in a slow circle (an old childhood habit) I see a world so stormbeaten and spare it seems devoid of all mystery: bare alders on the north ridge, scrubbed by rags of cloud; spruces in the west, with the rain wall coming; more alder in the south, and more gray rags; once-gold meadowgrass to the east, lying flat and gray as a carcass on a freeway; in the middle of the carcass, the dead brown patch of yarrow. That's all there is. That's really all there is. And as the day darkens and Gretchen says so long, all there is does not seem sufficient to get us through this time of molting.

The rain hits hard. I pick up the ax and raise it high, thinking to sink it deep in the chopping block so Tucker can't pull it and hurt himself later. And only then—ax in mid-air—do I remember. *Cleave the wood and there am I . . .*

I slam it down. The ax buries itself like it will never come out again, but the huge spruce block barely shudders. And I feel heartsick. All that work, all that splitting, and not once did I remember. I tell myself that the words were apocryphal, but immediately recognize this as a kind of lie: there was nothing false about the way they resounded when I read them. Knowing I've missed an opportunity, knowing I've the concentration of a creature raised on burnt toast with eyeballs and *hoohoohoos,* knowing that if enlightenment requires my assistance, that if mindfulness is something we must generate ourselves, that if some kind of transmundane Nibbles doesn't show up with the bike pump and restore my lost dimensions, I am doomed, I slouch off toward the cartoon-filled house, hear a gasp down the driveway, turn to see that Gretchen hasn't yet climbed in her car—and that she's radiant. Her face has bloomed. When she points, agape, toward the meadow behind me, I realize I've been listening, for some time, to a strange thrumming in that direction.

I turn.

And were it night, and were we shepherds, we might have dropped to our knees in the face of such beauty. But, things being as they are, we just walk, rubberbooted, toward it, drawn like oil through a wick up into a burning lantern that makes sudden, perfect sense of the valley's dark, rain-washed gray. The beauty thrums, allows our approach, turns to and fro, thrums louder. We are nearly upon it before it moves. And though it is a hundred beings, two hundred wings, that rise up before us, it is one deft gesture that pierces the rain: one mind, cleaving the whole dark valley, as the hundred sun-bright goldfinches rise from the dead brown yarrow.

FIRST NATIVE

for my father

ONE OF THE SIGNS OF A TRUE ARTIST, ACCORDING TO THE ASIAN EPIC MAHABHARATA, IS A WILLINGNESS TO WORK PATIENTLY AND LOVINGLY WITH EVEN THE MOST INFERIOR MATERIALS. I MENTION THIS BIT OF LORE IN CONJUNCTION WITH THE STORY OF MY FIRST LARGE NATIVE TROUT, BECAUSE THE FLY ROD WITH WHICH I CAUGHT THAT TROUT WAS, ESSENTIALLY, A NINE-FOOT-LONG OPPORTUNITY TO SEEK THIS SIGN OF THE ARTIST IN MYSELF. THE ROD WASN'T MINE. NEITHER WAS I AT THE TIME. WE BOTH BELONGED TO MY DAD, ACTUALLY. BUT ONE DAY WHEN I WAS ABOUT HALF THE ROD'S LENGTH, THE DAD WE BOTH BELONGED TO PLACED THE ROD IN MY HANDS, STOOD ME ON THE BANKS OF OREGON'S DESCHUTES RIVER, SHOWED ME THE SALMON FLIES CRAWLING along the sedge grass and alder leaves, said, "Good luck," then thrashed off through a current too swift and deep for me to wade, out to an island, where he began to work the far riffle—

—leaving me utterly alone and utterly stunned, with this double-David-lengthed rod in my hand, this gigantic green river in front of me, and this gigantic opportunity, the first in my life, to find out whether there was, according to the Mahabharata, any sign of the artist in me.

I didn't know, that day, that my fly rod was inferior. With nothing but a stumpy green glass spinning rod to compare it with, I'd have been equally delighted with a Leonard, a Powell or a pool cue. Which is lucky. Because a pool cue is, basically, what my father had given me. It consisted of three yard-long, luminous, hexagonal lengths of Tonkin bamboo, the world's finest. The same bamboo, after American B-52's turned the Tonkin Gulf into a moonscape, was worth its weight in gold. My rod, however, was a pre-War effort: priceless raw material converted into a fishing instrument by Yankee craftsmen who'd taken the same degree of care, and produced the same weight of implement, as the makers of some of our finest garden hoes. Time and past owners had enhanced the rod further: it had cracked and yellowed varnish, dark red wrappings on the guides that weren't electrical-taped, black bloodstains on the hook-chewed cork handle and a most beautiful blue-green corrosion all over the reel seat. Its action brought to mind things like spaghetti, wilted lettuce and impotence. The scrinchy, out-of-round reel and antique braided flyline upped the weight total from hoe to shovel. But what did I know? And, not knowing, what did I care? It is faith, not knowledge, that leads us into paradise, and at age nine I had perfect faith that my reject rod, reel and line were the most magnificent tools and the Deschutes the most magnificent river that any sort of Dad & God combo could possibly have bequeathed me.

My paradise, though, had its raunchy edges. To pursue what

needed pursuing I had to step through a bunch of waxy-leafed vegetation that only retroactively identified itself as poison oak. Then,
like some nine-year-old prefiguration of a contemporary fundamen-
talist homophobe, I had to catch this small, helpless, male homosexual salmon fly—or I assume it was male and homosexual, since it
was riding around on the back of its dead ringer, who in turn was
riding the slightly more voluptuous-looking back of what I took to
be the female, since the probe-thing coming off the middle male,
the straight one, I guess you'd say, terminated in her *fuselage,* I guess
you could call it, and she seemed perfectly serene about this. Anyhow, I nabbed the little humper up top, he seeming, in terms of the
future of his race, the least gainfully employed. Drafted him, you
might say, which makes me think: why would anyone *want* to join
the military? Because the instant I drafted this guy I impaled him.
No boot camp or nuthin'. Just impaled him, from one end clear out
the other, on a #10 barbed steel bait hook. No apology, no prayer:
that's where I was, in terms of the spirit world. But the little trooper
I'd just skewered—think what you like about his sexual orientation
—was about to enact a Passion Play that I would never forget . . .

That he remained alive with my whole hook running through
him didn't affect me at first. That his little legs kept kicking, and that
the legs, or maybe they were arms, that weren't kicking started
hugging my finger—even that didn't affect me much. But when I
pulled his little arms off my finger, swung him out over the river,
and he, seeing the wild waters below, suddenly opened multiple
golden wings in the sunlight and tried, hook and all, to fly, he
finally hit me where I live. And homophobe, hell, it was *way* worse
than that: I felt like this nine-year-old Roman asshole who'd just
crucified a little winged Christian. When he hit the water and, still
fluttering, sank, a cold stone filled my throat. I have tried, however
awkwardly, to pray for every creature I have knowingly killed since.

. . .

AND YET—WHEN I DRIFTED MY LITTLE WINGED CHRISTIAN into a foam-flecked seam in the lee of my father's island, things happened that would very soon lead me to martyr many, many more such Christians. What can I say? We all live by sacrifice. As Tom McGuane once put it, "God created an impossible situation." But then salvaged it, I would add—or at least made the impossible lovable—by creating native trout.

For the first long instant of contact with my first great native, I saw nothing—just felt the sudden life pulsing, punching, shouting clean into the marrow of my know-nothing, nine-year-old hands. But those little white hands, to keep feeling that wild electric pulse, suddenly forgot all about the things they did or did not know and began to work the ginked reel, dorked line and impossible rod with the passion and patience of some ancient craftsman straight out of the Mahabharata. Neither my hands, nor I, have been quite the same since. And when the fish, still invisible, turned from the quiet seam and shot into the white-watered heart of the river, my fly rod was never the same either: it was five inches shorter.

That native's first long run turned the whole hollow canyon and me into I don't know what—a oneness, music, a single-stringed guitar, maybe; and the way that blazing blue river played us, the sizzling song the line sang in the water, this alone would have indentured me to the Deschutes for life. But then my native revealed itself —the rainbow, the whole shining body flying up out of the water, filling me for the first time, then again and again, with so much yearning and shock and recognition and joy that I can no longer swear I remained in my body.

Every fisherman knows the basic alchemy: you place an offering on a steel point; you throw it in the river; your offering sinks despite the beating of its wings; you feel terrible, yet dare to hope a miracle will take place; then one does: the river converts your meager offering into an unseen power that enters your whole body through your hands. An old metal reel you mistook for tackle starts to shriek like a wounded animal. Your old rod breaks but keeps lunging. Your heart does the same. Then, with no wings at all, native life comes flying up out of the river—and that's when a hook's point pierces *you*. A barbed point, you realize later, because even when the day ends, the change in you does not. By the time you hold the native in your hands it is you who has been caught; you who shines, and feels like silver; you who came, long ago, from water; you who suddenly can't live without this beautiful river.

NOT ROCKING THE BOATS

> *There are also enough rocks on earth to kill*
> *the world's population several times over.*
> —Lieutenant General Daniel
> Graham, former director,
> United States Defense
> Intelligence

I INTEND NEVER TO WRITE A HOW-TO PIECE ON FISHING. MY REASON FOR THIS IS SIMPLE. IT STANDS SIX-FOOT-SIX IN HIP BOOTS, WEIGHS 240 FLABLESS POUNDS, HAS FLAMING RED HAIR AND HUGE RED HANDS AND IS PRONE TO SUDDEN OUTBURSTS OF VIOLENCE. ITS NAME IS JEREMIAH RANSOM. ITS FRIENDS CALL IT "JER."

JEREMIAH IS A MILITANT. HIS CAUSE IS FLY-FISHING. AND HIS PRINCIPLE MILITARY THESIS IS THAT THE HOW-TO FISHING PIECE IS THE MOST OVERDONE, FORMULAIC, UNCONSCIONABLE branch of sporting literature in the world today, rivaling grocery store romances, quick-money and slow-sex manuals, and Jesus Is My Friend & Your Enemy books on the all-time list of paper wasters.

How-to fishing pieces come in two sizes: the article and the book. Jeremiah's opinion of which of the two is worse depends entirely on which of the two he has most recently been reading. He maintains, however, that the fly-fishin' cognoscenti (i.e., he and his drinkin' buddies) unanimously agree that, in either form, the only beneficiaries of the how-to-ists are the how-to-ists themselves, the fishing tackle industry and the hordes of wildflower-stomping, water-whacking rubes they lure to the riverside. The cognoscenti also agree that the how-to-ers' inevitable victims are untrammeled waters, fishermen who love solitude, the literature of fishing and, of course, the fish.

Ransom divides how-to fishing writing into two categories: "redumbdancies" and "traitor tales." He claims the redumbdancy is the more common form, better measured in raw tonnage, "like sewage," than by lists of titles. These are the books and magazines that tirelessly rediscover all of the stalest, most rudimentary angling advice known to man. Jeremiah speculates that were the nation's TopTen fishing writers to swap jobs with, say, the TopTen basketball reporters, NCAA and NBA coverage would suddenly scintillate with headlines like "How to Handle Those Pesky New Velcro Shoe-Fasteners," "Ten Ways in Which Tall, Fast Players Are Preferable to Short, Slow Ones," "Some Advantages of Outscoring the Opponent" and so on. His point is pretty well taken. No writers of sporting literature come close to fishermen in their relentless dedication to telling the rankest beginner what to do over and over to the exclusion of all else. To read the redumbdancy writers with anything like interest, one must either be a complete novice to fishing (and preferably to English) or the proud possessor of what Hercule Poirot calls "the head of a sieve."

The redumbdancy writers' primary crime, Jeremiah maintains, is aesthetic: their work is simply and unrelievedly *boring*. But when their tired rehashings are published on glossy, nonrecyclable paper, Ransom holds that they have bumbled their way to the more serious sin of "tree-wastin'," a crime he suggests should be made punishable by a fine ten times the amount of the royalty check, with proceeds going to his Columbia River Dam Dismantlement Fund—an organization of one, whose funds have so far been used solely to supply its founder with beer. Second offenses, he maintains, should earn double the fine, with an additional court order that all unsold or discarded copies of the slick-papered work be returned to its author to be personally used for toilet paper.

That's Jeremiah at his most mild. It is the traitor tales that tilt his needle to the militant side. These, according to Jeremiah, are the "Machiavellian scribblers," the "big-name commercial fly fishermen," the "lunker pimps" who see trout, salmon and steelhead not as prey or challenge or mystery or blessing but as potential ads to push their guided float trips, books and autographed rods and flies. All the fly fisherman's most cherished secrets are fair prey to the traitor: the finest hatches; deadliest techniques; spawning grounds; witching hours; the little-known, fragile river, lake or stream. By mass-marketing and technologizing what was once a secretive craft practiced in beautiful secret places, Jeremiah feels they've converted the solitary streamside epiphany into "a fur and feather fashion show with a fish clientele," and changed the rivers themselves into "a buncha wet bowlin' alleys." In so doing, they have made themselves one large, red-headed enemy.

"But what can anyone really do about these traitors?" I once naively asked my friend.

"Two things," he replied. "Number one, boycott 'em. Don't buy their books or magazines. Don't patronize their shops or resorts or guide services. Don't join their private clubs. Don't even *glance* at their gorgeous damned catalogs or you'll be sucked into the vortex. And number two: rock 'em."

Being a pacifist by habit, if not always by intention, number two did not quite register. "Rock 'em?" I said blankly.

Jeremiah nodded. "Most famous Western fly waters are big, so most famous traitors hit 'em in drift boats. Look in the mags, find out what they look like, watch for 'em. And when you see one float by, *rock* him!"

"*Rock* him?" It still hadn't quite sunk in.

He nodded again—and indulged in a bit of how-to-ing of his own. "Basalt's okay. Granite's better. Biggest damned chunk you can throw. Aim for their cameras. Aim for their writin' hands. Scare the feces out of 'em! If enough of us keep it up, they won't be back to *that* stretch of river."

I finally got it. This is definitely the place to point out that not all of Jeremiah Ransom's fishing strategies are put into practice by me. I tried my best to dissect his rock 'em advice. I said, "What is this 'traitor' obsession of yours? What about clear-cutting, overgrazing, over-irrigation, strip-mining? What about drift nets, pesticides, the Army Corps of Beaverbrains, nuclear wastes?"

"All disasters," Jeremiah said with a shrug. "But none of 'em are hypocrites, because none of 'em've got the gall to call themselves *fly fishermen.*"

I told him I wasn't about to rock anybody. I told him he was like the Crow Indians who cheered the arrival of the U.S. Cavalry because they figured the bluecoats would help them win their old feud with the Sioux. He reddened some, but repeated, *"Rock 'em!"* I told myself he couldn't be serious. Myself was not convinced.

It is undoubtedly foolish to speculate on the psychology or psychoses of a man six-and-a-half-feet tall, short-tempered and well aware of where you live. But since Jer knows (I hope) that I only wish him well, I'll risk it:

Jeremiah is the fly-fishing son of a fly-fishing bum. He was born in Butte, Montana, where his mother taught school and his dad painted signs. It was his mother who named her son after the fierce Old Testament prophet (sample prophesy: "O earth, earth, earth!"). And it was his mother who ran off with a barnstorming evangelist, abandoning her son to his father and fate at the age of four (second sample: "Mine heart within me is broken [and] all my bones shake . . . For the land is full of adulterers [and] the pleasant places of the wilderness are dried up."). For the next fourteen years Jeremiah and his father painted signs in the small riverside towns of Oregon, Idaho and Montana, their meanderings determined not by commercial opportunity (which was always meager in the towns they preferred) but by rainfall, snowmelt, and stone-fly, may-fly and caddis-fly hatches. Jeremiah says he was raised on the Bighole and Madison, the Clearwater and Salmon, the Metolius, Rogue and Deschutes of the 1950s, but "raised *by*" is more like it. And I believe it's perfectly possible for a lonely man to make a surrogate wife, or a lonely boy a surrogate mother, of a river. I think Jeremiah ended up with a dozen or more beautiful mothers, all of whom he loved with a fierce, blood-simple love. I believe this is why, seeing the same mothers today, he spends so much time seeing red.

I have never seen a man show a more anthropomorphic courtesy to wild waters. I've seen Jeremiah converse with his favorite rivers—not mumble to them, or to himself, like the rest of us, but come right out and say stuff like, "You're lookin' lovely today." He'll ask after the health of the headwaters and mouth as if discussing chronic migraines or tooth decay. He'll commiserate about dam releases and irrigation draw-downs as if he's talking take-home pay and property taxes. He'll stop and listen while she answers. I've seen him stop fishing—when the fishing was *good*—to stuff his archaic wicker creel full of other men's monofilament snarls and beer cans and Styrofoam. I've even seen afternoons when *all* he did was fume and curse and wander the riverbank, helplessly picking up trash.

Ransom may be a Luddite, but he isn't a moron. He's seen what dams, logging, mining, cattle, corporate farming and all the rest of it has done to rivers. But he's a man with a peculiarly human love for water. He's also a fighter of that archaic Western school which holds that fights are things you conduct with your fists. And it just isn't possible to duke out a papermill, aluminum plant or dam. So maybe the most punchable instruments of the changes he abhors on the waters he adores really *are* the fly-fishing popularizers he calls "traitors."

HOW-TO PIECES HAVE NOT ALWAYS OCCUPIED SO LOW A PLACE on the literary or cultural totem poles. The first known how-to-ists —Babylonians and Egyptians of around 3500 B.C.—engraved stylized fishermen demonstrating proper technique on the sides of urns and vases, a huge improvement over contemporary magazine how-to-ing in that, if a customer later decided they'd purchased inept or hackneyed advice, they nevertheless got a handsome container for their shekels. Around the fifth century B.C. the Chinese Taoists began to indulge in a bit of how-to-ing—a rather Chinese-sounding verb. But there was little danger that most Taoist advice (for instance, Chuang-tzu's recommendation to "Take an enormous hook, bait it with fifty bullocks, sit down on a mountaintop, cast your bullocks into the Eastern Sea, and wait . . .") would make much of a dent in the fish population—or in the bullock population, for that matter. Homer's ancient Greek advice on chumming and surf-fishing in the twelfth book of *The Odyssey* is certainly accurate enough to draw blood. But Homer had the courtesy to surround his angling didactics with one of the greatest epics ever written.

Something else to consider before one starts slinging rocks at writing hands is the uncanny link between how-to fishing writing and the English language itself. The longer I study our language and literature, the more convinced I become that our tongue has a life of its own, that this life has a voracious love for random piscatorial theorizing, and that this love overrides our own feeble likes and dislikes whenever it chooses. Consider this passage from John Bunyan's *The Pilgrim's Progress:*

> You see the way the Fisherman doth take
> To catch the fish; what Engins doth he make?
> Behold how he ingageth all his wits,
> Also his Snares, Lines, Angles, Hooks and Nets . . .

The crabbed grammar, oddball spellings, bizarre list and rhetorical tone make these lines a paragon of the how-to species to come. But what makes the passage almost frightening is that it's surrounded by an allegory of killjoy Christian dogma that gives Bunyan no context for mentioning fishermen or their "Engins" at all. What I mean to imply is that, thanks to our language's own renegade love for fishing jabber, the prose or poetry of anyone writing in English is in constant danger of disfigurement by sudden irruptions of nonsequacious angling advice.

"Fish!" exclaims Annie Dillard, out of deep left field, in her unballasted best-seller, *Pilgrim at Tinker Creek:* "You can lure them, net them, troll for them, club them, clutch them, chase them up an inlet, stun them with plant juice, catch them in a wooden wheel that runs all night . . ." and so on. But can we really? Can Dillard? And if not, why is she so excitedly telling us these things? It appears Bunyan is not the only pilgrim victimized by this odd English-speakers' malady.

"Blue dun; number 2 in most rivers for dark days, when it's

cold," intones the estimable Ezra Pound, apropos of *nada,* in his inestimable tome, the *Cantos:* "A starling's wing will give you the colour or duck widgeon, if you take feather from under the wing/ . . . can be fished from seven a.m./till eleven; at which time the brown marsh fly comes on . . ." What we have here is an absolute *non*angler, in a nonaquatic poem, suddenly tossing us untested tips by the pound. To what end? My guess is, Ezra hadn't a clue. My guess is, English did it.

The second-largest-selling single volume ever printed in English is, for no sane reason, Izaak Walton's *The Compleat Angler*—an arcane, pious, derivative how-to fishing book that virtually no one ever reads: yet century after century, compleat nonanglers march like body-snatched zombies out to bookstores, see the title and purchase the tome as insurance against the day they may need to review how best to catch swallows with a fly fished from a church steeple, or how to catch pike using live ducks as bait.

For a final example of the random how-to outburst, consider this archaic plea for catch-and-release angling:

> Canst thou put an hook into his nose? or bore his jaw through with a thorn? Will he make many supplications unto thee? will he speak soft words unto thee? . . . Shall thy companions make a banquet of him? shall they part him among the merchants? Canst thou fill his skin with barbed irons? or his head with fish spears?
>
> Lay thine hand upon him, remember the battle, do no more.

Wonderful advice, centuries ahead of its time. But in what famous fishing tome does it occur? Why, the forty-first chapter of the King James Book of Job!

I rest my case. And I, for one, could never bring myself to stone the pen-hands of Dillard, Pound, Walton or the King James scholars—and would use only smallish rocks to maim the hand of Bunyan. All of which brings us, somehow, back to Jeremiah and his obsession.

MY REASONS FOR OUTLINING THE HOW-TO PHENOMENON ARE not polemical. Polemics are Jeremiah's department. I just want to tell the story of a fishing trip Jer and I took with our mutual friend, John Rawlins, and one can't begin to describe fishing with Jer without first describing his obsession.

The trip took place in June of last year, when—after a cold, sodden, typically late Oregon spring—Ransom blew into Portland during a sudden hot spell and invited John and me to "sashay on over" to the Deschutes with him to fish the most ferociously overdescribed and overpopulated of all Western trout-fishing possibilities: the salmon-fly hatch. We met in Portland at noon, and as Ransom had no air-conditioning, it was hot in his car till we reached the Cascades. Then as we shot through Blue Box Pass and began the long nosedive to Warm Springs, Ransom negated the alpine air by launching a harangue on the havoc the how-to-ers had been wreaking on his dear Deschutes. I should have known he was incapable of "sashaying" anywhere.

It is worth mentioning that Ransom was at the wheel, that he drives a rusted-out 1976 Dodge Coronet 440 with original shocks and what look like original tires and that he is one of those fanatically earnest motorist-monologuists who refuses to tear his eyes off your face for such rhetorically purposeless purposes as glancing at the road. Jer is also a proponent of his defunct hero Edward Abbey's long-distance-driving method ("If you don't drink, don't drive. If you drink, *drive like hell!*"). Well into his day's second six-pack, he was ending most every sentence with an exclamation point typed on the accelerator—which exclamations, though nicely wed to his discourse, bore no correlation to the contours of the road.

John Rawlins rode shotgun, his part in the discussion being to stomp an imaginary brake pedal located beneath, or sometimes on, the glove compartment every time things got too centrifugal for him, and to interject the occasional salient, "Uh, Jer, you're in the wrong lane!" or "Speed trap!" or *"Jerthere'salogtruck!"* I, meanwhile, rolled from side to side in the seatbelt-less backseat, providing Ransom a face to yell into. With an eye to highway safety, I experimented with different facial locations. If I sat on the right side I found that Jeremiah turned to face me constantly, so I moved left, thinking this would force him to holler at my reflection in the rearview mirror. When his furious foreplay reached the climactic topic of summer steelhead, guided jet boats and electronic fish locators, though, he turned around 180 degrees to fume at me, leaving John—without warning—to man the wheel. So I returned to the right side, and camped there.

Since I was conscientiously matching Ransom beer for beer, my recollection of his rampage is hazy. I am, by the way, a wine man. Macro-brewed American beer makes me belch, then fart, then puts me to sleep, then gives me carbonated nightmares, then wakes me with a sprained bladder, aching head and killing thirst. But I recalled reading somewhere—perhaps in a how-to fishing piece— that the limp bodies of drunks sometimes survive even devastating car wrecks. So the open containers, in my case, were a kind of safety equipment.

I ACHIEVED THE DESIRED STATE OF LIMPNESS BUT WAS UNABLE to put it to the test, for we arrived, unwrecked, at the rim of the canyon. We then managed—by pissing for ten or so minutes, by donning backpacks, by trespassing and by hiking down two tortuous

miles of snake-and-poison-oak-infested deer trail—to reach a stretch
of river sporting thousands of salmon flies and, incredibly, no fishermen. The two-mile descent, plus two quarts of springwater, plus
two peanutsanderbuttwiches (as we call them back home) negated
enough of my eight beers to make the word *fly-fishing* pronounce-
able, though the act remained inconceivable. Jeremiah, though,
scarcely needs a pulse to handle a fly rod. Getting his neoprenes on
frontways taxed him for a time. He couldn't get to his fly boxes,
either, till he realized his fishing vest was on inside out. But he
missed only two guides in threading up his rod. And no sooner did
he weave into the river and cast into the evening breeze than he
began letting out a series of fish-on hoots that hit John and me like a
full pot of French roast . . .

Within minutes all three of us were hip-deep in one of those
mythic zones, early in the hatch, when every big rainbow in the
riffle is chasing salmon flies across the surface. It was our further
good fortune that a salmon fly imitation is a concoction so huge that
it is mistakenly raped, on occasion, by male muskrats. I remained too
road-glazed and beer-gummed to focus on objects the size of junipers or Jeremiahs, let alone the size of dry flies, but all I had to do
was slop these mammal-sized things out there, not drop the rod or
fall in the river, and wait for the attack. Once I got used to it, it only
doubled my pleasure to find that, according to my vision, I was
fishing two flies on two rods on two Deschutes Rivers at once.

Like anything worth describing, this evening was indescribable. The canyon wall was twelve hundred feet tall and complicated.
The latter-day light was doing reddish things to the rimrock. The
redwings were keening, the chukars *chuk-chuk*ing, the canyon wrens
nabbing salmon flies big as themselves, landing on twigs, then glar-
ing at us with four translucent wings flickering like flames out their
beaks, making them look, in that rapturous red light, like little apos-
tles unable to speak in, but at least able to stick out, a mouthful of
glossolalian tongues. The wind was shirtsleeve warm and rife with

the scent of sage. The river was luminous, glass-green with runoff, specked with endless fallen bits of sun. And its trout were identically green-backed, identically sun-sided and so abusively hungry they'd sometimes porpoise yards across the surface before savaging our flies.

For two solid hours we did nothing but hook and play and lose and catch native rainbows ranging from the size of my (modest) forearm to the size of Jeremiah's, and the Jeremiah forearm-sized ones had us running up and down the long glide, kicking water all over each other, crossing lines, cursing like kingfishers and jabbering out the very words the apostolic wrens were too full of salmon fly to say. We were playing fish simultaneously so often that finally, when our three lines were braided and broken once again by frantic trout, John and Jer introduced me to a little square dance routine they'd once worked up on the cutthroat-infested waters of the upper Yellowstone:

We started out side by side, cast simultaneously and waited till we'd all hooked fish. We then moved in shoulder to shoulder, John started twanging out an imitation Jews' harp rendition of "Bloke in a Poke," and Jeremiah, eyeing the zigs and zags of our trout, began unzigging them by making like a square-dance caller:

"Swing that Fenwich past my nose! Watch that leaper, yikes! Dos-à-dos!

"Now two rods high an' one rod low, cross 'em quick! *Shit!* Thar they go!"

I joined in with the washtub-bass part: *"Whoong, bugga-whoong, bugga-whoong whang-whoong!"* John kept harping: *"Ninga-ninga-nang, ninga-ninga-nang nanger!"* Ransom drawled, "Pass me that chopstick from Taiwan! Oooo! watch them redsides scoot along!" and we linked and unlinked arms, swapped poles and partners, reeled each other's reels, managed somehow to keep all three fish on and laughed so hard I could no longer even see double—

So I'd no idea why all of a sudden I was *Whoong bugga-whoong-*

ing all by my lonesome, with a rod in each hand, neither one mine. I turned upstream to see what my partners were gawking at . . .

And there were the boats, jammed with gear and silent fisher-men, nearly upon us. Three steel-gray drift boats, one ten-man supply raft, and on the side of all four vessels, in foot-tall Day-Glo pink letters you could've read a mile away:

JIM BURNETT'S FLYFISHING EXTRAVAGANZAS!

I glanced at Ransom. He was red. Pure red. I looked back at the boats, and at the oars of the last recognized Jim Burnett himself, the most famous of all the Northwest fly-fishing entrepreneurs—and the most prolific and overpublished of all the how-to when-to where-to "traitors."

Like a boat full of stones, my heart sank. But it takes a moment or two to leap from sheer beerblissful nincompoopery to self-righteous wrath, and we were standing in gravel far too small to crush a head, hand or camera (though it would have made an interesting sort of bird shot). Also, John Rawlins's mind was even quicker than Ransom's temper: before Jer could move, John stuck his rod under my arm (so that for a few seconds I enjoyed the other worldly and highly illegal distinction of playing three large trout at once on three different fly rods) and moved in so close to Jeremiah's left side—and throwing arm—that Ransom couldn't budge without first shoving his best friend in the river. Meanwhile ten strange faces not thirty feet away sat staring like confused cattle at a blissed-out square-dance caller transformed, at the mere sight of them, into six-feet six-inches of crimson ice.

Fortunately the river was fast. Two of the boats and the raft passed quickly out of range. But Burnett, the madman, started pulling on his oars, holding his boat and two clients right in front of us —right in the water we'd been fishing. "You're Jeremiah Ransom, aren't you?" he asked, amiably enough. But the water carried his voice to us with an intimacy that felt obscene.

"I'm Roderick Haig-Brown," growled Jeremiah.

"I'd like to talk with you, Ransom," he said.

"I'd like you to get the fuck out of our drift," said Jeremiah.

The clients turned pale. But Burnett remained calm. "You know," he said, "there isn't a guide on this river who hasn't heard of you. You crushed Cal Mason's gunwale with a rock last year."

One of my organs, I'm not sure which, rose up into my throat. This was the first I'd heard of Jeremiah actually practicing what he preached. Ransom said, "Cal Mason parked a jetboat-load of corporate assbites on a gravel bar I'd hiked in to fish. And right at dusk."

Burnett nodded. "Cal's an ass. I don't like him any better'n you do. But you should have asked him to leave, and smashed his boat if he didn't."

"I'm askin' *you* to leave," said Jeremiah.

"I'd like to talk," said Burnett. "We'll be camping just downriver. Come on down for a drink."

"I wouldn't drink in your camp, and there's nothin' to say," said Ransom. "The side of your fuckin' boat says it all."

"Cal's carrying a .38 revolver under his seat this season." Burnett told him. "Calls it his snake gun. My fuckin' boat couldn't quite say that."

My stomach somersaulted.

Burnett reversed his stroke. The boat shot away.

Jeremiah turned and waded ashore without a word.

John and I reeled in the fly lines. I'd lost all three of the rainbows.

I HAD DECIDED I WOULD NEVER FISH THE DESCHUTES AGAIN. I'd also decided I'd never fish with Jeremiah again. It was just after dinner, just after dark, and though we'd built a small, cheery illegal campfire and the Milky Way was pouring out its lovely nondairy product, I couldn't recall a gloomier end to a better day. And it threatened to get gloomier still when, up through the sagebrush, a flashlight beam wove its way toward us. A cop, I thought, come to nail us for the fire.

Then Jim Burnett stepped into the yellow dome of firelight.

"Peace offering," he said, holding up a fifth of Jack Daniel's.

John and I stood, thanked him, invited him in, so to speak, and introduced ourselves. Ransom stayed slumped against his boulder backrest. I noticed a few loose chunks of basalt near his feet—and immediately fantasized having to coldcock him to prevent a capital crime. But he remained so slumped that I decided I was being paranoid. Then John—Jer's oldest friend—walked over and sat paranoically close to his left side.

"You wouldn't drink at my camp," Burnett said to Ransom, "so I thought I'd bring a sip to yours."

"How Christian," quothe Jeremiah. *O earth, earth, earth.*

There was a long, awkward pause during which the famed how-to-er—forgetting the difference between backpacks and ten-man supply rafts—stood waiting with the bottle, apparently expecting one of us to produce a bag of cocktail ice and set of highball glasses. Because there'd been no conversation before his arrival, I'd been playing my B-flat tin whistle—a slow, improvised air in the minor key; "Pacifist's Farewell to the Rimrock Canyon," I'd been calling it. Seeing Burnett stymied, though, I turned my whistle upside down, plugged the holes with my fingers and held it out. He stared at it, then got the idea. "Want a toot, do ya?" he chortled. "I like a man who dudn't mind wettin' his whistle."

John and I chuckled. It wasn't all that funny, but I admire *any* wit in a person who knows that at least one and maybe all three of his companions hate his guts. And it got a little funnier when he poured, and I discovered I'd forgotten to plug the mouthpiece and so had to more or less chug the whiskey as it dribbled down my chin and shirt.

Burnett and I sat now, the bottle made some rounds, and I didn't know whether to be relieved or worried by the heavy losses Jeremiah inflicted on it. Burnett asked John and me what we did for a living. John—an untenured history professor at a podunk college —said he was executive vice-president of Georgia-Pacific, which inspired me to say that I sold phony life insurance policies to non-English-speaking Hispanics and Hmong tribesmen. Burnett looked so confused by this that John smiled guiltily and told him he was really a professor, and I told him I was really a writer. But now Burnett just gave us a crooked grin, believing neither one of us.

The crickets were nerve-rackingly loud, and the river was doing that weird thing it does at night, where the volume goes way up, then way down, for no reason. I felt so edgy that when the bottle floated my way I took some unsportsmanlike swigs. And they worked: in no time our camp turned into a cozy little Jack Daniel's ad as my insides inflated with that ninety-proof fondness for anything alive. I passed the Jack on to Burnett, who took a fair-sized slurp himself, then said, "What I came for, what I'd really like to know, is exactly what you all—especially you, Ransom—have against me."

His timing, in terms of blood-alcohol content, was perfect. I chirped that I had nothing against him, except the price of his trout flies. John chimed in, "Me neither, except I'd kinda hoped a real *Rey del Mundo*–type guy like you might bring along Maker's Mark or Old Heaven Hill instead o' Jack Daniel's."

Burnett grinned, said, "Next time."

Then Jeremiah sat up straight, cleared his throat, peered across the fire and growled, "I'll tell you what I've got against you, Burnett —if you've got some time."

Burnett said he had all night. Jeremiah growled, "I might need it."

He then proceeded to make what Burnett and John and I, to this day, refer to simply as The Speech.

"What I have against you idn't much," he began in a voice that was quiet, rusty and uncomfortably calm. "Only everything you publish, everything you say and do, every buck you make, every fish you hook, every goddamned thing you stand for."

Burnett nodded as if this made perfect sense and passed Jeremiah the whiskey. Ransom took his time with the bottle, taking on fuel, I felt now, and steam.

"What I have against you, Mister Jim Burnett's Fishfuckin' Extravaganzas, is that there isn't a trout of any size left in Oregon, Idaho or Montana that hasn't posed on the cover of some slick how-to fly-fishin' rag, and every one of those rags is in the back pocket of the tackle industry, and the tackle industry will soon be, if it idn't already, in the back pocket of the Multinational Techno-Industrial Megalith, and the Megalith fishin' rags of the future will brainwash a whole new horde of clones whose rods, flies, boats, clothes, vitamin pills, booze and sexual lubricants'll all be made of nothing but space age plastics and petroleum-derived plumbagos that only Megalith executives an' famous fishermen like yourself can afford. What I have against you is that you're a goddamned imperialist in neo-prenes, an' if you and your co-conspirators have your way there'll come a day when every blue-ribbon stream in the country will be a private fishin' club. Then when you an' your jaded clubsters get tired of catching one- an' two-pound natives, you'll stock your waters with laboratory-designed, hatchery-bred mutants that grow faster'n lymphatic cancer an' write books an' articles damning as idiots anybody who didn't do likewise. What I have against you is that before you're through with it the only difference between trout-fishing and *golf* will be that golfers knock a manmade object *into* a hole with a graphite stick, while fisherman with graphite sticks pull manmade objects *out.*"

When I turned to the butt of this outburst and saw him simply listening with an equitable little scowl of concentration, I began to like him. Burnett's name may have been on half the fly gear in the Northwest, but no self-obsessed Techno-Industrial dandy could have endured a blast like that and still sat calmly listening.

Jeremiah stopped for a moment to sort of smile at the fire. But it was an acrid-looking thing, that smile:

"I can see it. I can *smell* it! I can smell the day comin' when there'll be two kinds of water left—million-dollar-dues fishin' clubs and open sewers. And the word *river* will be changed to *water-course,* and they'll map, diagram and number every riffle an' hole, an' each hole will have its own armed guard, electric fence an' gazebo cock-tail lounge, an' the fish in the holes will have brand names an' built-in microfiche scorecards you plug into your Jim Burnett UV-proof Stereophonic Extravaganza Helmet to read who all caught that fish, an' *how.* I can smell the day comin' when you an' your all-star cronies'll be merrily scrawlin' formulaic drivel 'bout catchin' some twenty-seven-inch model of the new Riverbuster Rainbows (division of DuPont) that took a number-eighteen Flotofill Caddis (division of ARCO) at five-forty-three Rocky Mountain Standard on the seventeenth hole of the Henry's Fork (division of Wise Use International) where it doglegs to the southwest, an' your god-damned Riverbuster's dorsal scorecard will tell you it had only been caught thirty times before, only nine times by famous fishing writ-ers, only eight of whom photographed it, x-rayed it, pumped its stomach, released it an' described the whole fuckin' rape in butt-boringly technocratic braggadocios with names like 'Fishing the New Thrombopolystyrene *Ephemeroptera* on the Dogleg at the Henry's, which they'll publish in slick 3-D snotrags with names like *The Global Village Angler,* with the entire pukin' performance also available on video and CD.

"An' that's only the future. What I have against you *now* is the dozen nouveau riche jerks you drag along every time you *do* a river, every one of 'em forkin' out three hundred clams a day for the honor of your bad company an' pimp expertise, every one of 'em K-notes deep into the gear you shovel at 'em in your crapulous chain of shops, every one of 'em believin' there's no honorable method, no honorable thought on rivers, no honorable rod that's not a Jim Burnett Extravaganza Method Thought an' Rod so 'Buy it, buy it, buy it, you'll be the Cutting Edge!' you tell 'em. An' meanwhile *you've already designed the prototype rod, reel an' line that'll outmode every goddamned thing you just sold 'em!* What I have against you, Mister Jim Burnett's Riverfuckin' Wetdreams, is that this time next year you'll be hypin' some new IBM microelectronic *Pteronarcys* or *Acroneuria* you operate with a toggle switch on the butt of some nine-thousand-dollar Jedi Jim Zukonite Fly Rod that sends electrolytic impulses down the line to the fly, causin' it to go through every life-stage of the bonafide insect, includin' screwin' an' dyin'! What I have against you is the way you blather the name an' videotape the sacred body of every piece of water you've ever shat beside so that a mob of munchkins totin' Jim Burnett Moron Outfits comes crashin' along after you before the turds have even dried! What I have against you is the way you strut uninvited into our camp an' try to ingratiate yourself to us with a bottle of mass-market booze that's about as Down-Home Phony as you are an' cost maybe a thousandth of what you made this very day. What I have against you, Burnett, is *you make me puke!*"

With that, Ransom crossed his arms like a chief in a Hollywood powwow and glared so hotly at the fire that it flared.

There was a desperate silence, during which I kept my eyes on the flames, feeling half like applauding, half like begging Burnett for forgiveness and half like simply leaving that stupid camp and canyon forever. I know that's three halves, but my feelings were more than full.

I finally glanced at John, though, just as he happened to glance at Burnett, and was surprised to see his eyes bulge before he covered them with one hand, commencing an obviously doomed struggle not to laugh. I then turned to Burnett—and saw that he was smiling at Jeremiah in *exactly* the way that Stan Laurel used to smile at Oliver Hardy. "Well, golly!" he said, smacking his lips a little. "Gosh, Jer, if *that's* all that's botherin' ya, *heck.* No problem."

Jeremiah looked up in amazement.

"Hey guy!" Burnett said. *"No biggie.* We'll iron 'er out in a jiffy!"

John and I exploded. Jeremiah scowled, trying not to join us. "Have another swig on Jedi Jim!" Burnett chortled, tossing Jer the bottle. *"Fly-fishin' helmets!"* he wheezed. "The dogleg at Henry's!" he rasped. *"DuPont Riverbusters!* That's good! That's really good!"

John and I laughed ourselves sick. Even Jeremiah finally chuckled a little. Then, as often happens with hysterics, they vanished as fast as they'd struck. The tension was back. The crickets grew shrill. The volume knob on the Deschutes started twisting up and down again. The bottle made a final circle, with a half swig in it that everybody but me was too polite or nervous to down. Then Burnett said, "Well, gentlemen? Is it my turn?"

This took us all by surprise, though Ransom tried to hide his by snorting, "Your turn to *what?* Empty *our* wallets, too?"

Burnett kept smiling. But what came out of his mouth had teeth. "All of what you said was eloquent," he began. "Maybe a quarter of it was true. But the other three-quarters, much as I enjoyed it, was a crock. Of course a crock makes for good comedy—it was a hell of a speech. But I don't think you *know* it's comedy, Ransom. And I hate to see a good man base his life on a crock."

Jeremiah turned his totem color. "You can't bullshit your way out of it," he said.

"Can I try?"

Jeremiah snorted, but nodded.

Burnett thanked him, took a moment to consider, then said, "What I have against *you,* Jeremiah, is the way you make a virtue out of your powerlessness and a soapbox out of your ignorance, then stand up and pass judgment on people whose lives and work you know nothing about. I'll be *damned* if I'll sit here listing my good deeds in self-defense. Nobody resembling me and no business resembling mine has been attacked here. I admit I've helped popularize some places I wish I'd kept quiet about. But I've also helped popularize catch-and-release and slot limits and wild trout and special regs. And the very crowds you hate are all that's *saved* some of the places we both love."

Jeremiah maintained an operatic frown.

Burnett said, "You've never set foot in one of my fly shops, have you?"

"Damned right I haven't!" Ransom snapped.

"You've never met even one of those 'corporate assbites' I *drag* out here to fish, either, have you?"

"Just seein' 'em on the river's bad enough," Jeremiah growled.

Burnett laughed. "Some muckraker *you* are, Ransom! You live in a time warp. Anybody ever tell you that? You're so busy living up to some big dangerous throwback-to-the-old-days image there's no place to even *begin* talking with you about what fishing really is, or what it should be, or what you or I should be doing to change or save it. And I'm a fool to make this offer—I ought to let you and that horse's butt Cal shoot it out in Zane Grey fantasy land. But I invite you, no, I *defy* you, to pack your things and come with me *right this minute,* and see for yourself who my clients are, and what they do for a living. I defy you to float the river with us tomorrow and watch our whole little circus in action. And when we drive back to town I invite you to inspect my books—that's right, my *finances,* buddy—and see for yourself what a ruthless imperialist I am. I defy you to come find out whether you're the crusty ol' sage of the canyon you take yourself to be, or a man who owes me a second look, and maybe, just maybe, even a fraction of an apology."

With that, Burnett stood, pulled out his flashlight and said, "Well?"

Jeremiah was scowling prodigiously—at a rock. But when he began to scratch his head I realized it was a scowl of indecision.

It didn't last long. Glancing at John and me, he said, "You guys mind if I bail out on you?"

"Not if you leave us the car keys," I said.

"Looks to me like he double-dog-dared you," said John.

"We'll miss your driving," I added.

Jeremiah started packing. Five minutes later they were gone.

BY MORNING THE WEATHER HAD TURNED COOL AND GRAY, SO for John and me it was big black nymphs, hard work, a lot of missed strikes and fewer, smaller, more sedate trout. At least none of them were DuPont Riverbusters.

During the long hike out of the canyon it struck John that while we were slaving like mules, Jeremiah was lounging in Burnett's drift boat watching the rimrock slide by, munching gourmet food. "Maybe *we* shoulda cussed him out, too," I said.

"Or rocked him," John grunted.

I nodded. "Coupla thunder eggs upside the head and he'd probably have *given* us his boat."

"And the keys to his Mercedes," John added.

JEREMIAH FLOATED THE RIVER WITH JIM BURNETT. HE ALSO returned with him to Portland, drove straight to the original of the "crapulous chain" of fly shops, poked around the shelves and warehouse, took a look at the books, chatted with employees and customers and was moved by the whole experience to retract "maybe 15 percent of The Speech." A sizable percentage for a man I'd never known to retract anything. And Burnett had that "wee fraction of an apology" he'd wanted.

Ransom said there were three reasons for his 15 percent change of heart: one was that Burnett's employees liked their boss, liked working for him and would have been papermill workers, unemployed loggers, bankrupt farmers and the like if it weren't for the fly shops, so "the Industrial Megalith had 'em by the shorthairs anyhow." The second reason was his discovery that for every "disgusting fat cat" that patronized Burnett's shops there must have been half a hundred John Q. Publics with ten bucks in their pocket and that crazed look of the hopeless river-lover in their eyes, and Burnett's employees were as courteous to the John Q.'s as to the fat cats. The third reason was that "in a pseudo-democracy like ours—where money buys the brainwashing machinery, machinery buys votes, an' votes buy politicians—our rivers an' trout an' salmon an' steelhead need payin' jobs, such as being floated an' fished an' caught an' released, so they can buy their own damned votes. Burnett understands that, an' pays the conservation tithes an' offerings that make it all work."

I was amazed. This was the first political statement I had ever heard Jeremiah make (discounting such pronouncements as "Impeach the fucker!" and "Shoot that assbite!"). What really turned his head, apparently, was learning about a statewide angler's lobby that Burnett had helped invent, fund and spearhead—a lobby that had many times delayed, and in two cases actually stopped, the construction of dams. "He stops *dams!*" Jeremiah kept repeating. *"Dams!"* This obviously came as a shock to a man who believed the only way to stop an adversary was to punch it.

Burnett celebrated his 15 percent gain in popularity by giving Ransom fifteen free trout flies, then taking him and a couple of employees on a beer bust, after which he coerced Jer into a taxi cab with him (another Ransom first) and invited him to spend the night in the enormous R.V. that doubles as his guest house. A lifelong army-surplus pup-tent camper, Ransom claimed the aluminum walls of the R.V. had given him horrendous nightmares, and probably the beginnings of Alzheimer's, too. As usual, beer received no part of the blame.

The following morning, Burnett—perhaps a bit cocky over his 15 percent success—invited Jeremiah to read through a few of his unpublished manuscripts and state his opinion of them. The ensuing conversation went on well into the afternoon, and grew, even according to the mild-tempered Burnett, "molten." The main bone of contention, predictably, had been Burnett's continued habit of naming and publicizing good places to fish. His argument, he said, was that more fly-fisherfolk meant more conservation voters, more protection for rivers, hence, in the long run, better fishing. But Jeremiah kept countering this argument with volcanic rhetorical assaults that boiled down to: "An' more cloned yahoos on every river rock. An' more millions for *you,* you greedy asshole." Jer must have been in top form, too—because, unless he's had some flagrant environmental motivation, Jim Burnett has not published one of his patented pieces on a little-known water or a fragile fishery since.

The culmination of these many wonders should have come the next evening, when Jeremiah "Rock' Em" Ransom and Jim "Tell 'Em How & Where" Burnett actually went a-fishing together (never mind where or how). To Burnett's amazement, though, Jeremiah spent the entire evening rise wandering forlornly through the bushes, stuffing streamside garbage into his old wicker creel.

It was this experience that inspired Burnett to launch his now rather infamous "Streamside Eyesore Elimination," or "SEE," campaign. Providing all customers with free "Jim Burnett SEE bags made of tough, brush-resistant fibers" (i.e., chicken-scratch feed bags), Burnett offered half a dozen of the "hot new Flaming Jeremiah steelhead flies" as a reward for every bag brought back full of genuine streamside dreck. What he neglected to mention was that Jeremiah himself had carefully designed these flies—to *spook* steelhead. Burnett earned himself a letter of commendation from the governor of Oregon, and a tremendous amount of free advertising, too, since the bags soon became as common a sight in riverside logjams and willow thickets as the trash they were meant to contain.

But Jeremiah uses them. And he appreciated Burnett's attempt enough to send a note—which hangs on Burnett's office wall *above* the governor's. It reads,

> Dear Jedi:
> Though I am unable to deduct further percentage points from The Speech, I have come, to our mutual misfortune, to consider you a friend. In honor of this, and your bags (in which I plan to stuff the occasional rude guide and littering fisherman), I hereby vow to throw 15% fewer rocks.
>
> Yours in Rivers,
> Jeremiah

My One
Conversation with
Collin Walcott

for Glen Moore, Ralph Towner and Paul McCandless

IN THE MID-1980'S, DURING A SEVERE AUGUST DROUGHT, I
STOPPED BY TO GAB WITH MY NEIGHBOR, JON (WHO PRO-
NOUNCES IT "YAWN"), AND HAPPENED TO ARRIVE AT HIS
HOUSE JUST AS HIS BALDWIN UPRIGHT PIANO (YAWN CALLED IT
HIS "AX") WAS HEADING OUT THE DOOR INTO THE LOCAL
PIANO-TUNER'S VAN. AS I GRABBED A CORNER AND HELPED
LIFT, I LEARNED THAT A JAZZ QUARTET CALLED OREGON WAS
GOING TO BE PLAYING AN OUTDOOR CONCERT THE FOLLOW-
ING NIGHT, AND THAT YAWN'S AX WAS HEADED OFF TO SERVE
AS ONE OF THE TWO "CONCERT GRANDS" THE BAND HAD RE-
QUESTED. WHEN I LEARNED THAT A FREE TUNING WENT WITH
THE LOAN, I SAID, "HEY!"—AND A SHORT TIME LATER THE
PIANO-TUNER'S VAN WAS JOUNCING UP MY MUD-RUT DRIVE-

way, destined to make my motheaten, hymn-beaten, five-owner Jansen upright Oregon's second "concert grand."

In defense of these pianos I should explain that we lived, geographically, on a decidedly rural portion of the Oregon coast, which implies that, culturally, we lived in what the national jargon would term a vacuum. On Forest Service maps we were a green thumbprint with a few blue veins (the creeks) running through us. On highway maps we were nothing at all—solid color without symbols or words. But there, nevertheless, we were, smack in the middle of Downtown Vacuum, our various oddball houses sprouting like Cubist mushrooms from the abandoned dairy pastures, clearcuts and river valleys. And somehow or other these internationally renowned musicians had found us and decided, despite our pianos, to play some music.

The place Oregon played was called Cascade Head—a twelve-hundred-foot "mountain" whose eastern end is actually a ridge buried in the Coast Range, and whose western end is actually a cape amputated by the Pacific into a serrated series of basalt cliffs and inaccessible coves. The concert took place at a little arts center named Sitka (after the local spruce trees), in a grassy outdoor alder-and-spruce-ringed bowl.

Because it was necessary to park at the bottom of the Head and hike a steep half-mile to reach this bowl, the arriving faces had that benign quality faces get when the psychic umbilicus connecting humans to cars is severed. And they grew more benign when, in a building behind the concert bowl, they discovered a local restaurateur catering wine and imported beer, and the baker from the co-op serving up delectable carbos. Meanwhile the local ocean was serving up a low summer fog that crept eastward through the trees like a spectator with no ticket. The fog cooled things fast, but with most of the rest of North America smoggy or humid and pushing 100 degrees that day, I heard no complainers. We sat on green grass in gray light, those who'd brought blankets sharing with those who hadn't. The band was on time, and already warming up.

For a while I bustled around the crowd like a demented father, pointing out my enstaged and honored piano to everybody I knew. My friends mostly gawked at it, then winced, so my pride soon grew containable. I sat, and began to check out the band.

Though I'd heard many, maybe all, of their recordings, I'd never seen Oregon in person. I eyed Glen Moore first, since he was the guy standing closest to my Jansen. He was wearing bright red pointy-toed genie slippers and even brighter maroon pants, but to judge by his smile he'd done it on purpose. Instead of plucking, tuning or even touching his stand-up bass, he just goofed around with a friend's baby daughter, zooming her low over the stage, *nnnrowwing* her round and round the spotlights. His bass, at least, looked ready for action: it sported a snarling gargoyle head and appeared to be at least a thousand years old.

Ralph Towner stood with his back to us, adjusting the valves or something on a Prophet 5 synthesizer, tuning six- and twelve-string guitars, blowing warm air through a flügelhorn, playing deft warm-up scales on Yawn's Ax. (I noticed Yawn not ten feet away, chest puffed, eyes glistening, pointing out his shining Ax to other concert-goers. But Yawn had an excuse: the Ax really is a nice piano.) When Towner finished the Prophet 5's valve job and showed his face, he looked a little as if he'd been working swingshift at United Grocers. But half an hour or so into the concert his fatigue, or whatever it was, had vanished, and I realized the United Grocers' look must have been merely the pre-fix appearance of a man whose body has become hopelessly addicted to the making of music.

Paul McCandless, in contrast to Moore and Towner, looked alert and fiery from the start, even in dirty, unlaced tennis shoes. His name and face brought to mind some indomitable, straitlaced, nine-teenth-century Scottish missionary who'd set out to convert the heathen world to God knows what, but by a stroke of luck had instead been converted himself, to unlaced heathen horn-playing.

Then there was the percussionist, Collin Walcott—a man whose name had me expecting a contemporary of Dickens, Trollope or Thackeray, but who instead sat buddha-style in the middle of things, his long bald head shining, his face solemn and focused, his manner comfortably, contradictorily Oriental. He had a synthesized drum set just to his north—the first I'd ever seen—its heads and cymbals full-sized in sound, but no bigger than tea saucers. He had five different tablas to his south, a sitar to his east and a bewildering semicircle of rattles, chimes, clackers, bells, whistles, finger-drums, triangles and unnameable noisemakers to his west. He was the first Western "jazz" percussionist I'd ever seen sit flat on the floor like an East Indian. And after a night of watching him play in that position, the thought of the standard drummer perched on a steel stool, convulsively whacking with both feet at a high hat and drum, seemed a trifle inane.

THE CONCERT BEGAN IN A COOL GRAY DUSK. SUNSET CONsisted of a few minutes during which the fog and white alderbark turned golden. Then it grew dark, the cool turned decidedly cold, and we listeners began to need the music not only as a source of pleasure but as a source of heat. A little later the no-see-'ums came out in clouds, convening mostly beneath the spotlights, so that the band needed their music to transcend the fact that they were being devoured alive. A little after that the baby girl Moore had taken on the pre-concert zoom got tired and needed the music to calm her to sleep. A heater, an insect-antidote, a lullabye: Oregon's music served many purposes that night. But what it did last it did best. What it did last—so it seemed to me—was bring on its own annihilation. But we'll cross, or stumble into, that chasm when we come to it.

There is something uncanny about live music, about watching

living, breathing musicians as their music is being born. For all its technical perfection, a recording is just what it says it is: an accurate but lifeless replica of a living event. It leaves out the flickering hands, bending bodies, skilled, exerted breathing; the sharp, almost desperate inhalations by the horn players; the *screek* of the pick against the wound strings of the guitar; the nods, fleet smiles, deft understandings flickering back and forth between performers. These visual nuances are satisfying in themselves, but also guide a live listener toward the intent of every silence and sound. And there is a cumulative effect to the best live music. One piece sheds light on another, like stories in a strong collection, till your ears begin to master a lexicon. And when song after song reaches climax after climax, energy is not only generated, it's congealed, distilled, intensified, like sunlight passing through a magnifying glass. The sounds burn clear through the mind and hit you somewhere deeper. That, at least, is the alchemy concert-goers hope for. What can't be described, of course, is what a band does to put a listener in this state. We call it *music* but so what? *Music* is just a word for something we love largely because it consists of things that words can't express. Likewise, the *heart* is just a word for something in us that music sometimes touches. But once these two somethings, heart and music, do touch, there is only one of them.

Music is the food whose peculiarity it is to enter us through the ears. Music is an inexpressible from outside us touching an inexpressible within, causing the frenetic persona that normally wedges itself between outside and inside, creating twoness, to vanish. Gospel musicians used to shout out certain words when they felt inexpressibles touching, maybe *hallelujah,* or *amen,* which literally means simply, "It is so." These were magic words once, both of them. Then people learned to shout them when they weren't feeling anything in particular, and the words took revenge by becoming hokey as hell. They still are hokey. But during Oregon's performance that night I longed for the presence of such a word: beery shouts and

clapping seemed far from sufficient to acknowledge the beauty of
what we were receiving.

Maybe two hours into the concert Oregon played a Towner
composition called "The Rapids" that had inexpressibles touching
all over the mountainside. It is so. In fact it is, or was, so much so
that just as the music was fading, a green brilliance flashed through
the fog, and just as we began applauding there was a polite peal of
thunder. Everybody laughed. Like a shouted *hallelujah,* genuine
"thunderous applause" at a genuine Oregon concert on the Oregon
coast seemed hokey. But it happened. And right afterward, when I
sniffed the air, I sensed more about to happen. Something electric
was going on. Something meteorologically electric. It hadn't rained
in two months, and the satellite picture in the paper that morning
had shown a North Pacific cloudless clear to Japan. But as a Cauca-
sian I am part Asian, as a part-Asian I'm part Hindu, and when my
Hindu part sniffed the air and saw more faint green flashes, it began
to suspect that the fog was now much more than fog, and that Indra,
the Rainmaker, was hiding in it, drawn by the music, listening
closely.

WE FOUND OUT LATER THAT THERE HAD BEEN A LONE BACK-
packer up on Cascade Head that night. Knowing nothing of the
upcoming concert, this young man had toiled up a swale to a point
maybe a quarter-mile beyond and five hundred feet above our little
declivity in the spruce and alder grove, pitched his tent in open
meadow, cooked his dinner on a tiny propane stove and leaned back
against the ridge to study the stars—when astonishing sounds began
to pour up out of the fog. He had no idea who or even where the
musicians were. But the long swale's acoustics, he said, were great.
And because he was perched above the fogline, he was aware of
things we never suspected down in our bowl. He saw, for instance,
the way the Head jutted out into the Pacific, its entire seaward face

crumbling, thanks to old storm batterings. He saw that the general source of the music was not—as it seemed to us—a cozy, sheltered glade, but a tenuous, fogbound fold in that same battered, seaward face. And he saw the moment when, far out in the ocean, gigantic whorls of vapor began to rise up off the fogbank, drift inland and upward toward the summit of the Head and gather there, darkening, congealing, intensifying, till they became a towering, blue-black entity that bore no relation to vapor. This thunderhead, he said, formed above the sea off our solitary headland like a listener created by the music itself. And when it moved in to listen more closely, when thunderhead met Cascade Head and they too began trying to become one thing, the entire sky above our niche began to spark and rumble. It is so.

The band began a song called "Taos"—a composition as indescribable as any piece of music. To get a handle on what happened next, I'll describe something that isn't music, which this music was something like. Let's say that "Taos" is a wordless narrative describing a seven-minute-long natural event. Say it takes place in uninhabited desert, perhaps somewhere (as the name suggests) outside Taos, New Mexico. Say it takes place, like our concert, late in the evening. The sun is just vanishing. The sky is cloudless. Things are cooling after a day of sweltering heat. The shadows, once long and black, turn blue, then gray as the sun vanishes, then grow indistinct . . .

The music begins, like everything on this planet, with the water: Walcott's tablas dripping a steady, assonant stream of drops, Moore's bass *tok-tok-tok*ing in high, percussive overtones, Towner's Prophet also pouring out something percussive, quiet and wet. It sounds as though there is a seep, a tiny spring, hidden in the scorched rocks and warm shadows. And when McCandless kindles a little tin whistle we realize there's a bird, too—some solitary, nameless desert bird the music brings so near to life that we feel its heartbeat. The bird drinks at the seep, then seems to go wandering, and the mood is so benign, the chords so simple, that you think the song is about almost nothing—a little divertimento. But then the overtones end, the bass gropes deeper, the tablas give way to an insistent, staccato cymbal beat, the bird keeps flitting along, and though there is no increase in volume and no dissonance—nothing diminished or augmented or even minor to warn you—there comes a moment when you realize that the day has ended, the desert nights are cold and the little bird's flitting is in deadly earnest. What is it looking for? Or who? Moore's bass stays deep, the volume low, the mode insistently simple, almost heraldic, as in a medieval chant. The whole band joins in a chord that seems to believe in but can't quite find resolution. The tin bird cries out in panic now. Then the cymbals crash, the mouth of an immense desert cave comes into view and the bass erupts—two astounding, tympanic tones rising from the depths of the cavern. The bird's cries grow frantic. And finally it comes: resolution, the same tremendous bass notes, but doubled, booming out in fours now, and the flickering cymbals are the wingbeats of the little bird, the piercing tin whistle its joy, and the synthesizer the answering voices of its thousand sisters and brothers, bursting from the cave's mouth in a cloud. Again and again the four tremendous bass notes. Again and again the ecstatic birds, swirling round their lost brother in a cloud that finally vanishes, with a beautiful echo, back into the cavern . . .

There is the description, the handle. Here is what happened as the music was played:

The very first time Moore's bass groped deep, all around us, all over the Head, the thunder joined in—the pitch, the timing and tone, the volume of the peal all so perfectly wedded to the music that some of us couldn't take it in. The acid-retreads among us gaped reverentially at the bass's gargoyle head. The scientists peered up into the trees, trying to make out the gargantuan hidden speakers that would let them chalk it up to the marvels of technology. But the next time the bass dove for the cavern notes, the thunder was there again: a perfectly pitched, perfectly played crescendo. This time no one missed it. Towner turned an incredulous face toward his campadres. McCandless, mouth full of whistle, bulged his eyes and nodded. Moore threw back his head and laughed. Walcott just played on. Brilliant green flashes shot through the cloud. And to the end of the song the guest musician, the thunderhead, played its part to perfection. Call it weather, call it coincidence, call it Khizr or Indra or anything you choose, we heard it as pure music, it came from all over that mountain, and it turned us inside out. Then the music became visible: just as the desert birds began swirling back into their cave a real wind swirled down upon us, the real trees began to churn and the early dying leaves from a thousand alders whirled round us like birds. The song ended, the air filled with ozone, and our bodies remained so full of the sense of listening that the music in us refused to die. *It is so.* We cheered ourselves hoarse, applauded till our hands stung like hail. Then Moore, sensing too late the impending downpour, said, "If you'd like to hear us again, you can catch us in October—in Greece."

LIKE THE AUNTIE WHO GIVES YOU THE SAME DANG PAIR OF socks each Christmas, the god Indra, when pleased, can think of just one gift. Cascade Head gets a hundred inches of rain per annum, the stage had no roof and we wanted more concert, so a greater godly gift, under the circumstances, seemed like no rain at all. But gods will be gods, and when musicians please one they must accept the consequences, though their instruments, amps and bare heads be exposed to the sky.

Trying to dispel some of the energy they'd brought down upon us, Oregon set out on a courageous but ill-advised coda—a contemplative little piece, with Walcott on sitar and Towner on guitar. Thunder smashed it into meaningless fragments. Wind blew the shards away. The first few drops fell, enormous and warm. Then came the downpour, the cold gusts, the crowd's insane, frenetic cheering. The stage was a puddle in seconds. Spotlights started exploding. An alert technician doused everything electric but the lights. Most of the audience fled, whooping and shouting, but a score or so of us altruists and piano-owners ran down to the stage, hoping to help.

It was a deluge, a real Ark-launcher. Everyone was soaked through in seconds. A couple of tall guys jumped up, grabbed the whipping canvas canopy, pulled it over the stage and lashed it, but the wind drove the rain straight in under it. Water ran down the amplifiers, drenched the instruments, stung our faces, and despite our incurable elation we could see that, for the musicians, it was a disaster. Walcott cased up his sitar first, Towner his guitars. A stage-hand packed up the Prophet 5. Moore—with admirable carelessness —tossed a tarp over his priceless gargoyle and turned to help Mc-Candless, the two of them popping woodwinds into cases quick as bagboys sacking grocks. My friend Yawn was a marvelous sight, staggering round under the bank of exploding spotlights like King Lear in Act Five, roaring, *"My Ax! O God! My Ax!"* till a bunch of brawny volunteers muscled it into the piano-tuner's van. I checked my own piano: its top was off and nowhere to be seen; a microphone was dangling down inside; a soggy blanket had been draped over the treble cleff, but I could hear rain dripping like coffee through a filter, thumping the soundboard, soaking the felts. Moore hadn't played a note on it. I was going to need that free tuning. I didn't care. I stretched the sopping blanket down over the bass clef —just to keep the damage symmetrical—and wandered over toward Walcott.

He was hunched in the midst of his forty or fifty instruments, piling, covering and desperately packing them away. Out on the lawn a few Zorbas were still dancing and screaming, and a woman in a sopped T-shirt, bouncing in bra-less stereo, shrieked, *"The ultimate Oregon concert!"* It came out sounding like a faked hallelujah. In the face of the real storm, even words of would-be ecstasy felt wordy. Walcott looked miserable. A lot of his life was splayed out in the rain. There would be warping and water damage. I asked if there was anything I could do. He looked up and, in a tone incongruously calm, dry and New Yawkish for a man so wet and Oriental, said, "Yeah. Make it stop."

I nodded, then solemnly set about doing a pseudo-Hopi anti-rain chant as I hopped in a puddle on one foot.

Walcott seemed marginally amused at best.

But a minute or so later, the rain stopped.

THAT WAS MY ONE CONVERSATION WITH COLLIN WALCOTT. And there won't be another. The following December, right after we'd all failed to "catch them in Greece," he was killed in a car wreck en route to a concert in East Germany. It is written that "the Believing Mind is the Buddha-nature." And I believe. But when I think of Walcott sitting cross-legged amid his instruments like a serious child surrounded by toys he lived only to give away, I feel nothing but loss. Yes, the Believing Mind is the Buddha-nature. But in disguise. And what a disguise! In the face of a real storm, even buddhistic words feel wordy. Yet my instruments, my toys, are words. And when I learned that this wonderful maker of music was gone, I was moved to make some sentences in an attempt, however hopeless, to give as Collin Walcott had given.

THE CLOUDS, THAT AUGUST NIGHT, DISPERSED SHORTLY AF-ter the music ended. And in bright sunlight the following morning, that solitary backpacker came down off the Head, looking for some sign of the marvels he'd witnessed. He found an old cedar stage covered with fresh-fallen alder leaves. He found, in the grass, the fast-fading imprints of a few hundred human bottoms. No native tribe ever left a cleaner camp. And after the grandeur he'd witnessed, this cleanliness confused the backpacker. How much had he heard? How much had he dreamed? Would anything he'd heard remain free of dream later?

Spotting the Sitka caretaker, he rushed over and cried, "Last night! That *music!* Who *were* those guys?"

But when he was told, "A band called Oregon," he just shook his head and laughed. Laughed, then failed, as I have, to tell how for one long song, one sweet seven minutes, he'd watched them play, like an instrument, an entire headland and sky.

THE KING OF EPOXY

Out beyond ideas of right-doing and wrong-doing
there is a field. I'll meet you there.

—Rumi

I

IN EMPTY DESERT, IN THE NORTH OF AFRICA, AN ARCHAEOLO-
GIST STOPS DIGGING. HE'S WORKED IT FREE NOW. HE STOPS
DIGGING, GRIPS THE STONE AND HEAVES IT UP OUT OF THE
HOLE. IT SINKS SLIGHTLY WHEN IT LANDS IN THE BONE-DRY
SAND. HE HALF-LIFTS, HALF-SLIDES IT AWAY FROM THE HOLE,
MAKING SURE IT WON'T SHIFT OR ROLL.

THE STONE IS FOUR OR FIVE TIMES THE SIZE OF THE AR-
CHAEOLOGIST'S OWN HEAD, AND SEEMS FRAGILE LIKE A HUMAN
HEAD, TOO. SOME KIND OF SANDSTONE, HE'D THOUGHT AS HE
WAS DIGGING, BUT NOW THAT HE'S FREED IT HE REALIZES IT'S
TOO SOFT—THAT IT'S NOT STONE AT ALL, BUT A SAND-COV-

ered, fibrous gray clay. He is very hot and dusty. No shade at the
site. No water either, after he downs the warm dregs of his canteen.
But when he looks at his find he's neither tired nor thirsty. Because
it's not just head-shaped. It *is* a head. The clay head of a monkey.
Yes. Clearly no ape or gorilla, despite the size. Wrong proportions,
wrong eyes. It's a monkey head, all right—and a huge one. Some
monkey god, I suppose, he thinks. Not my department, but there
were such things once. He wishes he knew more.

He sees an obvious imperfection: a hairline crack runs most of
the way across the face. But he's far too grateful to ponder flaws. It's
a miracle that he discovered this head at all. It was two miles or more
from the ruins he'd come to study, and half a mile from his camp at
the oasis. There was nothing around it, no context at all. He'd
simply seen, during his early morning walk, an incongruous lump of
gray sticking out of barren sand, hiked over, whisked away a few
grains of white and realized he'd found an ear. The excavation had
been child's play. He'd felt like a kid at the beach.

He rolls the monkey head into his lap, wanting to fondle it like
a baby. It immediately begins to crush his thighs. He spreads his legs,
lets the sand take the weight, tries to ponder his find, but realizes his
thirst and hunger are getting serious. He knows better than to challenge the desert. He has to return to camp soon. But the head is far
too heavy to carry back. And when he contemplates leaving without it, he feels a flood of emotion so intense it verges on grief. He
sits still for a long moment, gaping at the crude clay face, trying to
make his powerful feelings go away. "Don't be absurd," he finally
tells himself. But he moves like a mother putting a feverish infant to
bed as he gently shimmies the head down into a sheltering nest of
sand. And his voice is the same mother's as he whispers, "I'll be
right back."

He stands, turns in a slow circle, scans the mirage lakes on the
horizon, looks for man- or camel-shapes, interlopers or thieves. But
of all the shapes shimmering in the false waters, just three remain

constant: those of the stunted date palms, back at his camp by the well.

He sets out for the palms.

II

THE ARCHAEOLOGIST IS BACK AT THE SITE, OR WHATEVER HE should call it: back at his unlikely hole and infinitely unlikely head in the vast expanse of white. And he's feeling . . . he's feeling . . . well, he's not sure what he's feeling. *Ecstatic remorse?* Is that too contradictory a term? Because he had eaten beneath the palms, and brought two full canteens back to the site; brought his campstool and collapsible worktable and parasol, too. He was rested, shaded, comfortably seated, ready to ponder his find until dark if he liked. But when he'd lifted the great head up onto the table, a big fragment of mouth and chin had sheared off at the hairline crack, exploding, when it hit the tabletop, into a thousand gray crumbs. And then his own mouth had fallen open as he'd seen that his find was not a monkey head after all—or not just a monkey head: the soft gray clay was a crude outer layer, and as he proceeded, with bare fingers, to pick more pieces from the break he began to make out a far more vivid face, a *red* monkey face, hidden beneath the original gray.

Following the fracture line, picking and prying, the archaeologist exposes a band of red all the way around the head and finds that there are *four* faces in there: four symmetrical, simian faces, joined at the cheeks and ears, sculpted into a single big earth-red egg of clay. The inner clay is terracotta, or something like it. Each face appears to be identical. Each appears to be intact. And each faces a different quadrant. He wonders whether they were aimed, originally, in the four cardinal directions. A way-marker for ancient visitors to the oasis? Some more esoteric religious object? Not his department, but he wishes he knew more. Whatever their ancient purpose, they're still beautiful, and far more intricately sculpted than the outer head. If only he'd photographed that original crude face! The gray material, whatever it is, disintegrates completely as he removes it, and his colleagues back in the States, the difficult ones, anyhow, were never going to swallow an undocumented, or gray-powder-documented, tale of an outer sculpture added for no apparent purpose but deception. Not after they hear that he destroyed that layer, without hesitation, to reach what was inside!

But to hell with colleagues, he thinks. To hell with cameras. He can't stop himself now. He's working fast, and the soft outer layer—the "deceptive material," as he now thinks of it—is coming off so readily he doesn't even need tools. He finds he can remove large chunks with his bare hands, that the more tenacious stuff can be scraped out with his fingernails, that they're gifted, these fingers of his. He never would have guessed, having never turned them to such a task, but it's as if they've known in secret how to do this odd work all along. The scraping sets his teeth on edge and gives him gooseflesh, but the gooseflesh counteracts some of the heat. And he has water, and parasol shade, a satisfied stomach, a good surface upon which to work.

There are just two things bothering him now. The worst, by far, is the gray dust rising from the original head material. It's getting in his eyes, coating his arms, legs, clothing, and he's breathing it, too. He ties his shirt round his mouth and nose, but still can't help inhaling a little. And there's something troubling about its smell. Considering its extreme dryness the gray dust seemed acrid from the start. But as he's gone on working and added drops of his sweat to it, the smell has become downright fetid. And its not body odor, this is not his smell. This is a *swampy* odor. As if something organic has died and rotted. It smells like the water left in a vase after you throw out an old bouquet. Or (he wishes he hadn't thought of this) like the gigantic wood rats' nest he'd had to clean out of his mother's attic as a boy. Dried shit and mildew, dessicated food, urine-soaked nesting material—that's what *that* dust had been made of. And as disgusting clouds of it had filled the attic, he'd felt himself growing sick at once and had begged his mother to let him quit. But with eyes that stared straight through him to land on some agitated chapter of her past, she'd snapped, "Don't be ridiculous! Your father shot the last of those rats a decade ago. That's one thing he *could* do, was shoot." So he'd gone on breathing the stuff, had finished the job, then had sure enough fallen ill, and stayed that way, for weeks. There'd even been a period when he thought he might die.

And now this monkey dust, dammit, is reminding him of all that. Not as bad as that, certainly. Not nearly as bad. Yet, ancient as this sculpture is *(not my department; they'll carbon-date it later; still, wish I knew more)*, its very presence proves there were people here once, with all the auxiliary plant life, animal life, eating, bleeding and defecating that go with them. And he's inhaling the result! So a *real* particle mask. That's one thing he needs. And his goggles, too— because didn't he read somewhere that germs can infect us through the eyes? And the sun is getting low, it'll be setting in an hour or two, but he isn't at all tired, he'd love to keep working. So a light. His propane lanterns. That's the other thing.

Ever so cautiously the archaeologist lifts the four-faced head off the table, eases it down in the sand, and at the thought of leaving, grief strikes him again. "My *God,* you're a beauty!" he says aloud. "Wait here!" He then stands, turns in another slow circle, scans the horizon mirages once, twice, a third time, and sets off at a sand-hampered run for the camp beneath the stunted palms.

I I I

HE'S BACK, AND HE'S EQUIPPED. HE HAS HIS GOGGLES AND mask and not just one but two lanterns; two extra bottles of propane, too. And thank God or Industrial Man or whoever's responsible, he's thinking, for particle masks! Because the dust is really flying now, and really *reeking,* too, and it smells so much like that damned wood rat dust from boyhood it's almost funny. The fibrous outer gray, he now believes, is an ancient practical joke—a thick layer, he's almost certain, of carefully sculpted animal dung! Sun-dried, perhaps, or kiln-fired, but the smell, he is positive, could not come from any clay. "You were a shithead!" he laughs, meaning the original gray monkey. But it's a weird, wracked laughter, like a sob in its intensity, for the smells of ancient leaf and flesh growth, leaf and flesh death, leaf and flesh rot, are getting to him. He never stops working. In fact he can't recall ever having worked so fast or well. But the smell is dredging emotions that have him babbling as he labors—about his too brief, too simple link to his father; his too long, too intricate entanglement with his mother; about the ramshackle, mildewy, melancholy house in which she'd raised him, trapped him, smothered him in literal and figurative crap till he'd escaped to college; about her endless, adamant refusals to leave the stinking place, till she'd grown so old she'd begun, like the rats his vanished father once shot, to shit her nest—all of this is rising in the monkey dust. As is the smoke that flew, fast and black, from the house after she died, freeing him—without his having to enter the damned place even once—to order her possessions auctioned and the building razed and burned. *"Good-bye and good riddance!"* he yammers at the vanishing layer of gray. *"Good-bye and God damn you!"* he half-laughs, half-sobs, body coated, face masked, mind gray with the stuff. Yet even as he gibbers, even as he fumes, four solemn faces rise like russet islands from the stinking bank of fog. And the strange strength—*god almighty*—strange power in his hands—*where did I learn this!*—just keeps growing. He's conjuring features from a misshapen lump the way a pianist conjures life from lifeless black and white keys. And even as he babbles, a joyous confidence grips him, a working ecstasy that he with his three science degrees nevertheless longs to call "artistic" as the swamp layer, stench layer, old house/dead parents/diseased attic layer is being vanquished from his life forever—

Making it all the more killing when the entire cheek and eye socket of one beautiful Persian red monkey suddenly pops as if propelled from the mother egg, shatters on the table and falls in fragments to the sand.

IV

FOR A TIME HE JUST GAPES, UNBELIEVING, AT THE PIECES. Then he throws off his pith helmet, rips off his mask and goggles, sinks to the ground. *"Unforgivable!"* he gasps, amazed that he had succumbed to the compulsion to work so fast, that he'd used no tools, that he had grown so inanely confident. There is something that hurts, too, about the way the cheek broke not because of anything he'd done wrong but because of something crazy. It seemed to *fly* off. As if propelled from inside. It made no sense. Could a temperature or humidity change, caused by the inner layer's sudden exposure to fresh air, bring about that kind of breakage?

He suddenly starts with alarm, jumps to his feet. Something in the desert—a man, he fears at first, then some kind of owl, his North American ear decides—has let out an eerie cry. Turning east toward the sound, he sees no one, but notices, with a second start, that his shadow must be ninety feet long. Turning west, he sees a sun red and swollen, nearly touching the horizon. Always a shock, how fast the days depart here. No dusk at this latitude. And the moon just a sliver. "An Islamic moon," his sister used to call these slender sickles. His sister the romantic. Sister the would-be poet. Sister the actual greasy-spoon waitress, sacrificing everything for the nothing of beautiful words. Sister who wept and cursed him for razing their mother's damned house. Sister he hasn't seen in ten years. But the light, the very air, is reddening; the desert is impossibly aglow. And when he kneels back down beside the now luminous red monkeys —when he holds an eye fragment, like a stray word, up to a beautiful broken face—he finds himself close, for the first time in his life, to understanding his sister.

It will be next to impossible, this repair job. He sees that at once. The edges of the cheek and eye are fragile as broken saltine crackers. He'll have to take his sculpture home as is, hire experts to do the restoration. But he wants to assess the damage now. He therefore turns the fractured face westward, aims the setting sun straight into the break, hunches low, peers back into the hole—

and clutches his chest: inside the face, behind the fracture, is yet another layer of material, this one black as coal, shiny as marble, grainless as water. (An argillite? he wonders.) And as he shifts the egg slightly so the sun can pour in, he sees the inner black has been worked into a pair of lifelike wrists and tiny hands. Hands so exquisite, so meticulously carved, that he is sick, the instant he sees them, with the longing to see more.

He sits up, dazed, his mouth dry and open. He stares at the terracotta-colored sun. He feels something—a symmetry, a shape inside himself—and suddenly knows, by reason of this shape, that there was someone more inside his mother; knows that she contained a different person than the one who plagued him: knows that he, in his fear and childishness, made it impossible for that person to emerge. He knows, too, by reason of the shape in him, that there were things he and his sister needed—clues to themselves, even parts of themselves—inside his mother's house. And he'd sold those parts off unexamined and ordered the house burned to the ground.

He reaches in his pocket and pulls out his Swiss Army knife. He opens the knife's largest blade; holds the blade between thumb and forefinger as if it were a hammer handle; prepares to use the actual knife handle as if it were the hammer's head. He takes a few practice swings upon his thigh. He bends over the broken monkey. He forgets, once again, about documentation or cameras. He does not forget to whisper, partly to the monkeys, partly to his sister, *Forgive me.*

He gives the terracotta above the fractured eye a single firm tap. A fissure runs across the nose and into the other eye. He wants to weep when he sees this—yet it's exactly what he'd hoped for. He hits the eye socket again. More fissures run up the forehead to the top of the skull. He sets the knife down and, with bare fingertips and nails, begins removing red shards.

Shining, interwoven jet-black wrists and hands. This is all he can make out for a time. But to judge by the scale, these innermost monkeys are going to be full-body figures. And the combination of artistic detail and engineering, he can see already, is staggering. If, like the terracotta faces, these figures continue all the way around the "egg," there will be eight individual monkeys inside, fit together in there with the efficiency of slices in an orange; yet their upraised, dancing arms and wrists and fingers intertwine with an intricacy reminiscent of the mazes along the borders of old Celtic manuscripts. *"Illuminated,"* he finally whispers. *That's the word. What a craftsman, what a genius wove these hands together! But why monkeys, I wonder? So deep in the desert. The artist would have been a nomad—would have to have been, to survive. So why a jungle animal?*

He keeps tapping and pulling away terracotta, taking pains, as he goes, to keep the fragments in four separate piles, face by face, and in some kind of top-to-bottom order. He prays they can be reassembled later. He feels like an inexcusable vandal each time he strikes the red clay. Yet he keeps hammering, pulling out shards, hammering again, till he's working as fast as he worked on the original gray head—though with infinitely more doubt and humility.

"Except wait!" he suddenly whispers. "Wait wait wait. If the monkeys are truly ancient—and they look, they feel as though they are—then this *wasn't* desert. Because, that study. The hydrologists who discovered it was rain, heavy rains, that eroded the Sphinx at Giza. In ten, twelve thousand B.C. this was all forest, or savanna, they said. Like West Africa now. Where did I read that? Heavy seasonal rains, seasonal rivers, sparse but sizable trees, the full compliment of mammals. So you, my mystery monkeys, are from another world, really. In the time since you were created, every last thing about this place has changed."

The owl goes off again, scaring him almost as badly as the first time. What a voice! More than a little in common with a human scream, he thinks. A child's scream. A child playing, he tries to tell himself. Wild and troubling till you know what it is, but then a hint of crazed levity. Except it's *not* a child, he reluctantly reminds himself. And may not even be an owl. "What a home you chose!" he tells it. Not a tree, not a cactus, not a scrap of vegetation within miles except for those sorry palms. No water but the seep at the base of the tiny well. Why would any winged creature choose to stay in such a place?

"Wait," he says again, remembering the waterstained Sphinx, the vanished trees and rivers. And it hits him. "You were marooned," he tells the owl. *Your ancestors inhabited a grove in the ancient savanna. The rainfall slowly departed. The sands blew in. Your grove became an island in an untraversable expanse of white . . .* He imagines the owls, as their parched grove too began to wither, abandoning dead roosts and old nests, stealing the burrows of their prey. He imagines grazing mammals and their predators, the trees and their monkeys, all dying in the heat. He imagines the maker of the concentric sculpture watching these changes—the unstoppable desertification, steady disappearance of things utterly needed and known and loved. "Are these monkeys within monkeys your way of portraying those losses?" he asks the emptiness. *Were you heartbroken when you dreamed up your outwardly dead, inwardly beautiful sculpture? Or trying to heal the heartbroken? Were you laying a dead world to rest, or trying to portray some ancient belief about the world being an outer layer concealing something more real? What if—*

He feels a chill, despite the heat. He tries to laugh off the wildness of his thought. The laugh dies in his throat. It has occurred to him, with frightening force, that the original artist anticipated him. That he or she deliberately left half the work undone. That the monkeys are not a static sculpture but an interactive device, some kind of spiritual land mine, maybe, that has awaited him all these ages. And by finishing the sculpture, by opening it, he will set free— in himself, or in the world, for better or for worse—whatever it contains.

He shakes his head, whispers, "Not my department."

Then laughs at himself, and says, "But what *is* my department?"

Opening this monkey, a voice inside, or maybe outside, answers.

He reaches for a canteen, mutters, "Audio-hallucinations."

You were born for this, says the voice.

Long day, he thinks, taking a long drink of water. Too damned hot. Too many hours alone. The desert'll do this.

You were born, says the voice, *that the desert might do this.*

"Just work!" the archaeologist tells himself. Or hopes he told himself. But now his actual voice sounds more ephemeral than his hallucination. And the work itself has begun to scare him. He had intended originally, for instance, to keep one terracotta face intact, to show how deftly the concentric sculptures had been woven together. But as he studied, in the crimson light, the way the black argillite hands all joined one another, his own hands began to fight his original intention. And now he sees that his hands have won:

they're breaking up the last solemn red face no matter what he thinks about it. His archaeologist's heart aches as the last face shatters beneath his knife. Yet the artistic intricacy beneath the faces instantly quells that heartache. *Eighty* monkey fingers, each one long, slender, finely textured; each braided in among those of its neighbor. It's a labyrinth, a dance, a concatenation of fingers in there, and how they could have been carved without blunder into a substance as unforgiving as stone is almost frightening. The terracotta faces, perfect as they'd been, were a kindergartener's sculpture next to this.

The colors also begin to amaze him. Though he can cleanly pry the terracotta from any convex argillite surface, the red clay stubbornly adheres to the countless concavities. Because of this, the emerging black figures are everywhere outlined and limned by a glorious earth-red. The intricacy of this red/black entanglement—the contrast not only of color but of terracotta's dryness versus argillite's seeming wetness—creates illusions of liquid and solid, of earth and water, even of stasis and motion. It takes his breath away.

But the reds abruptly pale. The archaeologist turns and sees the sun out of round, dropping fast into the sand. Pitch dark soon but for the "Islamic" sliver. He's got no compass. Half a mile from camp. If he burns up all his propane, can he find his way back in the dark? What will happen if he doesn't go back? What will happen if he spends the night alone, in empty desert, opening up these monkeys?

The sun vanishes, the pink afterglow muting quickly to purple, then blue, then gloom. He notices a gravel in his neck and shoulders, born of bracing himself against the next scream of the owl. He notices the same old fetid swamp smell. He finds himself vividly remembering a fetish sculpture he once saw in a museum, a black wooden figure, head cocked at a neck-breaking angle, slit-lensed cowrie eyes, nostrils as obscenely flared as a vampire bat's, penis erect and sharp as an obsidian knife, the entire body streaked with human blood and feces. This sculpture, too, was thought to be what the museum curator had dubbed a "psycho-interactive device." Reading that term in the museum, he'd laughed at the whole notion. He now remembers the sculpture perfectly, but can't begin to remember why he laughed.

"What a relief," the archaeologist suddenly hears himself muttering, "just psychologically speaking, to reach this hard, clean argillite.

"It *had* to be hard," he hears himself adding, "to be carved this finely.

"So what I'm smelling now, surely," he hears himself continue, "is just the old gray stuff at my feet here. And on my skin. All over me, actually. That's the wood-ratty whiff I'm still getting. Sure. That's the—"

When the owl screams in the gloom and his adrenal glands spray him he jerks, several times, as if electrocuted. Yet while his blood is still screaming, his lungs still panting, he feels an impulse: shutting his eyes tight, he reaches in through the broken clay and explores, with his fingertips, the terracotta-smudged face of an argillite monkey till he can virtually see it. Eyes closed, heart still racing, he is not surprised when he feels the face begin to change. It becomes his mother's face, in life, then in death. Becomes his sister's face, in love for him, then in hate. Becomes his father's face, leaning over him the morning he vanished forever, the features fading now, but the thin lips clearly saying, *Look on the bright side, son . . .*

He releases the monkey face, opens his eyes, turns to the desert. He says, very calmly: "Fuck you, my father. And fuck your bright side. You ran, you coward. You left me so alone I've been just like you ever since."

Then, just as calmly, he says, "Fuck me, too. Away with me. Here I sit exposing the masterpiece, the life's work, the very vision, maybe, of some prehistoric genius. And all I can think about is a little childhood rat shit.

"What an ingrate!" he shouts. And it feels good to admit it.

Feels good, too, to think he might have scared that crazy owl. "What an imbecile," he adds serenely. "What a nincompoop . . ."

But his voice trails off as his attention turns back to the monkeys—turns so fully that he doesn't even notice, as red dust again begins to rise round his head, that a lifelong fear of dust is as gone as the sun.

V

HARD TO GUESS THE HOUR NOW, BUT THE OWL QUIT CALLING a forever ago. He's been hunched between his lanterns, working without pause, and the lanterns cast a hot, hissing light. But without their heat the night air might have chilled him, and without their brightness the precision of the artistry would have been imperceptible. And the speed with which the red clay vanishes, the strange skill in his hands—each argillite crevice carved clean with a few deft scratches, dust rising in an unfeared cloud—he never tires of this. He could work till he collapsed and never tire of this. Everywhere his fingers have journeyed, exquisitely carved argillite now shines. He finished exposing all sixteen hands and eighty fingers long ago. And when the sliver of moon set, leaving him no company but black sand and bluish stars, he'd taken it as a sign: selecting a single pair of arms, single torso, single pair of legs, he'd begun to free an entire individual monkey from the clay.

He'd started with the outer parts, worked his way slowly in. The deeper the crevices the greater the difficulty, but he's done the feet and legs, the torso and the shoulders without pause. It's gone so well, these long silent hours, that he's lost his ability to feel things like excitement or pride. That he's made the discovery of a lifetime no longer matters to the archaeologist. What the dust does to eyes or lungs no longer matters to the archaeologist. Archaeology no longer matters to the archaeologist. Only the monkey matters.

But as he finishes the throat and turns his attention to the face, he feels, for the first time in hours, some hesitation. Feels it literally: for in placing his hands on the monkey's face, he now feels his own face on the brink of some permanent change.

He removes his hands. Sits back to ponder. And finds himself picturing a faculty friend, an incorrigible old poet who he watched die, with great courage, of AIDS. In the last long minutes of what the hospital staff still defined as "life," his friend had seemed to be swimming from the presence of those at his bedside, heart-rate impossibly slow, breathing impossibly slow, eyes open yet unseeing. The archaeologist had been surprised as he'd watched. This death was almost soothing. The rhythms, the sounds and serenity brought to mind not a dying male, not a dying human, not a dying at all, really, but something genderless, slow and beautifully purposeful. A sea tortoise, maybe, setting forth on a long migration.

"*Migration,*" he whispers. He once heard migration defined as "a bridge"—a bridge that birds, animals and nomads crossed as the world behind them became uninhabitable. A bridge that vanished behind them as they went, leaving them no choice but the far side. He does not understand his conviction, but he feels sure that to remove the last of the terracotta, to expose the argillite monkey's face, will result in a similar departure of his own. And yet, looking down at the gray dust and red dust all over the sand, at his own gray- and red-dusted body, looking at the beauty of the black body he has already exposed, he sees it's already too late. Turning in a slow circle, gazing at empty desert and up at the night sky, he realizes that he's been migrating all night, that there is no other place, or life, to return to.

So cross, says a voice. Which he now hears as his own.

Obeying an impulse, he abruptly stands. Then, like so much terracotta, off go the archaeologist's shoes, the dust-filled socks, khaki shorts, sweaty underpants. "*Bismallah Allah!*" he sighs as he sits back down in the sand. Night air runs like water down his flesh.

And with the wonderful long nails he'd never have guessed an archaeologist would bequeath him, he begins to free the face.

He exposes the eyes—two bright obsidian beads.

He frees the pooched, serious lips—a simian parody of his own.

He culls hundreds, thousands of microscopic red remnants from the black facial fur, revealing a texture so fine that he begins to imagine, or to feel, individual hairs.

He loses all sense, as the red smoke rises from his fingers, that he is freeing these features. No archaeologist, no artist, no one at all frees these kinds of features. For they are the monkey's own features. It is the monkey, he knows finally, who must free itself. But now that this notion has dawned on him it's once again hard to work, for the face is nearly out now, and behind those serious little lips are some very sharp teeth! He laughs quietly. Fear of dusty, fecal diseases for the archaeologist. Fear of teeth for him. It's always something! But he keeps working.

Time passes, or maybe stops. Terracotta swirls over his arms, belly, chest, settles on his back, his head, his thighs, weds with his skin, and stains him. His once-white body is a ruddy brown, his tireless hands are the same color, his hair has thickened, curled, blackened, and his eyes—he can't remember what color they were as the archaeologist, but he knows, without need of mirrors, that they've the sheen of obsidian now.

He grows aware of a rhythm in his fingertips. His own excited pulse, he believes at first. Then realizes it's far too quick; that it comes from the stone beneath his fingers. With this recognition, his eyes begin to tear. Though he has longed for it to end this way, this is indeed the end. And there is never a way to steel oneself for the moment the entire black stone begins—as it does now—

to shatter . . .

A tiny hand grabs, then nearly crushes his wrist. Wet obsidian eyes stare out as if in shock. Then blink. Find his face. Focus. A second hand grabs the same wrist and pulls so hard he cries out. In an explosion of black shards, red dust and willpower, the monkey pulls itself from the stone. He gasps, loves, fears, he calls to it. The monkey screams in his face, flings his wrist away, turns to the desert. His face begins to crumble like old dry clay. The monkey peers out at the night with longing, turns back to hiss at him, peers out at the night. This division of attention agitates it. Not wanting to be watched, not wanting to be followed, it makes a charge at him, shrieking as it comes. Hoping it's a mock charge, he leans back, holds his hands up, palms out. The monkey shrieks and charges again. What, he wonders in his terror and heartbreak, would the archaeologist with his pith helmet and fear of Mama's attic have done at this moment? Wouldn't he have collapsed on the spot and fallen in his hole? Wouldn't the wind and sand have covered him and there his bones would have lain, awaiting the next guy with three degrees and a shovel?

Even he, after it's happened, can hardly say what happened: one instant it was stone, then it was his dreams and terrors come true, then it was free-standing, free-screaming, moving out into the desert night . . .

And then he was alone. Weeping hard now, not out of joy, or relief that his long labor was over, but out of useless, mothering concern for its well-being, and a useless mother's grief that it has left him so soon.

VI

HE WIPES HIS FACE WITH CLAY-COVERED HANDS, MIXING tears and red dust. He knows very well he's made mud, knows he's smearing it, hopes to hell it's making him hideous, hopes he's a downright fright. He then lifts his face to the sky, trying to defy every force or Being that made him. He mutters, "Being and nonbeing. Deserts, flesh and clay. Gray shit. Art. Was any least part of this *my* idea?"

When the usual silence rolls in off the desert, he can't help but hear it as a reply. It is so eloquent and still. And so huge. Not just a desert's silence. It comes down from the outermost stars. And picturing himself, suddenly, from that silence's vast perspective—puny mortal body, puny defiance, filthy face—he feels the already-dried mud streaks cracking into a ridiculous earthen grin.

With this grin comes a little strength. He is able to stand now, and dust himself. He is able, without looking back (for what's left now but archaeological rubble?), to leave the site. He is able to walk, very slowly under the stars, to the oasis, where he drinks water, bathes in water, even sings in it after a time. It's a while before he can eat. A far longer while before he can sleep. But after he does both, regains his strength, tends to every needful, then every idle, then every frivolous matter he can think of, swearing all the while to endure *none* of this, ever again—

he of course returns, the first quiet evening,

to dig up the next stone.

VII

AT LAST YEAR'S NATIONAL ARCHAEOLOGISTS CONVENTION AT the University of M——, the finale was, as usual, a banquet at which the year's highlights in the field were celebrated. Because archaeological data is subject to so many kinds of tests and methods of interpretation, this fete tended to be as much a roast of, as a toast to, those highlighted. So many men and women long to be their own scientific heroes or solo schools of thought—and an academic's myopia offends no one on earth as much as another myopic academic. The podium at this annual affair was often, therefore, held rather like a small Christian citadel under verbal Moorish siege. And

among the invited speakers at last year's banquet, none aroused more
of this "siege" anticipation than an archaeologist from a large mid-
western university—a fellow often known, behind his back, as "the
King of Epoxy."

The nickname came about as the result of his discovery, during a 1990 sabbatical in North Africa, of a small cache of absolutely
devastated terracotta and some slightly less damaged argillite shards.
A prehistoric rubbish heap, a sane colleague might have concluded.
But from a small portion, perhaps an eighth, of his argillite rubble
this man had managed—with the help of several cans of PC-7 brand
epoxy—to construct (or, as he claimed, to reconstruct) a small standing monkey. To convincingly construct it, we must admit, for the
archaeologist himself was a man of no known artistic ability, and his
monkey turned out to be a graceful, lithe little form.

This monkey sculpture created a small, perhaps deserved sensa-
tion. Had the man then written a paper describing his find—had he
amplified, in a straight-forward, responsible manner his epoxy tour
de force—he might have done his field some small service. What he
did instead was maintain an inscrutable silence. There was more
restoration work to be done before he spoke, he claimed. He then
proceeded—with even more prodigious feats of epoxying—to turn
perhaps a quarter of his terracotta rubbish into a monkey mask. A
mask so unconvincing, it must be added, that it appeared to everyone but the archaeologist himself to be virtually *made* of epoxy.
Hence his nickname.

These two projects alone took three years. And during his
PC-7 orgy our hero—once a promising scientist, a decent teacher,
perhaps a future departmental chair—published nothing whatever
on any topic. What's more he shirked faculty meetings, grew increasingly cryptic in speech and manner, joined some obscure Sufi
order, began to dress, upon occasion, like a Muhammadan tribes-
man and became increasingly cavalier in his teaching methods—
hence, of course, increasingly beloved by those shameless opportun-

ists, his students. At the end of a fourth year of academic silence, during which he was rumored to have completed yet another epoxoglyph—this one, it was whispered, an out-and-out gray blob bearing no resemblance to monkeys or to anything else; a blob, what's more, with a strikingly offensive odor—the Epoxy King had at last published the much-anticipated paper on his black argillite sculpture and terracotta monkey mask. Anticipation turned to disbelief, however, when this paper insisted that his black monkey *and no less than seven others like it* had originally been contained inside the red mask with *exactly three others like it,* that "the four masks were in turn sheathed in a crude head made of fecal material" (!), that this entire "concentric masterpiece" had been discovered *intact,* but that it had promptly been destroyed *by the archaeologist himself* (!) in order, as he put it, to "free a living archetype trapped for thousands of years in its center . . ." (!!!)

Well then. Getting back to our banquet: it was an understandably roguish curiosity on the part of the convention planners that resulted in the King of Epoxy's invitation to share his thoughts on archetypes, concentric art and who knew what other monkey business. And more than a few convention-goers were in their cups by the time the King was introduced, so it was hardly a surprise when a ribald babble filled the room: "Where's his Bedouin get-up?" "Where's his gray fecal sheath?" "Do archetypal monkeys eat archetypal bananas?" That sort of thing. But the Epoxy King's kind smile as he strolled to the podium, his seeming serenity and his unprecedented lack of props, papers, videos, pictures and slides created a surprising quiet by the time he bent to the microphone. He might actually have helped salvage his lost reputation—had he refrained entirely from words. He did not.

"It may be wrong, here in the desert," he began (invoking an immediate wave of confused laughter), "ever to speak or to act as if time can be long or short, or as if there could be real urgency to any human undertaking. It may also be wrong to share anything as dry and adamant as desert truth with anything as fleeting and moist as the human mind . . ." (A catcaller here tossed a modifier or two at the Epoxy King's own mind.) "But for years now," he continued, unperturbed, "time itself has felt short to me, and precious. Sometimes I fear it's simple dread of mortality that creates this sense of urgency. But at other times I feel that, no, it's something far deeper than mortal dread that compels me to speak of desert things. So I speak. From the shining blackness at my very center, I speak—even while wearing my archaeologist's suit."

His long, absorbed pause was met with perfect silence. There was palpable despair in the audience now. The man seemed without question to be perfectly sincere. He also seemed, without question, to be insane. Well. There may have been some question. The woman he'd come with, for instance—a rather wild-looking creature, hair like a gray lion's mane (his older sister, someone said; "a potter, or maybe poet")—looked pleased beyond measure with his every word. But she too, to be honest, looked insane. Of course there are iconoclasts and anti-academics in every scholarly crowd. "I think he's gay, or maybe trans," one man remarked afterward. "I think the poor brave bastard was trying to come out of the closet." "I believe he's got a touch," another woman later declared, "of what the Tibetans call 'crazy wisdom.'" To be fair to this fringe let us not judge the King of Epoxy's speech further, but simply set it down and have done with it:

"I agree with Thoreau," he had abruptly continued, "that there is something inappropriate about speaking of worlds other than the one in which we presently dwell. Yet all three worlds, we eventually realize, must be traversed. And with this realization comes a sense that building bridges between the worlds—even of mere words, or of sculpture—is crucial, and that our fear of attempting such bridges is a greater crime, spiritually speaking, than impropriety. Impropriety, in some instances, is an unavoidable smoke rising from the flame of yearning. Or a sculptor's unavoidable dust."

Another pause. Another perfect silence.

"Out of my own such yearning," the King concluded, "let me say this. Though I have sometimes called the monkeys *my* discovery, and though in writing of them I've attached my name to them, they have *never* been mine. Because you see my name on your programs and my body here before you, these very words appear in a sense to be owned or 'signed.' Don't let that fool you. Hear them just as they are spoken. Know that each of you, alone, is the archaeologist, and the naked artist. You are the stone's first sculptor, the sculptures themselves, and the wind, sands and time that buried them. You are the screams in the dark, and the silence before and after. You are man and woman, the monkey and its masks, the owl and the unseen Watcher. *Madness,* you might be thinking. Or, *Not my department.* And that's fine. That's humanity's privilege, its outer layer of gray. I mean to rush no one, and what is Real cannot *be* rushed, for there is no real place or time that It does not already occupy. I speak these words because, eventually, we begin to remember, and remembering, find these good things to hear. Peace be with you. And for this beautiful silence, thank you. Thank you very much. Truly. Thank you."

LIGHTHOUSE

ON A QUIET AFTERNOON, BENEATH A BLANK WHITE OCTOBER SKY, A SOLITARY GREAT BLUE HERON ROSE FROM THE POND BELOW MY HOUSE. THE HERON WAS NOT FLUSHED OR FRIGHTENED. ONE MOMENT IT WAS FISHING. THE NEXT IT STEPPED OUT OF THE WATER AND SET CALMLY OUT FOR ELSEWHERE. SITTING ALONE BY AN UPSTAIRS WINDOW, I SET ASIDE A BOOK I HADN'T REALLY BEEN READING, LIFTED A BATTERED PAIR OF BINOCULARS AND WATCHED TO SEE WHICH WAY THE BIRD WOULD GO.

AS IN ANY OREGON COAST VALLEY CUT BY CREEK OR RIVER, THE CHOICES IN DIRECTION FOR HERONS WERE TWO: EAST AND UPSTREAM, OR WESTWARD AND DOWN. I'D JUST CONCLUDED THAT THIS BIRD WAS HEADING DOWNSTREAM TO fish for sculpins on the tide flats when its wingbacks began to show blue against the green-black ridge of spruces behind it, and I realized it was turning, angling almost imperceptibly to its left. It continued on around till it was headed south, right for my upstairs window and me, and passed so close that for a moment I could see the baroque little ostrich feathers at its breast, the oval nostrils in its dagger beak, the unreadable winter ponds it used for eyes; it passed so close that, had the window been open, I may have heard not just its wing beats but its breathing; it even seemed to study me for a second—though it may have only glimpsed itself, reflected in the window glass. At any rate it flew on, maintaining the same counterclockwise tack, till for a moment it seemed to have chosen the swamps and frog ponds in the headwaters to the east. Then, slowly but implacably, round it came again, northward, westward, southward, eastward, not circling really, but climbing upward in a wide, lazy spiral. As if fed up with the options available to coast-stream herons. As if refusing this time to accept either the upstream or downstream choice.

There were no other birds in sight. The afternoon was silent, the sky a pure white sheet. A moistness so faint and fine it seemed a quality of the light was sifting down. The trees were motionless, no wind or updrafts, so I knew the heron was gaining altitude solely through the labor of its wings. Yet its flight seemed leisurely, almost effortless. I watched for a very long time, measuring time's passing not by a clock but by the diminishing size of the heron's silhouette. By the fourth revolution round the valley the silhouette was pure black, and about the size of a high-flying raven; by the seventh revolution it was a flicker; by the tenth it was something impossible —an insane bushtit, a suicidal winter wren. Yet it went on climbing.

My vision was 20/20. The binoculars were 8 × 30. When— still looking through them—the heron's pickax head and anorexic legs had at last turned invisible and even the broad, three-foot wings had become something no bigger than a pair of batting eyelash hairs, it occurred to me that the bird's height no longer bore any correla-

tion to the landscape: should it turn west and simply glide, its momentum would carry it miles out to sea; should it turn east, it had
gained sufficient altitude to coast past the headwaters of a stream two
or three times the length of the one in this little valley; should it turn
north or south it could easily have sailed, without another wing
beat, over the thousand-foot ridges, and far past the mudflats and
rookeries bordering the neighboring bays. Yet it kept rising. So I
kept watching.

I watched till the heron's flight ceased to make any kind of
ornithological sense. I watched till it began, against that white paper
sky, to look like a geometry problem—not a bird in flight, but a
pulsing point coiling round and round a fixed axis on an ever-higher
plane. The spiral remained incredibly precise: its axis continued to
be the little pond in the meadow, and each circle remained just
about the size of the bowl-shaped niche in the valley that now lay
thousands of feet below. I recalled watching golden eagles ride up
desert thermals as if they were elevators, becoming the size of gnats,
then no-see-'ums, vanishing in the blue the instant I blinked or
glanced away. I recalled a red-tail I'd seen catch a rat one cold
winter morning, and carry it up into a cloudbank to escape a flock
of marauding crows. But those sightings had been bare-eyed, and
those birds had been predators famed for their soaring. This was a
wading bird—a flop-winged mud- and water-lover who even
through binoculars no longer resembled anything but a pulsing
speck of dirt or lint or dust. What was it doing? What was I seeing?
Like all spirals, the one the heron was climbing seemed to corkscrew
toward some fixed and final point. But what point is there in a blank
white sky for a warm-blooded, fish-and-frog-eater to approach?
Maybe my heron's performance wasn't geometrical *or* ornithological. Maybe the laws of nature were on the fritz today, and the
metaphysical was getting physical, or the biological mythological.
Was I peering at the genesis of some preposterous little Greco-Ore-
gon myth starring this scraggy old tadpole-stabber as Icarus? Had

some crazed Bible Belt heron stumbled onto an ineffable but actual spiral ladder that led to the golden ponds of some bird-brained literalist Heaven? And was I the poor dumb Balaam whose evangelic or Audubonic duty it was to make an ass of myself reporting these mystic monkey-shines to the world?

Feeling giddy, feeling my heart beating as sloppily as my thoughts, I realized I'd been holding my breath for God knew how long, trying to steady the binoculars to keep my subject in view. Bracing the binocs against the window glass, I took several slow breaths to calm myself, tried not to think, tried only to watch. But even this was no longer easy. All I could see of the heron now was a pulsing mote spanning a space no wider than the dot on a typewritten *i*. Yet this mote was real: it had left fresh tracks in the mud by my pond. And I'd watched it so long and hard that I'd begun to get that feeling one gets when a skilled mime creates a door or wall out of thin air: I'd begun to sense concreteness where there was none; I'd begun to see the entire spiral, from the pond to the pulsing speck in the white. And having seen this pathway, having watched the bird work its long way up its impossible staircase, I next began to sense the bird itself as a kind of person. A thin old man. The keeper of a gigantic lighthouse, maybe, slowly climbing his enormous spiral stair.

THERE IS A DREAM I'VE HAD—A RECURRING NIGHTMARE, really—of an endless iron ladder. It always begins at the foot of my bed, always rises through a perfectly round hole that somehow appears in my bedroom ceiling and always shoots straight upward in a harrowing vertical line that narrows to a ribbon, then to a hair, and finally to nothing. The ladder is always empty: no angels, like on Jacob's; no other people; no passing birds, planes or celestial bodies. The sight of it always terrifies me. Yet there is never any question

that I will climb it. I always start off at once, before my fear has a
chance to build. I pace myself, climbing steadily, like the heron.

I've dreamt the dream so many times that I usually suspect,
long before it happens, how it's all going to end. To ward off intimi-
dation I'll tell myself to look nowhere but at the very next rung—
but I always forget this before long and look down anyway. The best
part of the dream is a period during which I'll feel purged, cleansed,
even joyous at how high I've climbed. The air is so cool, so pure,
and for a long time as I move upward the world lies below me like
the bottom of some vast, impossibly intricate tide pool. But as I
work my way higher the view loses its complexity and color, till the
sky below turns the same stark blue as the sky above, the earth
vanishes . . .

And there is empty sky, me and the ladder . . .

That's when I notice how cold I've become. And how tired.
That's when my bare feet and hands begin to stick to the freezing
metal. That's when I ask myself how I could have been so stupid as
to set out again without shoes, or gloves, or coat, or provisions. And
that's when I ask myself what end I'd hoped to reach, what I
thought I'd have done once I got there, who I was hoping to impress, and who on earth, who in heaven, who the *hell* is going to
help me now that I haven't the strength to get back down. But what
I ask myself makes no difference. There is me, there is the ladder.
There is up, and there is down. So I wrap my hands in my sleeves,
and climb.

I try my best, my very hardest. Then I try something beyond
that. I grow furious at the ladder, kindle my fury, burn it as fuel. I
grow terrified, but focus my terror and burn that too. I burn doubts,
hopes, yearnings, burn everything I can find inside me. Even
thoughts like *You idiot!* or *Please no more!* are good for another rung
or two. But though this emptying of inner pockets may carry me a
hundred, a thousand, even ten thousand rungs higher, the dream

always ends in air too thin to fill my lungs, with hands and feet so torn by the icy metal that I'm glad they're frozen, and a mind I wish would also freeze, so sick has it become with the realization that my ladder is no real ladder at all—that it's a man-trap, a mind-trap, a deadly abstraction: the straight and narrow offspring of a bad mathematician and a worse preacher babbling together about infinity. And I am a warm-blooded point suspended on that straight-and-narrowness, duped by it, doomed on it, no closer to any reachable human destination than I'd been on the very first rung.

For a long time I cling there, turning numb, cursing the maniac who created this impossible thing, cursing myself for braving it, wishing I'd the courage to let go. Then, quite by accident, I *do* let go—

to wake, gasping, in my bed, clutching at black air and blankets as if they'll somehow stop my fall . . .

BUT ON A QUIET AFTERNOON, BENEATH A BLANK WHITE October sky, a solitary great blue heron rose from the pond below my house. One moment it was fishing. The next it leapt up from the mud, set out in a slow, easy spiral and became, from my earthbound perspective, a series of shrinking silhouettes, a pulsing black splinter, a crazed religionist and finally the keeper of an enormous unseen stairway. Or at least the climber of the spiral of such a stair. I don't mean to make too much of this. I saw no white tower, no ship- or mind-guiding beacon, no light but the plain light of day. In the end I only stood, eyes burning, at the base of a vanished spiral, watching the slow, living throb of the dot on an *i* . . .

But the moist white light was still falling, and the black iota that was my heron was still beating like a heart when I lost it not against, but *in,* the milky whiteness of the sky. And I have not dreamt the dream of the iron ladder since.

JUST WIND, AND A CREEK

for Dylan Madenski

FOUR MILES UP A LOGGING ROAD, IN THE SOUTHERN WASH-
INGTON COAST RANGE, THERE USED TO BE AN UNEXCEP-
TIONAL YET BEAUTIFUL STAND OF ANCIENT SPRUCE AND HEM-
LOCK. ON ALL SIDES OF THIS STAND WERE ENORMOUS
CLEARCUTS—SKIDDER-SCARRED, SLASH-BURNED AND RE-
PLANTED IN THE LATE SIXTIES WITH THE TWO-FOOT-TALL
MONO-CROP THE U.S. FOREST SERVICE AND OTHER LESS DIS-
INGENUOUS LOGGING COMPANIES LIKE TO CALL "TREES."
ACROSS THE ROAD JUST TO THE SOUTH WAS A THOUSAND-
FOOT-HIGH, TWO-MILE-LONG RIDGE, ALSO CLEARCUT, AND
REPLANTED IN 1971. MY BIG BROTHER, EVERETT, AND HIS
FELLOW WAHKIAKUM COUNTY WORK CAMP CONS—VIETNAM
DRAFT-RESISTERS AND ILLEGAL ALIENS, MOST OF THEM—RE-

planted this vast ridge. And just a few days into their four months'
labor on it, Everett learned that our father was too riddled with
cancer to travel anymore. The only chance Everett had of seeing
Papa again would be by escaping from the camp and sneaking home.

The Mexicans tried it all the time. Vaulting the little wall,
sometimes in broad daylight, they'd make their way through the
clearcut hills and down into the comparative anonymity of towns
and cities. It was amazing how far even the old or overweight Mexican men could sometimes run. The guards loved them for it. What a
chance to work their dogs and off-road vehicles! But one in three of
those men never returned. *So,* my brother figured. *A .333 shot at a
farewell hug from Papa.* Good odds, these seemed to Everett—a lifelong baseball nut.

But Papa knew his oldest son well. That was why he asked him
not to try to escape, not to come see him, even forced him to say
aloud, over the prison phone one of the last times they spoke, "I
will *not* come. Yes, Papa, that's a promise."

It took our father many months to die. Everett spent every one
of those months replanting the two-mile-long ridge. So it was on
that ridge that he waged the war between his longing to see Papa,
and his promise not to see him. And all day, every day, that remnant
stand of ancient trees stood across the valley, doing whatever it is
that very old trees do.

They weren't much to look at as you passed by, down on the
road. Just two or so hundred acres of shaggy trees in a sort of bowl
on the side of a mountain. Trees whose bark was marked, moreover,
with the pink plastic tape and orange foresters' graffiti that so gaud-
ily announce impending doom. But on bright, clear days, when
there were no clouds anywhere, a little patch of mist would gather
over the bowl, just above the treetops. And the same bowl shape
sheltered the stand from gales blowing in off the Pacific, preventing
the trees from becoming storm-topped, letting them grow unusually

tall. So however humble they looked from the road, and however doomed, they were an untouched patch of intact creativity—a patch of what the world chooses to be where man has no say in the matter. And something about that manlessness called to Everett, beckoned to him as he slaved on his ruined ridge. But he had not been free to enter the grove, or to try to hear what it might be saying . . .

"Imprisonment—the bluntness and harshness of it—would be unbearable," my brother once wrote us from the Wahkiakum camp, "if you didn't learn to soften it by either training or tricking your mind. One prison favorite, for instance, is to make your confinement even tighter than your captors make it. Like say you're given a ten-foot cell. Okay fine, you think. And you use just six feet of it. That leaves you four feet of acreage to plant in imaginary beans or corn or alfalfa, four free feet of unexplored wilderness in which to go awandering any day you choose."

Everett grew skilled at such tricks. He learned to look at the length and unfairness of his sentence and laugh. He found ways to turn his longing for his girlfriend and their newborn son—a son he'd never seen—into a furious energy that obliterated the pain and fatigue of tree-planting. He even held his own in the struggle, the thousand times Papa's face passed through his mind, not to snap back into abject boyhood and run down off the ridge screaming, *"Don't die yet! Please, Papa! Not till you hold me."*

But the trees across the valley broke again and again through his mental fences. The sight of that old grove made the ridge he was planting more oppressive than a jail cell. And Everett wasn't the only one who felt this. As the weeks passed, the cons all reacted to those mist-topped trees, one way or another. One guy—oddly enough, a pacifist—said at least twice a day that he wished the loggers would whack the whole grove down. Everett knew what he meant: to have it gone would spare them the allure and beauty of it. Then there was the guy—a Jehovah's Witness, if that makes a difference—who swore up and down, one quiet August forenoon, that he'd heard music coming out of the trees. No one laughed at him. On the contrary, some dropped their hoedads and fir bundles cold, straightened their backs, turned to the grove and listened hard—till the guards finally noticed and snarled, "Get the fuck back to work!" Everett thought he'd heard something, too. Just the trickling, he figured, of a tiny hidden stream—yet the urge to see that trickle sang in his blood like the Sirens in Homer. Only the damned guards kept him lashed to the mast.

It made no sense, really. They were just trees, and maybe a tiny creek slipping down through moss and deadwood. His urge to explore the stand should have been nothing compared with his inability to see and touch his lover or baby son; nothing compared with his inability to be seen and touched by his dying father. Yet with so many vast freedoms missing, so many huge hurts, one hurt Everett could not tolerate was his inability to drop his tree-planting tools, hike over into that grove and spend a half hour or so just seeing what there was to see.

So on the day he was paroled—ten months after leaving that ridge, and more than a year after losing his father—Everett shocked his lover by telling her not to come pick him up at Wahkiakum, and not to bring the baby; shocked us all by making us swear, over the phone, not to surprise him, not to spy on him, not to celebrate his release with him in any way. "Let *me* come to *you*," he said. "I can't explain. It's just a feeling. But please. Let me be."

Say you're given a ten-foot cell. Okay fine, you think. And you use just six feet of it . . . My brother's decision upset and frightened the family. But his kept promise to Papa had upset my brother. There was a symmetry here. Thirteen months to the day after Papa died, Everett began his new life of freedom by exploring that symmetry: before traveling home to a roller coaster of great losses and great joys, he went to visit the forbidden stand of trees.

. . .

A GREYHOUND DROPPED HIM, NEAR MIDNIGHT, IN THE LOG-
ging town of Kashelweet, Washington. He slept in a plastic garbage
bag in a clump of hydrangeas behind the combination hardware/
grocery store, woke when it rained at dawn, stayed inside his bag
shivering till the store opened at seven, then bought a box of eight
Hostess applesauce doughnuts, a quart of Rainier beer and one ten-
inch white "emergency" candle. With these under his arm, he
hiked out of town.

On the way up the road he felt half sick to see three log trucks
coming down, each loaded to the hilt with hemlock and spruce
logs. But a few miles later his little grove eased, unscathed, into
view. And as the clouds broke open and the October day grew
bright, Everett saw once again that the only patch of mist for miles
around was the one hovering over that bowl of ancient trees.

He'd been planning for months to climb the ridge to the south
—the ridge that he and the other inmates had planted in corporate
fir. His hope was that by sitting up there awhile, looking crossvalley
at the grove, he could recapture the same old sense of confinement
and longing, hear the same siren call, then enter the grove to quell
it. As it turned out, though, the brush and scrub alder on the replanted ridge had a dangerously shriveled look—the result, most
likely, of a little bargain-basement defoliant that Weyerhaeuser had
snagged cheap from the government, courtesy of the doings in
'Nam. So Everett had no sane choice but to jettison his plan and
enter the grove point-blank.

He did. And just ten steps in, the light turned that eerie
stained-glass or undersea green caused by immersion in two hundred
vertical feet of life. Half a hundred steps in, the road and clearcuts
had vanished behind him. And the softness beneath his feet, the
silence of his footfalls, that nutrient-rich, fragrant, fern- and sorrel-

covered loam—it hit him fast: this was death he was walking upon. No mistake. The smell, the softness, the cessation of sound: this was natural death.

ANY APPEARANCE OF PIETY IN AN INCORRIGIBLE OLD REBEL like my eldest brother is not easy for me to picture. This is a guy who called his first sex partner "the piece that passeth understanding." This is a guy who calls Christians "POW's"—prisoners of worship. But in the heart of that grove, Everett did light his white emergency candle. Lit it, then sat "like some credulous damned peasant" there in the trees and logs and loam. He wouldn't have been ashamed to weep like the peasant, either, he said, if two-and-a-quarter years of prison life hadn't hardened his face into some sort of wallboard or plaster. Thanks to prison he settled for sitting, munching applesauce doughnuts, watching his candle burn. No bleeding-heart bullshit, no prayerlike mutterings, no beseechings or lamentations from Mr. Everett M. Chance, thank you. He'd come a long way, after a long wait, to do a simple thing, so he shut up, sat down and did it.

He looked around the grove, though, while his candle was burning, found himself bathed in the deep green light that had last year been denied him, and began to feel, now, why that denial had hurt: to see, in such light, the sinuous sunward and soilward groping of young trees and root-wads was to read a kind of poetry. A poetry of gesture, straining upward and downward; of two-way yearning, half for dark earth and half for the sky and light. And in the midst of the grove's two-way straining, there was nothing Everett had to force himself to reason out or to imagine or to believe in order to see life and death entwined, making a world *together*.

He couldn't help but see, for instance, that the table beneath his burning candle was the decaying body of a huge pre-Columbian spruce. There had been no burial or burning or embalming of this spruce tree's body, no ritual to disguise or spin the meaning of its fall. It lay in plain sight, and it lay lifeless. Yet all along its length, infant trees had sprouted: hundreds of them, rooting in the nutrients the tree had gained through its six- or seven-hundred-year life, feeding like piglets lined along the supine body of a thousand-nippled sow. What those piglet trees were feeding upon, Everett realized as he fed himself his doughnuts, is what we humans call a "corpse."

And with this thought, things began to happen. With this thought the memory of our beautiful father entered my brother's head, or the grove, so fully that in his pain he knelt. "Not to *pray*," he was careful to point out later. "It just hurt. Just felt like a shut-up-and-kneel type situation. And it felt weird to me to do even that. So once I did kneel, I popped open the quart of Rainier."

But to kneel, even beer in hand, in a kind of light that can reach you only after sifting down through two hundred feet of life, to smell the fresh-crushed sorrel and feel your kneecaps sink into ton upon ton of dark, death-rich loam, to see insect, plant and tree life springing from that loam, see constant composition springing from constant decomposition, is not at all like kneeling on church linoleum or cathedral flagstone or even in the dust behind home plate. This was a new kind of kneeling for Everett.

And it takes a ten-inch emergency candle a very long while to burn.

While enough, in my brother's case, to forget just who he was or wasn't, and what he didn't or did believe. While enough to forget, for instance, after kneeling "like a credulous damned peasant," not to take solace in the same peasant's feelings and beliefs. Everett knew damned well that the living and dead can't just meet when they please in some kind of Kwakiutl middle zone. He knew that, even if they could, a remnant stand of trees in a corporate rape site is no such zone. He knew, as he began madly washing down doughnuts and weird peasant feelings with gasping glugs of beer, that the loss of a loved one, whatever else it was, was a slammed door, a locked gate, a termination. Yet neither beer nor this knowledge could stop him, in the end, from actually mumbling a few outright peasant sentences. For instance:

"Papa, I'm back."

As if he had knelt in the ancient trees before.

And as if his father—who'd never even seen those trees—had never left them.

"I'm back," the candle, beer, prison, green light, root-wads, nurselog and silence ganged up and made him say, "And I kept my worthless promise. I didn't try to see you. So now I can't. Ever."

He tried to sound strong and caustic as he added, "Are you happy now?" But his voice broke like an old stick over the words. And after speaking them he paused—pure peasant again—actually waiting for some word or sign in reply.

Of course, he heard nothing. Or nothing but wind, moving through a billion spruce and hemlock needles, and a tiny creek some anti-war cons once mistook for music as they stood quiet on a nearby ridge. Just wind, and a creek. But at the sight of the nurselog before him, using all the structural integrity of its vertical centuries to hold up, in death, one silly candle and a thousand green children, Everett's prison-wall face began to slowly crumble, till he heard himself jibbering to the candle and to the dead log and to the still-palpable structural integrity of a vanished father, "I kept my god-damned promise, and now I'll *never* see you. That's where promise-keeping gets you! That's my fucking reward. And I'm not happy about it. Not one bit! It was wrong of you to make me promise, wrong of me to keep it, it stinks, it sucks, you were wrong! And now . . ." Another broken stick. "Now, God *damn* it, Papa . . ." And another. "Now you're gone . . ."

Yet even as my brother sang his honest heartbreak, his chest was heaving, his drought-stricken eyes were streaming, and the soul he swore to No-God he didn't own was slamming up and down in him like a salmon's tail in its redd as he felt a gone father's pre-

Columbian-spruce-sized pride in a son. "I'm *not* happy!" he told that pride. "Not one *bit!*" he kept lying to himself and to his father by the candle in the stand of trees up a road near Kashelweet, Washington.

"But you are, aren't you," he finally gave up and whispered as the wind moved through the billion needles and the unseen creek played its notes. *"You are,"* he repeated, listening, then faintly nodding.

And trapped, fifty-fifty, in his joy and his sorrow, trapped between the death-loam and the endless rising life, he found he could say no more.

RELIC

Atha dipa, Ana sarana, Anana sarana.
[*"You are the light, You are the refuge, no shelter but You."*]
—inscription on the box containing Buddha's ashes

I

ON A WINDLESS AUGUST NIGHT, DURING THE SEVENTH AND WORST YEAR OF THE RAIN DEARTH WE KEPT CALLING "DROUGHT" IN HOPES THAT SOME MORE APOCALYPTIC WEATHER SHIFT HAD NOT OVERTAKEN US, CECIL REEDER WOKE TO THE SOUND OF DOGS, RUNNING IN A PACK, SLAVERING AND KILL-HAPPY, RIPPING THROUGH THE BLUEBERRY HEDGE BENEATH HIS OPEN WINDOW.

CECIL'S FIRST THOUGHT WAS TO GO FOR HIS TWELVE-GAUGE, BUT HIS SECOND, ALMOST SIMULTANEOUS THOUGHT WAS THAT HE BETTER NOT WAKE BRYN IF HE DID. AT LEAST NOT BEFORE HE PULLED THE TRIGGER. THE TROUBLE WITH

"frontier justice" in the Reeders' small, southern Oregon coast valley was that by day you knew most of the dogs and all of their
owners by name, and most of these owners were kids. Yet by night
the same dogs, once they'd packed like this, usually didn't stop
running till they'd gutted one of the same kids' pet sheep or goats or
pigs. Cease Reeder was farm-minded first and community-minded
second—or maybe twenty-second—so he went ahead and started
for his gun. But Bryn was his exact opposite ("Why else do people
marry?" he would sometimes mutter). So the dogs were nearly out
of earshot, and Cease was *still* taking absurd, slow-motion pains to
slip out of bed without waking his wife—

when he noticed the sound of slow, heavy wing beats circling
the house; wing beats followed, at some distance, by the sound of
the panting dogs.

Cecil smiled into the dark and lay back down. They were after
the teak-brown gander. The same arrogant, half-wild old bird who
for six summers now had come up off the river when Cecil's corn
came ripe, staked claim to all forty acres of it, feasted on a few dozen
low-lying ears nightly, but payed Cease back by driving off every
other stray river duck or goose that tried to horn in. Every year
Cecil debated shooting and eating the gander once it fattened on his
corn. And every year the bird won his heart by leading these same
damned dogs on several goose chases, each of which nearly killed
them.

Cease fluffed up his pillow, rolled onto his back and basked
like a football coach in the sound of the opposition's tortured panting. He heard the gander lead them round the house and barn not
once or twice but five times; heard him coast over the cornfield and
plash down on the pool at the riverbend; heard the rainlike pitter of
dog bodies on corn leaves, the telegraphed groan of fence wire as
they squeezed through and under, the frustrated yelps and whines as
the gander began to swim the pack as close to death as their stupidity
allowed. But when the old river king began his usual irate sermon—

metallic honks, derisive hissing—Cease stopped listening and sank quickly back toward sleep . . .

. . . completely forgetting, as did the gander, that never before had the dogs come during a drought like this one. Cecil sighed, slid back toward sleep, began at once to dream, and so made no move as his drifting mind took in the sound of the pack crashing full-speed through the irrigation-robbed pool; gave no shout as he took in the gander's first and only squawk of genuine fear; felt no panic or remorse as the death-throe flapping and blood-drunk yelps washed over him.

It was the snarling fight for spoils that finally pierced his dream. He was stumbling, naked, down the porch steps as the dogs tore the tough old body to pieces. He was running, shotgun in hand, down long rows of sweetcorn as the last growls and splashes faded away.

AND WHEN HE REACHED THE WATER, THERE WAS NOTHING. No sound but the river's drought-sick mutterings; no skulking shadows; nothing to shout or throw a stone at. They'd carried the carcass off with them. And if they'd left a pile of teak-brown feathers, it was lost in shadows, or the river had spirited it away. The pool was moonlit, untroubled, perfectly still.

So still that it calmed him, soothed him completely, and he slipped home through the corn leaves grateful for the cool, moonlit blueness, grateful to sink back into bed, grateful for the moist predawn air that entered his window, filled his body, became his sleep;

So still that as he sat alone on his sunlit porch, the following morning, he found that the harder he tried to conjure some rough-edged impression of the gander's dying cry or desperate flapping, the more convinced he became that its death had been a dream.

II

CECIL REALIZED, OF COURSE, THAT HE COULD SOLVE THE dream-versus-death riddle directly by simply strolling down to his cornfield or river to look for evidence. But his body felt lazy in the morning sun, the fresh Darjeeling in his pot was too good to abandon, and this riddle was really a mental problem, anyhow. It fascinated him that the wall dividing memory from dream could so quickly and confusingly give way. To look for tracks, blood and feathers was a physical solution. He felt he should—by the exercise of memory and reason, and without leaving his teapot, porch, china cup or chair—be able to say, with confidence, whether the teak-brown goose had died.

Pouring a second cup of Darjeeling, Cease stuck his legs out in the sun, cocked his ears by habit toward the river, then quickly tried to uncock them, since one cranky hiss or honk would be an easy outward solution to his mental puzzle. There are few better ways of tuning in the senses, though, than to try to shut them off completely: he heard an ouzel chittering in the feeble rapid below the pool, heard the cheeping of the weaver finch in the rafters right over his head, heard the ratcheting of kingfishers over their nesting bluff a half-mile downriver, and the hollow *klook-klook* of a raven back in the logged-off hills. At the sound of the *klook*ing, though, his eyes stopped seeing, his hearing turned inward and a familiar voice was saying, "God's pet bird . . ."

Crutch's voice. Anthony Haynes Crutchfield the Third. Cecil's college roommate in the Long Ago; his oldest friend; now an annual visitor to the Reeders' farm. And on his last visit, Crutch had called every raven he saw—including the ones that were crows— "God's pet bird." When Cecil began to tire of it (which didn't take long), he'd argued that an old teak-brown river goose was the king of birds in these parts. But he'd never changed Crutch's mind about anything. "Coyote is God's pet dog," Crutch had said amiably, yet insistently, "and Raven is His talking parrot. Goose is too damned domesticated, Cecil. It's got no place in the Native Pantheon. You ought to know that. But Raven rides right there on the Big Guy's shoulder."

"God's talking parrot?" Cecil had shot back. "Sounds to me like *you.*"

Then Crutchfield had done what he always did when Cease tried to insult him: threw back his head and roared.

III

THAT LAST VISIT OF CRUTCH'S HAD BEEN EVEN MORE AWK-ward than usual. Fresh back to the States after yet another of the Indian pilgrimages that Cecil scrupulously insisted on calling "vacations," Crutch had arrived chockful of personal metanoias, sacred vignettes and pious enthusiasms, and had proceeded to bombard Cecil with all of them. Since Cecil was free (at least when Bryn wasn't listening) to tease Crutch mercilessly, this had all been tolerable enough. The truly clammy moment hadn't come till their last dinner together, during which Crutch, with an *extreme* outpouring of both Eastern devotion and Western affection, had presented Cecil with a leaf from the Bo Tree of Bodh Gaya—a direct descendant (so proclaimed the tacky Hindi/English legend on the red cellophane wrapper) of the tree under which Gautama Buddha had been sitting on the day he attained Enlightenment. While Cecil stared blankly and Crutchfield adoringly at the leaf there on the dinnertable, Cecil noticed a tiny folded note beside it. Unfolding this pellet, he read:

> For my favorite mossbacked Yankee iconoclast. But
> what powerful vibrations you emit! As I write this un-

der the Bo Tree, half a world away, I feel you cringing in your cornfields! Would it help at all to know, Cease, that at the moment Gautama sat down beneath this tree, "no one anywhere was angry, ill or sad," "no one did evil," "none were deluded or proud," and "the entire world became perfectly still, as though it had reached perfection"? Hmm. Didn't think so. Here's the truth, though, from this flawed soul but flawless seat: I love this leaf, and you too, Ol' Dirt Farmer. So why not unite my two loves and see what happens? That was my simple plan. You are a gift to me. Accept this gift to you.

With you at the Still Point,
Crutchfield

With a face as grimly straight as the Oregon/California border, Cecil had taken the leaf in hand and wheezed, "Thanks."

But Crutchfield knew him too well. "It's all right," he said, laughing. "I'm not offended. In fact, if you'd like to, tell us what you *really* think of it."

Cecil started to speak, caught a warning glance from Bryn, turned red as the Bo leaf's wrapper and said, "Nice."

Crutchfield burst into hysterics.

After a bit, Cecil managed to squeeze out, "Thoughtful."

Crutch nearly collapsed from mirth.

"It's a nice gift, damn it, Crutch!" he snapped. "Now let it lie."

Crutchfield laughed himself limp, but then sat up, looking suddenly (and to Cease, *dangerously*) sincere, and said, "Just hold on to it. That's my one hope, amigo. That you'll hold on to it, and hate it, but hate it honestly. Because it'll be a blessing to you if you do. Just wait and see."

"Be glad to hate holdin' on to it," Cecil muttered.

At which point Bryn could stand no more. "It's a *wonderful* gift, Crutch," she said. "He's touched. He's just too *thick* to know how to show it."

"There you go," Cecil said, relieved. *"Thick.* My true state in a nutshell. So what say we shuffle on out to the porch now, sit down at the Still Point or thereabouts, grow undeluded and nonproud as pie and have ourselves a tall cold one?"

THOUGH CRUTCHFIELD'S VOLUMINOUS POST-COLLEGE COR-respondence with Cease had long since dwindled to an occasional postcard, and though he dropped by just once a year at best, he had once remarked to Bryn, while the three of them were out hoeing three-inch-high cornrows, that he and Cease were "united by kar-mic connections so essential to our mutual inner balance that the endless differences of our minds are a constant amusement to us both."

For all her fondness for Crutchfield, Bryn felt a twinge of jealousy over the intimacy this declaration implied—till she noticed her husband wincing. "Friendship," Cecil had quietly replied, "in-cluding ours, Crutch, is just an obstinate determination on the part of any two random fools to explore some of the infinite number of ways in which everyone on earth disagrees."

As usual, Bryn was afraid that her husband had gone too far with his old friend.

And as usual, Crutchfield just roared with laughter. He then shouted, "Absolute emptiness and nothing holy in it!"

"What's he talking about now?" Cease sighed to Bryn.

"I'm saying you're my Bodhidharma!" Crutch cried—which did not exactly answer the question for Cecil. "To try to 'explain' us," Crutchfield further elucidated, "by referring to our push-and-pull, saltwater-taffy karma was just tedious of me. Your reductionist definition of friendship was the perfect response, Cease! A well-deserved punch in the shoulder! A needed slap from a more alert mind."

"And now a dead horse," Cecil muttered, "which you're standing there thwackin'."

"Another slap!" Crutchfield cried, delighted.

"Keee-*rist!*" Cecil groaned. "Can we move on to manure spreaders or trick tax deductions or jam recipes now?"

"And another!" Crutchfield exulted.

"But the hidden meaning *that* time," Cecil said, and he was serious, "was shuttup and hoe."

Crutch managed to zip it, but the huge grin he shot at Bryn fairly shouted that this last statement, too, hit him like some sort of cornfield sutra.

CRUTCHFIELD'S WORK, WHEN HE HAD WORK, WAS AS A FREE-lance cabinet-maker in northern New Mexico. But his true calling since college, maybe since high school, was simply his devotion to Gautama Buddha. Despite a couple of semi-disastrous, marriage-and-divorce-like relationships with two different living Buddhist masters, Crutchfield had continued to love Gautama in the same steady, unqualified way that boys love Michael Jordan or Joe Montana. For two decades he'd been known to all his friends but Cecil by the Buddhist name his first master had given him (Cease pretended never to remember it). He was also a celibate and proud of it, voluntarily poor and proud of it, an ascetic and proud of that, and he endeavored in his daily life and prayer to annihilate all three of these prides, manifest pure compassion and attain Mindfulness, Suchness, Oneness or some such Be-All-&-End-All the name of which, it seemed to Cecil, should not have kept changing from time to time.

Cecil, on the other hand, had for fifteen years owned fifty-six and farmed forty south-facing, solar-collecting, platter-shaped alluvial acres just six miles east of the Pacific Ocean and a bare quarter mile east of the summer fog line. This delicately beneficent piece of land—thanks to the westward bulge of that part of Oregon, to the unstinting help and outside income of Bryn, and to Cecil's own unstinting hard work and know-how—enabled the Reeders to produce what Cease called "the *only* gourmet North American sweetcorn grown anywhere west of the 124th meridian." And before Crutchfield, or anyone else, could question this assertion, he would add, "I am perfectly aware of the more westerly 'sand-corn' grown down around Eureka, for sale to a clientele so skewed by an infamous herb of the local clearcuts that they'd happily munch a bare cob. I am also aware of the corn-shaped fodder artificially produced in more westerly Alaskan greenhouses, providing flavorless but cornshaped counterpoint to the ubiquitous moose stews of that fine land. But if it's *gourmet organic sweetcorn* we're talking—corn to cause an Iowa ringneck to jump states, corn to woo a native Cornhusker . . ." (Bryn was from Nebraska) ". . . corn to draw down, from some celestial realm only Crutchfield can name, the teakbrown King of the corn-thievin' River Ganders, then you will not find it growing one *inch* further west, anywhere on this vast continent, than the western tip of Bryn's and my very own cornfield."

To sum things up in a geographical manner, Crutchfield was a man struggling, for the most part with pleasure, even in the pain, to incarnate a few Far Eastern aims and blessings so much farther east than they'd ever been before that his New Mexican neighbors, friends and clients would just give up in confusion and accept them as Western. And Cecil was a man struggling, with the same sort of arduous but overall pleasure, to grow a Midwest blessing so much farther west than it had been grown before that the Oregon coast yokels who bought it considered it Eastern, hence suspect, but devoured it with gusto nonetheless. And somehow, between Crutch's easternizing efforts and Cease's westernizing one, there was an overlap. And regardless of any heavy-handed things Crutch might say about "karma" or Cease about "two random fools," they both felt this overlap. Their friendship had survived a great deal in its two decades, including what Cecil, in a miffed letter to Crutch, had once come right out and called "your irritatingly folksy, irresponsibly credulous, alarmingly long-term Buddhist piety," and what Crutchfield, in an uncharacteristically free-swinging response to that letter, came right out and called *"your* knee-jerk penchant for a daily spasm of purposeless, objectless, ostentatious iconoclasm!"

While giving a toast at Cecil's fortieth birthday party, Crutchfield had tried to sum the situation up by saying that their friendship had survived twenty solid years of nonstop disagreement.

"On the contrary," Cecil had replied, "it has consisted of it."

IV

SO THERE SAT CECIL ON HIS SUNLIT PORCH, ENJOYING A SECond cup of Darjeeling and trying to solve, with his mind alone, the problem of whether the teak-brown gander's death had been dreamt or real. But in trying not to listen for the gander (an easy, outside solution to his inner puzzle), Cease had heard a raven; and in hearing a raven he'd thought, *God's pet bird;* and in recalling this nickname he recalled the name's progenitor, Crutchfield; and in recalling Crutch, his thoughts leapt to the Bo leaf.

Cecil was not alarmed by these leaps. This is the way the mind works. Especially, it seemed, on its second morning cup of caffeine. Yet Cease was farther from a solution to the Teak-Brown Gander Puzzle than when the Puzzle first began to puzzle him. And he was about to stray farther yet:

From the Bo leaf his mind leapt again—to a dull summer's afternoon, a few months after Crutch's embarrassing leaf presentation, when he, Cecil, had been smitten by an odd impulse. Coming in from his late-morning chores, he'd trudged up to his bedroom and taken the leaf from his top dresser drawer—a storage place he'd chosen (with characteristic perversity) because it was where he also kept his prophylactics; in fact, one wonderful sweaty night he'd grabbed the cellophane-wrapped Bo leaf from the drawer and slid back into Bryn's embrace thinking it *was* a prophylactic, instigating a giggle fit that rendered the genuine prophylactic useless—and so prejudiced him still further against the leaf.

On this quiet summer noon, though, he'd fetched the Bo leaf from its drawer, freed it from the offensive red wrapper, placed it on a table, put on his reading glasses, turned on his halogen-bulbed reading lamp and begun to study it (this had been the gist of his impulse) with the purest attention he could muster.

He hadn't tried to meditate upon the Bo leaf's tree, or on that tree's august lineage; he hadn't given more than an involuntary thought to the Buddha's connection to the leaf, or to Crutch's gushing descriptions of the vibes at Bodh Gaya. All Cecil did was try to summon, for the little dried leaf itself, the same sort of energetic, impartial curiosity he felt when, say, he picked up the binoculars to study an unfamiliar warbler, or stooped by a trail to memorize the features of a wildflower he couldn't identify.

The Bo leaf had looked, after his first such impartial study, like any unwashed, proletariat leaf. It looked exactly the same after his tenth such study. So Cease had resorted to touch: picking it up in the tips of his fingers, he felt its dryness, traced its wrinkles, compared the brownesses of its two sides, compared its veins with his own. He then tried diplomacy: grabbing its tiny stem as if it were a hand, he shook it, said, "Pleased to meet you," then double-crossed the leaf and endangered its only limb by rolling it between his thumb and index finger, causing it to spin in rapid circles. When the leaf showed no signs of dizziness or dismay, Cease shrugged, set it on the table and invited it to do as it pleased. But what it pleased to do, naturally, was evince such bland, unremitting defunctness and leafishness that narcotic concentrations of boredom began to build up in Cecil's brain.

It was this boredom (or so he explained later) that goaded him into carrying the experiment a step further: placing the Bo leaf on a piece of clean white paper, then placing the paper twelve inches beneath his keen green eyes, he thwocked himself, with a finger, in what Crutchfield called the "third eye," began taking slow, deep breaths and proceeded, while thus gazing at the leaf, to venture into his mind, wending his way through the thought-wads as if through choked salmonberry thickets, parting the prickly growth quietly, moving like a hunter hoping to surprise a grouse. What Cecil eventually hoped to discover was a clearing in there—some clear presence or absence of thought in which the leaf could make the most essential, pure impression possible. Holding the leaf in his gaze, expecting nothing, Cease made his way farther and farther in—

and *did* reach a clearing. And to his surprise, what the Bo leaf impressed upon him there was an even *more* profound sense of its defunctness and leafishness, its *complete* lack of remarkable attributes and, more interestingly, the recognition that this was exactly as it should be:

For if a truly Perfect Artist set out to create a material world, he thought, there in his clearing, *only a thoroughly material world could demonstrate that Artist's skill. A physical world with metaphysical leaks in it, an earth that grew less earthy in the presence of certain trees or leaves under which saints once sat, a world full of inexplicable evanescences and miracle-zones and Jacob's-ladders and Mary Poppins' umbrellas, would just be a bunglement—just a Hollywood concoction in 3- or 4- or, what the hell? 5-D, through which numinous downpourings and wizardly upwellings could sizzle and flash at any fool's will. Right?*

So, he concluded in his clearing, *if the Creator is perfect, and if creation is a perfect work of art, then the Bo tree and its leaves are neither more nor less opaque or perfect or holy or interesting or sacred or alive or*

*boring or dead than any other tree and its leaves. All of which makes the
Buddha's accomplishment (but don't ever admit this to Crutchfield!) all the
more remarkable, more universal, for it implies that he could have attained
the same goal beneath any old tree, including the Gravenstein right under
my window, or those shitty little Doug firs up on that Weyerhaeuser ridge,
or those beaver-chawed willows down by the pond or that big Port Orford
cedar Sonny Bragston totaled his dad's Ford Taurus against on Coquille
Road last week. Hell, given the fact that Enlightenment unites you with
Eternity, and so reaches back to your beginning and enlightens that, and
forward into your future and enlightens that, too, I'll bet ol' Buddha could
have attained it not only under any given tree but at any given instant,
including, if he didn't get hit, that Port Orford cedar at the instant Sonny
totaled the damn Taurus. In which case we'd now have two-man teams of
Buddha-freaks like Crutch making kamikaze pilgrimages to Coquille Road
in Ford Tauri by the thousand, so that one pilgrim could sit under the damn
cedar while the other smashed the car against it, trying to manufacture
nirvana like a damned Ford product!*

Gratifying insights, all.

But what they failed to do either individually or collectively
was increase Cecil's respect for his Bo leaf. In fact, for people to
wrap these deliberately mundane tree-droppings in red cellophane,
deny their god-given mundanity and sell them to pilgrims like
Crutch struck Cecil as downright predatory. And for Crutch himself to succumb to "special feelings" after having been thus predated
("I love this leaf, and you too Ol' Dirt Farmer") struck him as
nauseatingly naive, and perhaps even idolatrous . . .

All of which explains—so far as irresistible impulse is explain-
able (and of course it isn't, otherwise it wouldn't be irresistible)—
why Cecil suddenly succumbed to one of those "spasms of un-
founded, purposeless, ostentatious iconoclasm" Crutch had accused
him of earlier. So convinced had he become of the ordinariness of
his own and every other Bo leaf, and so offended was he by the
special treatment Crutch and countless other Buddhists gave the

things, that he felt he was purging the planet of a particularly perni-
cious snippet of delusion as he picked his old friend's heartfelt gift
up off the table,

   popped it into his mouth,

   and ate it.

V

BUT THE INSTANT HE SWALLOWED, CECIL BEGAN TO FEEL BAD.

   Not physically bad. In fact the thought of being rushed to a
hospital in order to have a life-threatening holy relic pumped from
his stomach rather appealed to him, in that it would confirm the
opinion he'd had of such objects all along.

   His bad feeling wasn't metaphysical in nature, either. If he'd
misjudged the leaf completely, if it turned out to be some dose of
homeopathic holiness that whacked him into a clearer, brighter, less
iconoclastic way of working with the world, then so be it, he
thought. More power to it.

   But if, as it now seemed to Cecil, the meaninglessness of the
Bo leaf rendered his consumption of it equally meaningless, then all
he had actually done was commit an act meaningless in every way—
except in its power to hurt his old friend's feelings. Shit. Crutchfield
had journeyed halfway round the world to see that bloody tree. And
when he got there, its leaves and trunk and roots had apparently
packed some sort of mystic buddhistic wallop that brought tears to
the poor bastard's eyes when he'd tried to describe it. Yet he cared
for Cecil so much that he had *given* him his dang leaf! The *only one
he'd bought!* The selfless son of a bitch hadn't even kept a back-up!

   And now Cecil had eaten it.

   "I'm a *moron!*" he groaned.

   Before he could kick himself harder, though, he suffered yet
another iconoclastic spasm: telling himself that friendship was sacred

even if the impending Bo turd in his belly wasn't—telling himself
that while two wrongs did not make a right, they *did* sometimes
make a wrong much harder to detect—he bolted outside and tore all
over his fifty-six acres, collecting every stone-dead Bo-sized tree leaf
he could get his hands on. He then returned to the house, dumped
his pickings on the same table and white sheet of paper, shut his eyes
like a bhikku at prayer, tried to conjure a clear image of the leaf he'd
eaten, then put on his glasses and started comparing. He labored
long at this task. When he'd narrowed his choices to an unseason-
ably brown specimen off a dwarf pear tree and a little tent-caterpil-
lar-killed unit off a young alder, he picked the alder leaf for its
greater apparent experience of the First Noble Truth (suffering),
wrapped it with surgical precision back into the lurid red wrapper,
chanted *"Om mani padme hum"* as he worked, and not facetiously,
either. He chanted it with feeling—feeling genuinely bad that
though Crutchfield had translated the holy phrase for him maybe
twenty times through the years, he could not for the life of him
remember what it meant.

By the time he'd finished these many labors, his desk drawer
seemed a rather pedestrian location for such a fussed-over leaf.
Prowling the house for some more auspicious location, he finally
decided on the little hexagonal Indian brass-and-glass display case he
called his "nimnam box," partly because the box was prominently
displayed in the library, where Crutch would eventually be sure to
see it, and partly because the box contained several more compre-
hensibly miraculous relics, the company of which Cease hoped
might rub off on the sham, recharging a bit of its devoured punch.
Among the sacred nimnams: 1) the meerschaum Cecil no longer
smoked—the miracle being that he'd ever managed to quit; 2) the
translucent green arrowhead miraculously discovered in a stand of
junipers beside a Utah highway when the ancient Budweiser can he
was pissing on rolled over and revealed it; 3) his daughter's and son's
first lost baby-teeth—the miracle here being the speed with which

the two kids had become a college freshman and junior, and the near-infinite extent to which he and Bryn missed them; 4) his hole-in-one golfball—and this was no par 3 piece of crap, mind you: this was the brand-new Wilson Staff 2 last struck on July 4, 1969, which ball had flown as if God, or at least his pet bird, had piloted it, carrying 260 yards in the air, bounding past three bunkers on the sun-baked, rock-hard fairway, crossing a massive, two-tiered green and rolling straight into the cup on a 299 yard par 4.

So the "Bo" (hoho) leaf was in excellent company. And Cecil was, he now felt, satisfactorily armed against the day Crutchfield might ask after the health of his gift. All he would have to do would be to keep a straight face—and at this he was a master.

BUT THE YEARS PASSED, THE ANNUAL VISITS CAME AND WENT and Crutchfield never asked.

V I

SO FROM THE VANTAGE-POINT OF HIS SUNLIT PORCH THE morning after the pack of dogs had, or on second thought maybe hadn't, killed the teak-brown gander, Cecil decided his impulse to devour the Bo leaf may have been the best response after all. Because weren't all such artifacts, on some level, shams? Wasn't it staggering to think how many credulous, Crutchfield-like devotees, worldwide and through the ages, had squandered money, effort, devotion, even genuine love tending their Buddha leaves, their Cross-shards, their Prophet hairs, and the ostentatious shrines that housed them? *What is there to learn from a dead leaf,* Cecil thought, *that a live tree can't teach us better?*

I can hardly believe, he thought, *that had the Bo Tree and the Cross both been burned to ashes on the very days that Buddha and Christ each left*

them, there would have been no pagodas or cathedrals, no mystic poets or
Zen patriarchs, no icons or koans, no Basho or Bach . . .

This—Cecil told Crutchfield and Bryn, when he came clean
about the leaf, a short time later—was as far as he could think. He'd
felt no need to think further, there on his porch. He'd been far too
pleased with the tea in his belly, the ripening corn in his fields, the
sun on his legs, the dangerous ring of the word *iconoclast* in his mind.
Considering the morning's puzzle solved, he poured a last splash of
Darjeeling, leaned back in his chair and gave good listen, fully expecting now to hear, down along the river, the grating cry of the
indomitable old gander . . .

VII

AND THAT WAS WHEN THE WEAVER FINCH FLEW AGAIN INTO
the rafters above him. That was when Cease noticed that—all
morning as he'd sat pondering—she'd been lining her old nest with
fresh-plucked, teak-brown down.

A Door

for Henry Bugbee

Clark Fork River, late September. My knees in a patch of forget-me-nots. The light reddening. Waning sun. I'm working a glide: it's silent water. And kneeling pays. A fish begins rising not two rod-lengths away. I flip out a mahogany-colored mayfly. The take, my strike and the leap are instantaneous, the trout and my face suddenly side by side, the only sound on earth the pulsing of its body.

We hear nothing so clearly as what comes out of silence. The trout's airborne pulsing is like a single spoken word in an empty room. There is no bottom-of-the-boat indignity in this airborne thrashing. Trading water for sky, meeting no fluid resistance, the trout's swimming becomes a spasm of speed, its whole heart and fear and body producing a sound like doves taking flight. The trout leaps again. I hear wings again. It leaps again. And now I feel them. My heart lifts, body vanishes, mind flies into a jubilant spasm, and I suddenly know a litany of things I can't possibly know: that the souls of trout too leap, becoming birds; that trout take a fly made with feather out of yearning as well as hunger; that an immaterial thread carries a trout's yearning through death and into a bird's egg; that the olive-sided flycatcher, using this thread, is as much trout as bird as it rises to snatch the mayfly from its chosen pool of air; that Tibetans, using this thread, snatch home departed lamas half-lost inside little boys; that the flycatcher that was the trout was the mayfly that was the river that was the creeks that were last year's snowpack that was last year's skies . . .

and that leaps are exhausting. Still kneeling in forget-me-nots, I forget. Played out, the trout turns on its side.

I step, half-lost, into the river. I ease the trout into my hands, unhook the fly. The fish streaks for the depths with every appearance of purpose. I stand in the shallows with nothing of the sort.

There are no rises on the glide now. My rainbow's leaping has spooked things for a time. If I were a younger man I'd say the show here was over and rush, before light failed, to the next likely water or showing fish. But there are desires the vaunted energy of youth conceals. What I often want now is to be more present where I am. There are tricks to this, as to any kind of fishing. Here is one . . .

When trout rise in rivers the rings drift quickly downstream. For this reason a fisherman must cast not to visible rise-rings, but to an invisible memory of where rings first appear. I've heard this called "the memory point." I knew of this point when I was young. What I did not know, then, was that one's best casts to it are not necessarily made with one's rod. Leaning mine against an osier, using eyes alone, I cast to a memory point now:

In the last hours of a September day, you can't see down into the waters of the Clark Fork. The sun is too low, the light too acutely angled. In the last hours of day the river's surface grows reflective, shows you blue sky and red clouds, upside-down pines, orange water-birch, yellow cottonwoods. Deer hang as if shot, by their feet, yet keep browsing bright grasses. Ospreys fly beneath you. Everything is swirling. In a snag, way down deep, you might spot a flycatcher. It's hard to believe that these clouds and trees, deer and birds, colored grasses are a door. It's hard to believe fish live behind it. Yet it was the clouds at my feet the rainbow troubled by rising. It was into the downward sky that I cast the mahogany mayfly. It was out of inverted pines and cottonwoods that the trout then flew, shattering all reflection, three times speaking its leaping word.

Not every cast hits the memory point. But when one does, this word just goes on speaking. It says that death is like the Clark Fork, late in the day. It says true words are eternal. It says eternity passes through doors as it pleases.

ACKNOWLEDGMENTS

I OWE A HUGE DEBT OF GRATITUDE TO ONE REEL PRODUCTIONS OF SEATTLE, WHOSE INVITATION TO TAKE PART IN THEIR ANTHOLOGY, *EDGE WALKING ON THE WESTERN RIM*, LED TO A MEDITATION ON THE NATURE OF MEMORY AND STORY, THE RESULT OF WHICH WAS THE "RIVER TOOTH" FORM. FOR THE ORIGINAL OCCASION, AND FOR PERMISSION TO INCLUDE THE RESULT, LOUISE DiLENGE, JUDITH ROCHE, THANK YOU.

BILL THOMAS'S EDITING HAS BEEN AN INDISPENSABLE INGREDIENT IN THIS BOOK'S MAKING, AND HIS LITERARY BROTHERHOOD AN UNADULTERATED PLEASURE. FEW THINGS SURPRISE OR TOUCH ME MORE THAN IDEALISTS LIVING IN NEW YORK.

KEVIN ODERMAN'S WRITING REMAINS A COMPASS, AND HIS MARGINALIA ("WHOOF" "YOU WHACKED!" "BLAH" "NOW *THAT'S* SOME WEIRD SYNTAX" "+") REMAIN, AS IN ALL MY BOOK MANUSCRIPTS, THE TERSE CARROTS THAT KEEP THIS MULE PLODDING.

FOR VARIOUS KINDS OF HELP WITH VARIOUS STORIES, THANKS TO ILENA SILVERMAN, DAVID FOSTER, LINNY STOVALL, ROBLEY WILSON, MELANIE BRINKLEY, FRANK BOYDEN, TOM CRAWFORD, GEORGE AND MARGOT VOORHIES THOMPSON, DENNIS HELD, CLAIRE DAVIS, TIMOTHY WHITSEL, ELIZABETH WOODY, HENRY BUGBEE, CYNTHIUS AND SUSAN, BRENDA LEMON AND CLARE ANN.

FOR LIVING WITH ME, DYING WITH ME, COLLABORATING ON EVERY HEARTBEAT, DAY AND DIAPER LET ALONE ON EVERY WORD, ADRIAN, HOW CAN I THANK YOU. MAY WE GIVE IT ALL AWAY BEFORE IT'S TAKEN. MAY WE ARRIVE AT SWEET NOTHING THE SAME BREATH.